LONGMAN STUDY GUIDES

GCSE
Geography

Steve Milner

physical
rivers
ice
coast

human
population
industry
development.

LONGMAN

► LONGMAN STUDY GUIDES

SERIES EDITORS: **Geoff Black and Stuart Wall**

Titles available

Biology
Business Studies
Chemistry
Design and Technology
Economics
English
English Literature
French
Geography
German
Information Technology

Mathematics
Mathematics: Higher Level
Music
Physics
Psychology
Religious Studies
Science
Sociology
Spanish
World History

Addison Wesley Longman Ltd.,
Edinburgh Gate, Harlow,
Essex CM20 2JE, England
and Associated Companies throughout the World.

© **Addison Wesley Longman 1997**

First Published 1988
Second edition 1997

ISBN 0-582-30486-5

British Library Cataloguing-in-Publication Data
A catalogue record for this book is available from the British Library.

Set in 9.75/12pt Sabon
Produced by Longman Singapore Publishers (Pte)
Printed in Singapore

CONTENTS

Population, industry, & development & interdependence.

tectonic activity

Industry

EDITORS' PREFACE

Longman Study Guides have been written by the people who set and mark the exams – the examiners. Examiners are aware that, due to lack of practice and poor preparation, some students achieve only the lowest grades: they are not able to effectively show the examiner what they know. These books give excellent advice about exam practice and preparation, and organising a structured revision programme, all of which are essential for examination success. Remember: the examiners are looking for opportunities to *give* you marks, not take them away!

Longman Study Guides are designed to be used throughout the course. The self-contained chapters can be read in any order appropriate to the stage you have reached in your course. The examiner guides you through the essential parts of each topic, making helpful comments throughout.

We believe that this book, and the series as a whole, will help you to establish and build your basic knowledge and examination technique skills. For additional help with exam practice and revision techniques, we have published a series called **Longman Exam Practice Kits**, which are available from all good bookshops, or direct from Addison Wesley Longman.

GEOFF BLACK AND STUART WALL

ACKNOWLEDGEMENTS

I am indebted to the following Examination Groups for permission to reproduce examination questions. Whilst permission has been granted to reproduce their questions, the answers or hints on answers are solely the responsibility of the author and have not been provided or approved by the groups.

EDEXCEL Foundation (London)
Midland Examining Group (MEG)
Northern Examinations and Assessment Board (NEAB)
Southern Examining Group (SEG)

Special thanks go to my wife, Phillipa, for her constant support, forbearance and encouragement.

STEVE MILNER

This book has been written as a course companion for use throughout your GCSE course in Geography. The first chapter gives advice about preparing for the examination including information about revision, examination questions, grading and assessment objectives. Chapter 2 focuses on the National Criteria for Geography, the syllabuses of the main examination boards and the skills you will need to demonstrate. There are also some exercises at the end of this chapter to practice the skills. You should read these first two chapters carefully as they give invaluable advice which will be useful throughout your Geography course.

The remaining chapters, 3 to 15, deal with key topic areas in GCSE Geography and all follow a similar format. Each chapter begins with a **Getting started** page which is an introduction to the chapter. This includes a **Topic chart**, a table which, at a glance, shows the breakdown of the chapter into key topic areas and identifies which examination boards cover the topics of the chapter. The chart can be used to check your study and revision progress over the two years. A Topic chart looks like this:

LONDON A	LONDON B	MEG A	MEG B	MEG C	NEAB A	NEAB B	NEAB C	NICCEA	SEG A	WJEC	IGCSE	TOPIC	STUDY	REVISION 1	REVISION 2
✓			✓							✓	✓	Weather measurement			
✓									✓			Climatic region and climatographs			
	✓	✓		✓		✓			✓	✓		British climate			

Key to the initials
London EDEXCEL Foundation (formerly ULEAC)
MEG Midland Examining Group
NEAB Northern Examinations and Assessment Board
NICCEA Northern Ireland Council for the Curriculum, Examinations and Assessment
SEG Southern Examining Group
WJEC Welsh Joint Education Committee

Each topic listed is then explained in the **What you need to know** section – the core of the chapter.

▶ Revise the ideas and places which summarise the topic and explain and illustrate the key ideas. Throughout the book examples from LEDCs and MEDCs are given. Make sure that you know that LEDC = Less Economically Developed Country and MEDC = More Economically Developed Country.

▶ Study the **case study** and **key issue** provided. Most case studies are about places and many of the case studies match places required by the only syllabus to set the places for you to know about, e.g. Japan, Amazonia, the Lake District and the M4 corridor (NEAB B).

▶ Learn the list of **geographical terms**.

▶ Consider the **student** and **tutor answers** to common GCSE questions. None of these are tiered at Tier F (Foundation) or H (Higher) but levels shown by the examiner tell you about the standard achieved!

To help you to practise what you have just learnt, there are then a series of tiered examination questions. Try to answer these to the best of your ability before checking your answers against those given in the answer scheme, where level 2 means an answer of around grade C standard. These practice questions can be done at whichever level you choose – F or H.

At the end of each chapter there is a **summary box** which briefly identifies the key points about topics covered in the chapter. You should check that you know, and understand more fully, each of the key points listed.

Best of luck!

Revision, examinations and coursework

 GETTING STARTED

The two timed written papers you will sit in the final examination will account for 75% of the available marks in nearly all GCSE Geography syllabuses. How can you best prepare yourself for these written exams? Successful preparation involves being able to do the following three things well:

1.   revise your notes,
2.   answer set exam questions, and
3.   cope with the exam room pressures on the day.

 WHAT YOU NEED TO KNOW

▷ **Revising your notes**

Though the examination is far from just a memory test and is very much about testing your skills (i.e. what you can do) and your awareness of people's values, you will need to *remember* some knowledge and some understandings of how things work from the course you have studied. You will also have to ensure you have fully mastered the *skills* learned during the course, including giving a *balanced view* of an issue which might be controversial.

Many students have difficulty in coping with working on their own; independent work is essential before the written exam. Effective independent work is about developing good working habits and generally being a rather organised person, capable of sorting out, planning, etc. Approach your learning and revision in an *organised* way.

'A good set of notes will provide a solid basis for your revision'

▷   First of all, make sure that you have a good set of classwork notes with everything completed, from which you can revise. If not, you would be well advised to talk to your teacher about the situation. Everyone could usefully profit from using a good geography *textbook* written specifically for GCSE. Use such a book alongside your class notes and this book. You may also find it useful to make a few notes on your *coursework* before handing it in; there may be an exam question on the topic you investigated! Notes on any *field courses* you have been on will also be extremely useful for exam revision.

▷   Take all these notes and organise them, first under **key headings** and then perhaps into an **order of priority**. Getting familiar with the actual **syllabus** you are following may help you do this, as it will include lots of headings.

▷   To successfully **revise** these notes you need to be both organised and have a definite plan of action. You also need a quiet and secure place to revise, preferably at home rather than in a library. Leaving all your revision until the last minute is foolish. But do not start intensive revision too early either. You could become so tired and bored that you go off the boil before the exams even start. The best time to begin revision is around twelve weeks before your first exam. From then onwards, you need to revise regularly, in small doses, according to a sensible **revision timetable** which you have sorted out yourself. This timetable should give enough time to cover all the work you need to, and leave some time for rest, relaxation and leisure activities. Your *geography* revision timetable should be part of a bigger, master one showing time you are going to give each subject. An example of what your personal timetable for geography might look like is given below (Table 1.1).

Table 1.1 A personal
Geography timetable

SUBJECT – GEOGRAPHY

Date	Time	Topic
1 April	7–9 p.m.	River studies and water supply
4 April	10–Noon	Farming in MEDCs
	2–4 p.m.	Farming in LEDCs
8 April	7–9 p.m.	Map and diagram skills
11 April	10–Noon	River studies and water supply
	3–5 p.m.	General principles of weather and climate
etc.		

Revise on a topic-by-topic basis, ticking off the topics as you cover them; concentrate on topics you feel least well-prepared for, especially the weak spots shown up in your mock exams. Restrict your revision sessions to no more than 2 hours, perhaps 1 to 1¹/₂ hours at a time. You are unlikely to help yourself by working too hard for long periods at a time, especially in the form of frantic, last minute cramming before the exam. Frequent, short revision slots, say of 1 hour, over the twelve weeks before the exam period, are far better than marathon swots of 3, 4 or 5 hours in the last week.

▶ You need to work out for yourself the revision *method* which works best for *you*. There are various possible ways of dealing with your geography topics. Revision should after all, only be going over and reinforcing what you have *already* learned earlier.

'Active revision can help you'

We learn best by *association*; unrelated facts cannot, for instance, be remembered easily. You need to organise what you wish to learn, and find *links* between things. You need to see the *pattern*, and learn in a network. An *active* approach is recommended. Revise actively by asking yourself questions and making notes and charts as you read. Never attempt to revise anything which you do not first understand.

Which of the following **revision techniques** works best for you?

1 Write down a list of *central points* as you read through a topic in your notes. After finishing the reading, try to remember all you can of the things which are linked with that point.

2 Write a *summary* of each topic, perhaps on a small card or on larger sheets which you can stick up on the wall in your room. Include important facts, the main ideas, relevant examples, etc. Carry any small cards about with you for regular reference. Noting down things you really must know, such as terms, on cards is a really good idea.

3 Read through your notes and use a *coloured highlighter pen* on the main points.

4 Read your notes on a topic; *put them away* and then try to write a summary (précis) of that topic. Check how good it is by looking back at your notes when you have finished.

5 Read your notes then enlist someone *to test you* with questions. Parents, brothers and sisters or fellow students may be willing to help. Testing, including self-testing (testing yourself), is one of the most effective techniques for revision. It pinpoints shaky areas in which you have difficulties, and that you need to work on, and it indicates those areas which you have understood and should be confident about. There are two main types of testing. One involves the quick and simple questioning by yourself, a friend or parent, at the end of a revision session that we referred to earlier. Learning the definition of technical terms is usefully done this way. The second type involves the use of exam questions.

6 Practice *answering examination questions* obtained from your teacher either using your notes and books, or without them. It may be a good idea to time yourself and see if you can write an answer in about the time which the examination will allow you. Preparing yourself for the examination by using exam questions can be a great help to you in understanding what is being asked for in the questions set. You need not always answer questions in full. Working out *rough plans* to long questions in, say 10 minutes, can be a very effective exercise. Studying specimen and past exam papers is essential to your preparation. Practice questions are given at the end of each of Chapters 3–15 in this book.

7   Some people like to express their notes as *diagrams* or drawings. Try re-presenting your notes in areas where your understanding is shaky. For example, building up a diagram or *flow-chart* showing main points of a topic might be a better way of understanding it than presenting it as a paragraph of writing. Fig. 1.1 shows an example of a simple diagram which has been worked up to summarise a passage of writing about the aims and work of the Tennessee Valley Project. Turning written accounts into diagrams is useful preparation. Lined paper is not necessary. Making notes on plain paper in the form of 'doodling' with loops and lines linking the information in a logical sequence may be helpful. Experiment using colour.

8   Try to develop little *memory techniques* to help you recall really important pieces of information. Acronyms like 'never eat shredded wheat' help some students to remember the four compass directions – north, east, south and west – in clockwise order.

9   Try reciting part of your notes on a topic into a *cassette recorder* and play it back to yourself from time to time. The best notes are those you make *yourself*. Have a go at *rewriting* teacher hand-outs, etc. in your own handwriting and in your own words. It should be clear that summarising is an important skill in effective revision. Being able to 'boil down' the material you have on a topic is excellent practice in trying to identify what is really important. It will help you to structure your thinking on the topic, and will provide an excellent set of *brief* notes for going over just before the exam.

Fig. 1.1

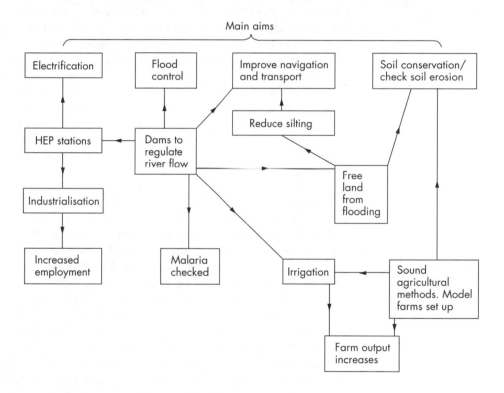

▷ **Answering questions**

One important aspect of examination preparation, is that you have adequate *practice* in answering the sort of questions set in the examination. Later in this chapter we describe the various *types* of question the GCSE uses. With most types, your answers in the examination are to be written in the question booklet. The important thing with all types of question is that you decide *what* the examiner wants from the question set, and give in your answer *nothing but that*. Read the wording of the question very carefully and try to decide what the examiner is seeking from you. Answering the question and nothing but the question must be your rule!

Does the examiner want *facts* and straightforward description, or *reasons* why something happens, or what *you think* about something (a values question)? Each question will contain some key words or 'action' words such as 'describe', which means the examiner wants facts; 'explain why', which means give reasons for, and so on. These 'action' words should tell you what the examiners expect you to do in answering the question. Here are the meanings of some of these words, which should act as *signals* in telling you what is wanted.

Compare   Show or find out what way two or more things are like each other (or are different from each other). Say or show that something is like something else. Examiners are looking for a description of differences and similarities.

Contrast   Bring out the differences between one thing and another.

Describe   Say what something is like, help the reader to form an idea of something, bring out specific qualities. Recalling the relevant facts about a topic or a saying that you see in a map or diagram.

Explain   Account for, give the meaning of something, make clear by giving reasons for something. You will be expected to show understanding of what you are writing about.

Comment   Summarise the various points on something, give an opinion, attempt to explain and criticise.

Discuss   Talk about something from several points of view, debate, consider, compare opinions, show the various views held, argue.

Criticise   Give an opinion on something and give your reasons. Students often concentrate on bad points and mistakes, but favourable points are just as relevant here.

Illustrate   Though it suggests draw, it actually means give specific examples.

'Answer the question actually set'

If you simply seize the geographical words in a question like urbanisation, population, migration, and take them as an invitation to write *everything you know* about them without doing what the other key words tell you to, then you will get limited marks. Make sure, as you write, that you are answering the question set. GCSE questions will be carefully worded and the examiner who will mark your paper will have a precise marking scheme. You will *not* get marks unless you give him/her exactly what the questions ask for. Imagine how you feel is you ask a spoken question and another one is answered.

You also need to give the right amount of attention to each part of structured questions. There is a *limit* to the number of marks you can gain not only from the *whole question*, but from each *part* of it. Give the examiners exactly what they ask for, and no more. The number of marks allocated to each part will be shown in brackets on the examination paper. This, together with the amount of space left after a question for your answer, is there to indicate the length of answer the examiner is looking for. Do not throw away marks by ignoring this!

Practise writing to time and finishing a paper; not finishing is a terrible waste of marks. NEAB syllabus A uses objective question papers, which include multiple-choice questions. These are not speed tests; you will be allowed ample time, say 1–1½ minutes to answer each question. They are precise thinking questions, a form of problem-solving, which are perhaps best tackled by *eliminating* one by one each of the wrong answers (known as distractors) given. It is valuable practice before the exam to understand *why* each distractor is not the best answer. Marks are not lost for giving a wrong answer so if you do not know the right answer and can only knock out, say three wrong options, then guess from the two which remain. This gives you a fifty/fifty chance of success. But please remember that *random guessing*, or trying to find a hidden pattern in the correct answer letters through the paper (e.g. 1A, 2B, 3C, 4D, etc.), will *not* pay off!

The main type of multiple-choice question used will be the simple **five-choice completion** question. This consists of a statement, a question or an unfinished sentence, followed by the five alternative answers. Some more complicated types – multiple-completion and matching-pairs – will be used. A **multiple-completion** question is one where one or more of the alternative answers may be correct, so an answering code is provided. **Matching-pairs** questions consist of a group of questions and a group of answers. You have to *match up* each question with the answer. If you are taking the NEAB syllabus which uses multiple-choice, do practise with *all the types* of multiple-choice questions used. Your teacher should be able to help with sample questions for this. You will also find some multiple-choice questions in later chapters.

Most of the advice given so far in this section applies equally well to all your subjects. In addition, there are a number of points which, in my experience as an examiner, geography students will find particularly helpful to follow.

▶   First, you will get no marks for vague answers. It is particularly important that you know the case studies of the specific places and events you have studied during the course. Be able to give *named examples*, *named places* and *named case studies* in the exam. For example, if you have studied farms as a system then make sure you know about one or more farm studies as examples, ideally in both developed and developing countries. Waffle is a waste of your time and energy; in particular try to avoid phrases like 'good climate' which really do not mean anything!

▷ Second, make sure you understand the *technical terms* used in geography and can explain them or use them correctly in your writing.

▷ Third, almost every question on a geography paper will have a map, a graph, a diagram, a photograph or a cartoon. Practise reading these and explaining what they show. When looking at maps, try to see some *pattern*. It is a very useful skill to be able to describe where things are on a map; these are called **distributions**. Distributions of things often form a pattern. Maps are easily obtainable and useful for revision purposes. The world distribution maps in a good atlas, a 1:50 000 Ordnance Survey map of your local area, and the weather maps in newspapers or on the BBC showing how a weather system crosses the British Isles, are all helpful. Learn also to draw maps and diagrams wherever you think it suitable, a map or diagram can often save you a lot of words.

▷ Fourth, geography is a great *integrating* subject which links and relates various aspects of the world. Some exam questions will *cross* topics and cannot be answered fully from your revision of one topic only. A good answer will require you to bring together your knowledge and understanding of more than one area of geography. For example, questions on the **growth of a town** will also require you to be able to say something about the **development of transport** in and around it.

▷ Fifth, and finally, ensure that you know how to answer the longer structured questions used by examining groups. Their degree of difficulty goes up and down, though it generally goes up as you work through the parts to the end. Develop your answering technique with these questions. Do not, for instance, look for more than the obvious in the easier opening parts; give the right amount of attention to each part, bearing in mind its mark limit and the space left for your answer by the examiner; and remember that writing *more* than you are asked for wastes valuable time.

▷ Succeeding on the day of the examination

Coping on the day means understanding yourself and your reactions; we are all different. Try not to go into the exam room tired from a late night, or worried about some detail you know you are unsure about and should have checked upon. Some people find a bit of last minute revision both useful and relaxing, but don't revise too much immediately before the exam. Try to keep calm on the day and to keep a sense of proportion about the whole thing – it is not a life or death matter after all! You can only do your best, everyone else will be nervous too, and examiners will be trying to give you marks, rather than to take them away. Make sure you have everything you will need on the day of the exam – a watch, sharp pencil, coloured pencil, ruler, etc.

When you receive the paper:

1   Read the instructions on the front page (the rubric) very carefully. Check you know the right answer to such questions. How many questions do I have to answer? Are any compulsory? From which section of the paper do I choose my questions? How much time do I have? etc.

2   Where you have a choice of questions, read through *each part* of every question before you decide which ones you will answer. Work through the whole paper first, making a mental note of those questions you like the look of. Do not make your choice on the first parts of a question only. There will be lots of marks for the middle and closing parts of longer structured questions. Choose questions on topics you have studied during your course and, preferably, go for those that look more straightforward to you!

3   Work out a rough timing for each question and stick to it! Make sure you answer all the required questions, even if incompletely. There are straightforward marks to be picked up at the beginning of every question; you need these! Do not answer more questions than you are asked for. The examiners may not pick out your best answer to mark, but rather the first ones they come to!

4   For the longer, more open, parts of questions you might write a brief plan of your

answer in pencil on spare paper, perhaps on the back page of your booklet. This should enable you to produce a better finished answer. Jot down the main facts, ideas, opinions, in pencil, then write them up in an organised order in ink and finally cross out your rough pencil plan. If you are short of time, answer the last question or part question in this kind of note form.

Finally remember to do exactly what the question asks. Try to leave time at the end for checking through your answers, correcting mistakes, rewriting bits, making small additions, etc. After it is all over, don't indulge in post mortems with fellow candidates outside the examination room! Now, forget about geography exams and concentrate on the next subject in your GCSE.

▷ Targeting the examination papers

The paper will be targeted at both your ability and at the assessment objectives in the syllabus.

One of the features of GCSE examinations is that they should be a worthwhile experience for you in which you can show what you know and can do, whatever your ability. Positive marking of positive achievements is what GCSE is all about! It must give you an opportunity to show your achievements and to be given high marks for good performances. This approach to assessment of setting more 'user-friendly' examinations for you all so you can each do your best and so distinguish yourselves from others is known as differentiation.

Generally, the idea in your coursework will be that a particular geographical issue, problem or question can be investigated at different levels and that this will show up in the quality of the final write-up. This approach to differentiation is known as **differentiation by outcome**.

Tiered papers

However, this approach is not considered the best way of giving you all chances in the written examination; the exam boards offer a choice of papers at two levels. The F (Foundation) Tier is targeted at those of you expected to get grades C to G while the H (Higher) Tier paper is designed to stretch abler students aiming at grades D to A*. You will see that there is a two-grade overlap (C and D) between the papers, so some of the questions might be the same on the two papers. Most questions will be different and targeted at different levels of difficulty. Differentiation will be largely through these differentiated tasks (known as **differentiation by task**). Some schools may decide to adopt this approach to differentiation for their coursework – different coursework tasks in terms of difficulty for different students.

Assessment objectives in geography

Every syllabus has assessment objectives which describe the achievements and/or abilities against which you can be measured by the examinations and coursework. The final grade you are awarded depends upon the extent to which you have met these assessment objectives. Geography has three broad assessment objectives – knowledge, understanding and skills. These are types of geographical learning which in practice are closely interrelated and often difficult to separate.

However, the examiners will set questions which focus on one or more of these three objectives. Questions focusing on **knowledge** will ask you to recall information about places and examples you have studied. They may also expect you to define and use correctly geographical terms. Knowledge and **understanding** are often integrated. Understanding of ideas, processes in the 'physical' and 'human' worlds, relationships within environments and of local and global patterns requires knowledge of locations and places. The attitudes and values of people towards the environment, developments and other people also fall into understanding.

Skills are assessed in the written examination papers and through the coursework, and amount to techniques needed to learn geography through enquiry and investigation. Mapping, photographic and graphic (diagram) skills are part of this approach. Most syllabuses break down these three broad categories of objectives into a number of knowledge objectives, understanding objectives and skill objectives. All syllabuses have to have between 30 and 40% of the whole examination assessing each of the three objectives. Individual parts of the whole examination may be less balanced in terms of their assessment objectives. For example, one of the written papers may be targeted so that it assesses much of the knowledge for the whole examination, which will mean that more than half the marks for that paper are for the assessment of knowledge. Check the syllabus and the examination you are studying with your teacher. It is useful to know if one of the components of the examination is targeted in this way. Does your syllabus figure in the table.

Table 1.2

Assessment Objectives	% total marks permitted for whole exam	Syllabuses with Maximum %	Minimum %	Individual papers with heavy targeting of objective
Knowledge	30–40	35% (NEAB B)	30% (most other syllabuses)	NEAB A Paper 2 MEG A Paper 1/2 SEG B Paper 2
Understanding (including values and application)	30–40	40% (WJEC; NEAB A and C)	30% (SEG A and B; MEG A; London B)	Assessed in all papers and coursework so rarely needs to be dominant objective
Skills (and techniques and application)	30–40	40% (SEG A and B; MEG A; London B)	30% (NEAB A, B and C; WJEC)	MEG A Paper 3/4 SEG A Paper 1 Coursework

You can see that all syllabuses have to have roughly one-third of the marks for each objective, so there is a lot of similarity between them.

▷ Types of Examination Questions

All written papers are offered at two tiers, Foundation or Higher. Some papers, namely SEG A Papers 1 and 2, NEAB C Paper 2, London A Paper 2 and Paper 1/2 on all three MEG syllabuses, offer a choice of questions. All other papers, in other words most, use compulsory questions.

Four types of question figure on GCSE Geography papers:

A Resource-based longer structured questions
B Resource-based short structured questions
C Objective (multiple-choice) questions
D Decision-making/problem-solving/issue evaluation exercise (using multi-part/ structured questions as in A and B)

Types A and B are by far the most commonly used as the table below shows (Table 1.3).

Table 1.3

Syllabus	Type of examination question Type A	Type B	Type C	Type D
London A	✓(Paper 2/4)	✓(Paper 1/3)	—	—
B	✓(Paper 1/3)	✓(Paper 1/3)	—	✓(Paper 2/4)
MEG A	✓(Paper 2/3/4)	✓(Paper 1)	—	—
B	✓(Paper 1/2)	—	—	✓(Paper 3/4)
C	✓(Paper 1/2)	—	—	✓(Paper 3/4)
NEAB A	✓(Paper 2)	—	✓(Paper 1)	—
B	✓(Papers 1 & 2)	—	—	—
C	✓(Paper 2)	—	—	✓(Paper 1)
SEG A	✓(Paper 2)	✓(Paper 1)	—	—
B	✓(Paper 2)	✓(Paper 1)	—	—
WJEC	✓(Papers 1 & 2)	—	—	—
NICCEA	✓(Papers 1 & 2)	—	—	—

You can see from the table that you have to be able to handle structured questions, whether short or longer. These questions are structured into various parts, usually develop a common theme or topic, and as far as possible are stepped for difficulty with more closed, straightforward questions, requiring a short answer early on and more open questions allowing longer, freer responses as the whole question unfolds. Higher tier questions will have more opportunities for writing in extended prose (that is, more than two sentences) as more of the latter type of question parts are set. Shorter answer questions will be at their most frequent on the Foundation Tier. These questions may be directly based on stimulus-resource material (this is, maps, diagrams, tables, photographs, etc.). Make sure that you use this data to the full when the question refers you to it or when the data contains information which can help your answer. Always study the data given carefully and thoroughly.

The more open, longer response question parts require you also or only to use your own knowledge learned from your course in geography and hopefully brought with you into the exam. For instance, case studies and examples should be introduced here. Many of these question parts are marked by an approach known as '**levels of response**' marking. You will be awarded a Level 1 mark if your answer shows a basic knowledge and/or understanding of the geography raised by the question. These answers are likely to be characterised by simple statements, brief descriptions, outline reasons, vague examples and perhaps a listing of points only, and will attract only a few marks. A higher quality Level 3 answer will get you full or nearly maximum marks. These will be good deep answers illustrated by examples studied, perhaps detailed case studies and giving full and well-argued reasons. There is scope for more extensive prose on higher tier papers. Developing and elaborating your answer with locational knowledge is one sure way of reaching a Level 3 mark. The marks available for a question part will be clearly indicated and this, together with the space left for your answer, should be taken as advice as to how much to write and how long to spend on that part. Those where Level 3 can be reached usually have at least 4–5 marks available.

One syllabus, NEAB A, has an objective items paper as was referred to earlier in this chapter. Answering successfully Type D exercises used by four syllabuses – London B, NEAB C and MEG B and C – calls on you to follow the advice just given on answering structured questions (they are assessed by such a paper), plus doing a little extra. Three of the four announce the title of the exercise early and issue an advance resources booklet, at least 2 weeks before the examination. You must, along with the help of your teacher, study and analyse these resources and their information, researching more information on the area of geography involved, and use them as a guide to the question paper to come. Pure recall of the information in the booklet will not be expected, but understanding will be. A copy of the booklet annotated by yourself cannot be taken into the examination room.

Examples of the four types will be used throughout this book.

▷ Making the grade

You will gain a particular grade when you reach the broad standard set for that grade. Papers are marked with great care, checked and re-checked. At the meeting where grades are decided, examiners with long experience judge where the borderlines between key grades such as C and D should be placed. Candidates getting a particular grade should expect to have reached a certain standard of 'USK' (understanding, skills and knowledge) in geography. Some of the abilities that candidates who get grades A, C and F are expected to display are given below. Use this information as a means of helping *you* to give the examiner what he or she is looking for, so that you end up with a good grade!

Grade A

▶   Candidates recall accurately detailed information about places and themes, across all scales, as required by the syllabus, and show detailed knowledge of location and geographical terminology.

▶   Candidates understand thoroughly geographical ideas as specified in the syllabus and apply their understanding to analyses of unfamiliar contexts. They understand thoroughly the way in which a wide range of physical and human processes interact to influence the development of geographical patterns, the geographical characteristics of particular places, and the interdependence between places. They understand complex interrelationships between people and the environment. They evaluate the significance and effects of attitudes and values of those involved in geographical issues and in decision-making about the use and management of environments.

▶   Candidates undertake geographical enquiry, identifying relevant geographical questions, implementing an effective sequence of enquiry, collecting a range of appropriate evidence from a variety of primary and secondary sources, using effectively appropriate techniques, drawing selectively on geographical ideas to interpret the evidence, reaching substantiated conclusions, communicating clearly and effectively the outcomes, and evaluating the validity and limitations of the evidence and conclusions.

Grade C

▶ Candidates recall accurately information about places and themes, at a range of scales, as required by the syllabus, and show a broad knowledge of location and geographical terminology.

▶ Candidates understand geographical ideas as specified in the syllabus in a variety of physical and human contexts. They understand a range of physical and human processes and their contribution to the development of geographical patterns, the geographical characteristics of particular places, and the interdependence between places. They understand interrelationships between people and their environment. They understand the effects of attitudes and values of those involved in geographical issues and in decision-making about the use and management of environments.

▶ Candidates undertake geographical enquiry, identifying questions and issues, suggesting an appropriate sequence of enquiry, collecting appropriate evidence from a variety of primary and secondary sources, using a range of appropriate techniques, reaching a plausible conclusion, communicating the outcomes, and appreciating some of the limitations of the evidence and conclusions.

Grade F

▶ Candidates recall basic information about places and themes, at more than one scale, as required by the syllabus, and show an elementary level of knowledge of location and geographical terminology.

▶ Candidates understand some simple geographical ideas as specified in the syllabus in a particular context. They understand some simple physical and human processes and recognise that they contribute to the development of geographical patterns and the geographical characteristics of places. They understand some simple interrelationships between people and their environment. They show some awareness of the attitudes and values of people involved in geographical issues and in decision-making about the use and management of environments.

▶ Candidates undertake geographical enquiry, collecting and recording geographical evidence from primary and secondary sources, drawing simple maps and diagrams, communicating information and outcomes by brief statements, and recognising some of the limitations of the evidence.

Finally, remember that each of you will have *up to* an extra 5% of the total marks for each paper and for coursework added to your score for your spelling, punctuation and grammar. The quality of your written English language is judged as follows by the examiner:

Threshold performance (approximately 1–2% of total marks added)	Candidates spell, punctuate and use the rules of grammar with reasonable accuracy; they use a limited range of specialist terms appropriately.
Intermediate performance (approximately 3% of total marks added)	Candidates spell, punctuate and use the rules of grammar with considerable accuracy; they use a good range of specialist terms with facility.
High performance (approximately 4–5% of total marks added)	Candidates spell, punctuate and use the rules of grammar with almost faultless accuracy, deploying a range of grammatical constructions; they use a wide range of specialist terms adeptly and with precision.

Watch your language and try to write in your best English! Present your work attractively, paying attention to handwriting, spelling, punctuation and grammar. In your longer answers use short paragraphs and simple, straightforward sentences.

▷ Coursework

What is important in geography cannot always be measured by written papers alone. Some skills are best assessed in a continuous way rather than a few hours on the day of the examination. **Coursework** is mostly testing **skills**, as Table 1.4 for the SEG syllabus A shows; 15 of the 25 marks from coursework are for skills, many of which cannot be tested in a written paper. Allowing marks for coursework is fairer to students who might suffer from exam nerves, and rewards work achieved during the course when there are not the same time limits on you. We all know that timed written exams have strong elements of a lottery. You may have a heavy cold or period, or the examiner may set the 'wrong' questions for you! By the time you get to the final written exam in GCSE, you will already have some marks under your belt from the coursework, so you'll not be leaving your entire fate to the 'do-or-die' lottery of the exam.

Table 1.4 SEG Geography syllabus A

Objectives	Component			Total
	Written component one	Written component two	Coursework component	
Knowledge	12%	18%	—	30%
Understanding	11%	9%	10%	30%
Skills	17%	8%	15%	40%
Weighting of each component	40%	35%	25%	100%

All syllabuses have either 20 or 25% of the total marks for coursework. It is clearly a very important element in GCSE, and is generally a very effective means by which you can differentiate your abilities from those of your fellow students.

Coursework can be made suitable to your circumstances, abilities and interests, either by the teacher planning the work or by organising things so you can choose your own topic and method of investigation.

Do *complete* the necessary amount of coursework! You cannot afford to lose marks by leaving work unfinished. The GCSE examining groups generally do not insist that all the coursework asked for in the syllabus be submitted before a grade can be awarded, but don't throw marks away! Make sure you submit for assessment the complete works.

Being judged on work done during the course does put strains and pressures on you, especially if you are the industrious type. Some of you have an enormous amount of work which is very demanding on your time. You will need to be very *organised* and to allocate plenty of time to coursework. Don't panic and don't let it get you down!

You will need to learn to work independently, and to organise your time. Remember coursework will be completed in your *own* time. Know *exactly when* coursework must be given in! Then produce a '**deadline diary**' for yourself, entering the dates when each piece should be handed in. Include all your coursework in *all* your subjects. Parents can help with this diary or you can ask your teacher. Next, plan exactly *when* you are going to do each piece of work and set yourself **check dates** by which time you should have got to a certain point in your investigation. If you can keep up to date, then you may avoid conflict over the use of your time for other pieces of coursework, revision and your social life. To keep up to date, you will need to be able to *motivate yourself* to get down to work and keep at it, pacing yourself correctly. Good working habits and support from your parents (e.g. by providing funds and transport if you have to go out to collect the data for your fieldwork enquiry) are of enormous help. Try to arrange a shelf and/or a series of files at home where you can keep your coursework as it accumulates.

'Time spent on planning now will save time later on'

Coursework is marked by your own teacher, according to strict guidelines produced by the examining group. Table 1.5 is an outline example from the NEAB. The marks are then moderated by an examiner who re-assesses some or all of the work from your school or college. This ensures that the marks conform to standards elsewhere. The examiner will change your teachers' marks, if necessary, to that everyone's work is marked according to the same standards.

Table 1.5 The mark scheme for the geographical investigation in NEAB syllabus A

Assessment criteria	Marks
A Planning and organisation: how well the candidates handled the investigation as a whole, including problem identification and the generation of hypotheses.	9
B Observation, collection and recording of data, and sorting of secondary data.	12
C Classification and representation of the information using relevant techniques and presentation, and description of secondary data.	12
D The skills involving the interpretation of the transformed data and the ability to analyse and make judgements leading to valid conclusions.	24
E Spelling, punctuation and grammar.	3
Total marks	60

The number of pieces of coursework you must do varies from syllabus to syllabus. The syllabus summaries table in Chapter 2 (Table 2.1) shows that four of the twelve syllabuses (London A; NEAB A and B and NICCEA) ask for one piece, three (London B; MEG B and C) ask for two pieces, and the other five offer a choice of one or two pieces. Whether it is to be one or two pieces, your coursework must include a geographical investigation supported by at least two days' fieldwork, spent collecting 'first-hand' data in a small area, usually in your local environment.

Geographical enquiry

Geographical enquiry is a part of everyone's GCSE Geography course. The enquiry skills involved in planning and carrying out a fieldwork investigation are tested in all the syllabuses. Every syllabus asks you to complete at least one geographical investigation, which may either be teacher-directed and already planned in outline, or more of your own choosing. There are *six processes* through which you must go to complete an enquiry, this is often known as the *enquiry sequence* or the *scientific method*, because it is how scientists think and work. Sometimes it is called the **research design**, because it is the way in which researchers carry out their work. Coursework in GCSE Geography is largely about *you* going through each of these processes and the teacher and examiner assessing your performance in each enquiry skill.

'Become familiar with the six processes of geographical enquiry'

The six processes of the enquiry sequence of scientific method are as follows:

1   Identifying a problem or hypothesis or issue or question
2   Selecting appropriate methods
3   Collecting relevant data
4   Analysing the data
5   Interpreting the data
6   Reporting findings and conclusions

The enquiry approach is a means by which a question, problem, hypothesis, situation, conflict or issue can be investigated methodically in a series of steps, starting with a defined aim and progressing to a conclusion, taking into consideration the information gathered during the investigation.

Writing up

The list above shows the stages through which your investigation should go. Writing up your completed investigation should include the following seven sections:

1   **Title** e.g. 'Does our town need a by-pass?' 'Rivers flow faster the further they are from their source'.
2   **Aims** Explain in your own words *what* you are trying to discover.
3   **Methods** Describe *how* you collect the data, both field and secondary (see below); explain *why* you collected it; comment on its suitability.
4   **Presentation of data** Use a variety of techniques (e.g. tables, bar charts, averages, etc.) to illustrate your data or a selection drawn from it.

5   **Analysis and interpretation** What does the 'presentation section' suggest; are there any trends, deviations from trend, etc?

6   **Conclusion** Summarise your finding, relate back to your aims.

7   **Appendix** Include your rough fieldwork notes and a bibliography.

An investigation should be planned in this order and written up in this order, using these headings. It will be marked this way, as Table 1.5 above shows. The vast bulk of the geography coursework calls for **enquiry** work. Your teacher will tell you if any coursework does not require the enquiry approach. No investigation should be left *entirely* to you. You will need your teacher's guidance in selecting the investigation (when it is not a teacher-directed one) and in deciding what approach, surveys and data collection are necessary.

Characteristics of 'good' coursework

Generally speaking, good pieces of geography coursework will have the following in common:

It adopts the 'right' approach

Geography coursework should be investigated involving student enquiry. 'Look-see-describe' fieldwork reports, full of copied material and 'stick-ins', are out! We have shown what is meant by an enquiry approach. Your written-up study should be arranged in the seven sections shown above; which incorporates the elements considered in Table 1.5.

Start with an explanation of what you set out to try to do; then describe your methods; then present the data you collected in diagrams, maps, etc. (it is a good idea to put your original data in an appendix at the back of the study); include an analysis of your results where you interpret and discuss your data; finish with a conclusion which is linked to your original purpose behind the work. Writing the work up in this way will show the examiner that you have adopted an enquiry approach. Try to have a clear, snappy title, perhaps best written right at the end when the work is done and in the form of either a question, a hypothesis (i.e. a geographical statement) which testing will either prove or disprove, or a problem/issue. For example, inner city areas are deprived areas or the growth of retail parks/out-of-town shopping centres reflects our changing lifestyles.

Fig. 1.2 Route to fieldwork investigation (NEAB syllabus C)

Stage of production	Student activity
Identification of the issues or questions	Students or class discuss the feasibility and planning with their teacher
Preparation	Students write up their introduction
Primary data collection, observation, recording, sketching, mapping, etc. Selection and collation of data/information	Students or class carry out fieldwork, collate and select data/information Students provide evidence of their own fieldwork activity Individuals write up and evaluate method
Representation and communication of results	Students may seek teacher guidance Students represent and communicate their results
Analysis and interpretation of results	Students analyse, interpret and draw conclusions about their findings
Completion and review	Students organise and complete the work and review their findings

It is actually based on fieldwork

This is vital *where the syllabus calls for fieldwork enquiry*. You should check with your teacher whether fieldwork *is* required or not. **Fieldwork** means that you observe, collect and record your data yourself, outside the classroom; this data will be firsthand information, known as **primary data**. Filling in questionnaires in the street, or taking measurements on the bank of the river, produces primary data. **Secondary data** is that collected by other people so that it comes to you second hand. Information which you might take from a popu-

'Remember the definitions of primary and secondary data'

lation census, or from Meteorological Office weather records, can be used to *support* your primary data in a fieldwork enquiry, but to be a fieldwork enquiry there must be primary data with it! Some coursework for GCSE *can* be based on secondary data alone, but this will not then be a fieldwork investigation.

Such secondary source enquiries based on sources like directories, published maps, official statistics, etc. and conducted entirely in classrooms or at home make suitable second pieces of coursework where the syllabus calls for two pieces.

It includes the various types of geography which the examination board says it will give marks for

It will be impossible for you to gain the marks set aside for values or skills when these are missing from your coursework. Your overall coursework should incorporate a lot of practical skills work, including as many suitable techniques of presentation as possible, and some work which shows your understanding and awareness of people's values. Investigations which consider a conflict of interest between two groups of people, like residents and a business community, might fit the bill.

It is very largely your own work

It is important that both you and your teacher can *sign a declaration* that this is so. This should not stop you from regularly consulting your teacher about how a fieldwork investigation is coming along, about *what* you might do next, etc. Your teachers cannot do the work for you but they are there to help and guide you! Equally, it is quite acceptable for data to be collected in groups and for you then to pool and share it, providing the *rest* of the work – the presentation of the data, its analysis and the conclusions drawn from it – is your *own* personal work.

It is of a suitable length

It is quality rather than quantity that counts in GCSE! Syllabuses recommend that coursework should be kept down to between 2000 and 3000 words, including your maps and diagrams. This is no more than between eight and fifteen sides of A4 paper. You must not forget that though coursework studies should not be long in terms of pages of written work, they should be long in terms of *time you spend* on the work. Coursework does carry a large percentage of the final marks for the examination, at least 20%.

Submitting coursework

Finally, a word about the actual *submission* of your coursework. Try to make everything you submit as impressive to look at as possible. The presentation of your work is very important. Research has shown that examiners give the same work higher marks when it is written neatly and is legible, than when it is in a mess. Here are a few tips to help you to present your coursework decently:

1   Make sure each section is completed, and has a clear and proper heading.
2   Check that all maps and diagrams are correctly labelled and have a title, a key, a scale, etc.
3   Read the whole of your coursework through at least once, watching out for careless errors. Check that the introduction and conclusion describe the study accurately, that you have stated your findings clearly and that the points you make follow on from one another sensibly. Make sure that your work demonstrates what it is supposed to. Rewrite any bits you are unhappy with.

The different syllabuses and their central themes

▷ **GETTING STARTED**

This chapter looks at GCSE Geography generally across all the various syllabuses. Whichever syllabus you are following, it is essential that you work through it. We include a summary of the content, and the ways in which each of the syllabuses will be assessed. Make sure you know which syllabus you are studying!

All syllabuses will be assessed by a combination of written papers and coursework (fieldwork), but the nature of the written papers used and the requirements of the coursework are not the same in every syllabus. Syllabuses are also different in their content – the topics you study, and in the way in which you look at them. There are a number of different approaches to geographical study, but there are some common elements which all the syllabuses have to meet. This chapter deals with these, and they apply to all 12 standard GCSE syllabuses.

▷ **WHAT YOU NEED TO KNOW**

▷ **The central themes of GCSE Geography**

You will studying one of twelve standard syllabuses, IGCSE or one of a number of short course versions. Geography is a broad subject which can be approached slightly differently depending upon which syllabus you are studying. Nevertheless, all syllabuses have to meet the National Criteria, the government guidelines for learning and assessing geography which try to answer questions like; what is important in school geography? and; how can your achievements in these important aspects of the subject be best measured?

All syllabuses have to:

1   deal with ideas, issues and places and the links between them

Fig. 2.1

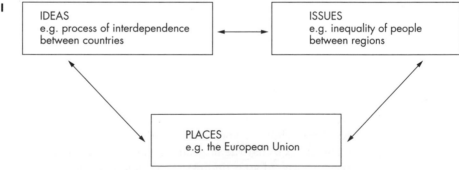

2   cover physical, human and environmental geography in a balanced way

Fig. 2.2

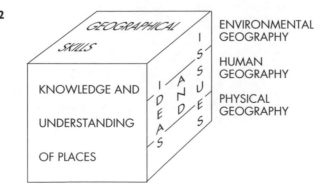

3   study the interrelationships/interaction between people and the environment

4   show that geographers study change and difference, and that different places offer people different opportunities, challenges and constraints

5   study examples set within the UK, other areas of the European Union, other MEDCs (more economically developed countries) and within LEDCs (less economically developed countries)

6   study the characteristics and interdependence of places (e.g. what is the place like? why is it like that? how is it changing?) and the interlinking of business activity across the world

7   cover examples at each of the five scales in geography (global – world-wide patterns; international – between countries; national – a whole country; regional – a large area within a country; local – in a small area within a region)

8   develop geographical vocabulary, i.e. terms

9   study attitudes, values, conflicts and decisions about how environments are used and managed

10   developed map and diagram skills, consolidate the geographical enquiry skills developed in National Curriculum Key Stage 3, and study in a way which links them with places and geographical themes (ideas and issues).

Fig. 2.3

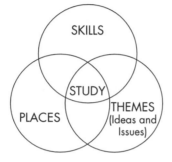

These are the central themes of GCSE Geography which you should all understand. They are common to all GCSE Geography syllabuses.

▷ What makes a GCSE Geographer?

You can see that GCSE Geography courses deal with the real world. Geography is real, alive, and relevant to what goes on around us all of the time, whether in the newspapers, on the television, or in the community we live in. Most problems, themes and issues in life have a *geographical* aspect to them, that is they have a *spatial* aspect. Put another way, they have a *location in space* over the earth's surface, and may have a *pattern of distribution* over the earth. Geography is largely about those modern problems and burning issues which have a major geographical (spatial) slant. To do well in GCSE Geography you need to learn to think as a geographer and see the world as geographers do. Geography is a *way of viewing* the earth's surface; something you should be learning to do during your GCSE course. This list of central themes of GCSE Geography above gives examples of the way in which geographers think. It is a thinking subject and not a descriptive, factual 'quiz programme' subject. Locating places on maps might be a popular image of what geographers do, but the subject is so much more than spatial general knowledge. Geography has changed.

Facts in GCSE Geography are no less important than ideas and skills, as Chapter 1 clearly shows. To do well you must learn some facts about different places. Geography is a study of places, as the central themes list indicates. It is fine knowing about differences in lifestyles between MEDCs and LEDCs and being able to describe what it is like to live in say Calcutta, but you must also know *where* Calcutta is.

The 'graphy' of geography means the graphic means of communicating our knowledge and understanding of the *earth*, which in turn is the 'geo' of geography! Graphic communication is absolutely essential in GCSE. Geography is about maps as well as chaps! Maps are spatial drawings of the earth as the home of people; map-making is the geographer's very own skill. Geography would, in fact, not be geography without maps and a number of other skills, collectively called **graphicacy** – i.e. landscape drawings, ground photographs, air photographs, plans, diagrams, etc. These are used to *present and analyse* locations, patterns of distribution, movements of population, land use and weather.

Geography is a very broad subject which bridges the humanities and the sciences. The National Criteria lay down that all GCSE syllabuses should have **human**, **physical** and **environmental** elements. Topics which link and integrate human and physical geography fit well in GCSE. Central theme 3, given earlier, is about the spatial relationships between human activities and the physical or natural environment. For instance, around Mt St Helens in the USA, the scene of the volcanic eruption in 1980, the *physical* environment influences people's activities considerably. On the other hand, in the inner areas of large cities, *people* attempt to control an environment which *they* have created. In GCSE you should try to take a whole view; human and physical aspects together. Geography will help you make sense of the confusing world in which you live by enabling you to understand certain fundamental concepts. It should constantly remind you that we not only depend upon the natural environment and the earth's resources, but also upon other people and other countries. The economic well-being of all countries depends on their ability to trade goods and services internationally. Individual people, groups of people and countries are all **interdependent**. GCSE Geography expects you to realise that we are all citizens of the same world, so that our own lives influence and are influenced by conditions and events in other parts of the world. Chopping down the rainforests of the Tropics will affect every single one of us! GCSE Geography should help you to develop a **global** view of the world as well as to deal with more parochial (local) matters.

Being a good geographer in the late 1990s and beyond means being interested in *anything* you see, hear or read about the things that are happening to places and environments. Your answers in the written examination will be all the better for references to recent events reported in newspapers, on the television, etc. Geography teaches about living and is a good preparation for adult and working life in our rapidly changing world. It can be a particularly useful preparation for life in *multi-cultural Britain* and a *multi-ethnic world*. Avoiding bias, stereotyping of people, discrimination and racial prejudice are clear intentions of GCSE.

In GCSE Geography you will investigate *questions* about the world and society which require *solutions* which must be found by *people*. This is one good reason why I teach it! Questions of an environmental nature might include how we should manage the earth's resources. Seeking solutions to such questions involves taking *decisions*, which inevitably brings into play certain *values*, *attitudes* and *feelings*. Everyone holds certain 'values' to be important, whether they are those *making* the decisions or those people *affected* by the decisions. Considering the values and attitudes which various people hold is an important part of GCSE Geography. In real life all decisions have benefits and costs, winners and losers. Few decisions can avoid an element of *conflict*, with groups supporting one outcome and other groups opposing it. GCSE Geography brings this whole aspect of 'values' and 'conflict' into the forefront of discussion. Values and attitudes questions fall into the understanding type of assessment objective. The three types of assessment objective/ability – USK (Understanding, Skills and Knowledge) – were introduced in Chapter 1.

▷ The different GCSE Geography syllabuses

Below are summaries of the main features of 12 standard GCSE syllabuses, the IGCSE and 5 short courses in geography (Table 2.1). Pick out the syllabus you are studying and take a special note of the features stated.

Table 2.1 Syllabus summaries

SYLLABUS	LONDON A	LONDON B	MIDLAND (MEG) A	MIDLAND (MEG) B (AVERY HILL) / also WELSH JEC B
The approach to Geography	Based on key ideas within units and themes. Core and optional element of both key ideas and units.	Based on key ideas and environmental issues within units and themes.	Based on broad key ideas and expressed as topics and headings within units. Each heading has a required context for study.	Key idea-based, some issue-based and expressed as key questions within units. Skills emphasised.
The content of the syllabus	Two units in each of four broad Themes (A–D), each with required studies at a specified scale: A People and places A1 Population A2 Settlement B People and work B3 Agriculture B4 Industry C Landscapes: Challenge and Management C5 Valley landscapes C6 Coastal landscapes D Environmental systems D7 Climate, weather and water D8 Soils, vegetation and ecosystems	Units within four themes, each with required studies: 1 Issues in natural environments 1.1 Drainage basin 1.2 Coastal management 1.3 Environmental hazards 2 Issues in rural environments 2.1 Primary activities 2.2 Recreation 2.3 Rural–urban links 3 Issues in economic development 4 Issues in urban environments 4.1 Their internal structure 4.2 Urban journeys 4.3 Population changes	Four units with eleven topics: 1 People and the physical world: Plate tectonics; rivers; coasts. 2 People and places to live: Population; settlement. 3 People and their needs: Qualify of life; economic activities; energy. 4 People and the environment: Resource development and the local environment; management of environments; global environment.	Four units containing eleven sections: 1 Climate, the environment and people. Weather and climate; natural environments; an issue of international/global concern. 2 Water, landforms and people. Hydrosphere; natural landforms; study of a distinctive landform. 3 People and place. Inequalities in urban areas; improving urban environments; urban–rural interaction. 4 People, work and development. Patterns of work and development; work and development process.
How you will be assessed overall	Two written papers and coursework. Paper 1 (Foundation) or Paper 3 (Higher): 1 hour for 25% testing core key ideas from A1 to C6. Short answer questions with no choice. Use of OS map extract. Paper 2 (F) or Paper 4 (H): 2 hours for 50% testing core and optional key ideas in either A1 or A2, B3 or B4, C5 or C6 and D7 or D8. Answer 4 of 8 long structured questions.	Two written papers and coursework. Paper 1 (Foundation) or Paper 3 (Higher): 2 hours for 50% total marks on a no-choice paper of three short structured questions and three long structured questions. Paper 2 (F) or Paper 4: a 1¼ hour decision-making exercise carrying 25% of marks and based on an issue in a pre-examination resource booklet. Second copy issued in examination.	Two written papers and coursework. Paper 1 (Foundation) or Paper 2 (Higher) lasting 2 hours. For 45% of total marks. Answer four questions, one from the two set on each unit. Paper 3 (F) or Paper 4 (H) lasting 1¼ hours for 30% of assessment. A no-choice, two questions paper assessing skills, including OS mapwork.	Two written papers and coursework. Paper 1 (Foundation) or Paper 2 (Higher) carry 45% of total assessment and are 1¾ or 2 hours long respectively. Assesses three of four units by answering one stepped question of two from each of three units. Paper 3 (F) or Paper 4 (H) carry 30% of assessment and are 1½ or 1¾ hours long respectively. A compulsory stepped problem-solving exercise on an issue derived from the fourth and previously announced unit.
The assessment of coursework	One fieldwork investigation (Paper 5) of around 2500–3000 words on a syllabus topic in the form of a question, issue, relationship, problem or hypothesis. Investigation to be teacher-assessed and externally moderated for 25% according to five criteria. There are no tiers for coursework which is targeted at all grades.	Two coursework items (Paper 5) based on different key ideas. Item A must be fieldwork-based (up to 15 hours total work) though item B can be fieldwork and/or secondary data-based (up to 10 hours work). Teacher-assessed and externally moderated for 25% (15% item A and 10% item B) using four assessment criteria. There are no tiers for coursework which is targeted at all grades.	Either one longer or two shorter pieces totalling up to 3000 words and supported by fieldwork. Carries 25% assessment and must be investigative in the form of a question, assertion or hypothesis, and relate to syllabus content. Teacher-assessed and board-moderated against three marking criteria.	Two pieces required, one fieldwork-based and together worth 25% of assessment. The first known as the Study carries 15% of total marks and should be a hypothesis investigation. The second known as the Cross-Unit Task carries 10% of total marks and should synthesise units, especially human and physical geography through an appropriate research, problem-solving or decision-making exercise. Teacher-assessed and board-moderated according to a Knowledge-Understanding-Skills mark scheme.

Table 2.1 (cont)

SYLLABUS	MIDLAND (MEG) C (BRISTOL PROJECT)	NORTHERN (NEAB) A	NORTHERN (NEAB) B	NORTHERN (NEAB) C
The approach to Geography	Key issues and ideas written as questions for enquiry within themes and sub-themes.	Concept-based with concepts expressed in three interrelated themes as key ideas under topic headings. Each idea can be studied at a range of scales.	Essential place-specific with prescribed places and spatial areas at various scales linked by five interrelated themes.	Focuses entirely on stated contemporary geographical issues. Each issue studied in an effect-cause-management sequence (key questions).
The content of the syllabus	Five themes containing sixteen sub-themes: 1 Physical systems and environments: Geomorphic processes and landforms; Atmospheric processes and climate; physical environments and systems. 2 Natural hazards and people: Nature and distribution of hazards; processes responsible for hazards; effects of hazards on people. 3 Economic systems and development: Economic systems; economic activity, growth and change; international disparities, trade and interdependence. 4 Population and settlement: Population distribution, structure and change; location and function of settlements; land use within settlements; growth and decline of settlements. 5 People's use of the earth: Earth's resources; exploitation and management of natural resources; resolving issues.	Nine topics within three themes are: 1 Challenge of urban environments: A Patterns and processes of growth B Patterns of land use C Dynamism D Challenge of change 2 Managing natural environments: A Environmental systems B Managing the living world 3 Impact of economic change: A What is economic change? B Changes in location of economic activity C Economic growth and decline	Five themes of: Physical geography; Economic activity; Transport and trade; Population and settlement, and Environmental issues studied within the following regions of the following three prescribed areas: • The UK – Lake District; East Anglia; M4 corridor. • The European Union – S. Italy; Ruhr; Mediterranean Spain; Rotterdam; Rhine. • The Wider World – Amazonia; Ganges Delta; Japan.	Eighteen issues grouped into six Key Areas: A Natural hazards: Unstable plate margins; storms, river floods. B Fragile environments: Deforestation; soil damage; threatened landscapes. C Population issues: Famine and starvation; ageing; international migration. D Urban issues: Rural-urban fringe pressures; inner cities; transport. E Resource issues: Water supply; resource depletion; UK power generation. F Development issues: Inequality; swing to services; new agricultural revolution.
How you will be assessed overall	Two written papers and coursework. Paper 1 (F) or Paper 2 (H) for 50% of total marks and lasting 2¼ hours. Answer two from three structured questions set in an EU/UK, LEDC and MEDC context and two questions from four set on Themes 1–4. Paper 3 (F) or Paper 4 (H) is a no-choice decision-making exercise worth 25% of total marks lasting 1½ hours and set on an issue related to Theme 5. Pre-examination resource booklet available.	Two written papers and coursework. Paper 1 of 1 hour for 25% of marks at either Tier F (50 objective test questions) or Tier H (60 objective test questions). Paper 2 of 2 hours for 50% of marks at either Tier F or H. No-choice structured question paper.	Two written papers and coursework. Paper 1 of 1½ hours for 35% of marks at either Tier F or Tier H comprising four no-choice structured questions on UK including OS mapwork. Paper 2 of 2 hours for 40% of marks at either Tier F or H comprising five no-choice structured questions, including a global scale question.	Two written pages and coursework. Paper 1 of 1½ hours for 25% of marks at either Tier F or Tier H consisting of an issues evaluation exercise of short-answer and structured questions devised from an advance information booklet. Paper 2 for 50% of marks at either Tier F or Tier H (1½ hours or 1¾ hours respectively) comprising six long structured questions, one per Key Area. Choose three for answering.
The assessment of coursework	Two pieces required, together worth 25% of total marks. A geographical investigation supported by fieldwork for 15% and a coursework unit or a portfolio of coursework pieces (based on primary and/or secondary data) for 10%. Should be question-based for the following sub-themes: Geomorphic processes and landforms; land use within settlements; an environmental or planning issue. Teacher-assessed and board-moderated according to a Knowledge-Understanding-Skills and Application mark scheme.	One fieldwork-based small-scale geographical investigation based on a key idea and up to 2500 words in length. Can include secondary sources. Teacher-assessed with inspection of work by moderator for 25% of marks according to four criteria plus spelling, punctuation and grammar. The investigation will not be tiered for difficulty, and will be targeted at all grades.	One fieldwork-based small-scale geographical investigation related to any part or parts of syllabus and up to 2500 words in length. Can include secondary sources. Teacher-assessed with inspection of work by moderator for 25% of marks according to four criteria plus spelling, punctuation and grammar. The investigation will not be tiered for difficulty and will be targeted at all grades.	Either a single investigation involving fieldwork and decision-making of up to 3000 words based on an issue or question or one or two items both derived or developed from syllabus, one which involves fieldwork and the other decision-making (together no more than 3000 words). Teacher-assessed with inspection of work by moderator for 25% of marks according to six criteria plus spelling, punctuation and grammar. Coursework is not tiered for difficulty and will be targeted at all grades.

Table 2.1 (cont)

SYLLABUS	NORTHERN IRELAND (NICCEA)	SOUTHERN (SEG) A	SOUTHERN (SEG) B	WELSH JEC A
The approach to Geography	A thematic syllabus with predominantly 'physical' and predominantly 'human' themes presented as key ideas, some issued-based.	Based on key ideas within 'physical' Geography topics and 'human' Geography topics with interaction between them stressed as are geographical skills.	Based on key ideas and issues within themes and topics. Geographical skills and environmental awareness highlighted.	Based on key ideas/questions, some issue statements within topics and units. Each topic also expressed as specific learning outcomes.
The content of the syllabus	Three 'physical' themes: A Atmosphere B Earth's structure and landscape development C Ecosystems Three 'human' themes: D Population E Economic activity and development F Settlement Key ideas within each theme have specified locations for their study.	Seven 'physical' topics: 1 Tectonic activity 2 Rocks and landscapes 3 Rivers 4 Ice 5 Coasts 6 Weather and climate 7 Ecosystems Six 'human' topics: 1 Population 2 Settlement 3 Agriculture 4 Industry 5 Managing resources and tourism 6 Development and interdependence	Four topics with three themes in each: A People and urban change: Population distribution; towns and cities; migration and urban growth. B Leisure, recreation and tourism: Tourism and the economy; provision of leisure activities; management of recreation and tourist environments. C The physical environment: Atmospheric processes and climate; tectonic activity; water. D Economic development: Levels of development; changing levels of economic activity; economic and environmental pressures.	Two units, each divided into four topics: 1 The fragile world – physical systems and environmental issues. A Ice, rivers and the sea. B Weather and climate patterns. C Physical–human interactions and their management. D Exploitation of fragile environments. 2 The interdependent world – economic activities, global inequalities and places. A Changing patterns of economic activity and their consequences. B Urban development. C Global trade interdependence. D Global inequalities in population and resources.
How you will be assessed overall	Two written papers and coursework. Paper 1 of 1½ hours for 40% of total assessment at Foundation Tier or Higher Tier. Comprises three compulsory multi-part questions, one on each of the three 'physical' themes. Paper 2 of 1½ hours for 40% of total assessment at F or H Tier. Comprises three compulsory multipart questions, one on each of the three 'human' themes.	Two written papers and coursework. Paper 1 of 2 hours carrying 40% of total marks at Foundation or Higher Tier. Comprises two sections: A – Geographical Skills including OS mapwork; and B – answer three from seven short structured questions on 'physical' topics. Paper 2 of 1½ hours for 35% of marks with six long structured questions on 'human' topics at F Tier or H Tier. Choose three to answer – Topic 1 or 2, 3 or 4 and 5 or 6 as above.	Two written papers and coursework. Paper 1 of 1½ hours for 25% of marks at F Tier or H Tier. A skills-based paper including an OS map extract and involving decision-making on a pre-released theme. No-choice structured questions. Paper 2 of 2 hours for 50% of total assessment at Foundation or Higher Tier. Four longer structured questions, one per topic set; all four questions to be answered.	Two written papers and coursework. Paper 1 of 1¾ hours for 40% of total marks at Foundation or Higher Tier. Four compulsory, structured questions assessing Unit 1 (The fragile world) content. Paper 2 of 1¾ hours for 40% of total marks at F or H Tier. Four compulsory, structured questions assessing Unit 2 (The interdependent world) content.
The assessment of coursework	One fieldwork-based investigative study of up to 2500 words worth 20% of total assessment, and involving decision-making, problem-solving or hypothesis-testing. Teacher-assessed and moderated externally by the council using four assessment criteria. Entry tiers not applicable to coursework generally but work undertaken to be appropriate to each individual's ability.	Either a fieldwork investigation of 2000–2500 words or a shorter fieldwork investigation and an additional coursework item (may be secondary source-based) totalling 2000–2500 words. Worth 25% of total marks and may be 'physical', 'human' or both, and for fieldwork must be a local/small-scale investigation of an argument, problem or assertion. Teacher-marked and board-moderated according to five criteria plus spelling, punctuation and grammar. Coursework common to both tiers but to be appropriate to student's ability.	Either a fieldwork investigation of 2000–2500 words or a shorter fieldwork investigation and an additional coursework item (may be secondary source-based) totalling 2000–2500 words. Worth 25% of total marks and may be 'physical', 'human' or both, and for fieldwork must be a local/small-scale investigation of an argument, problem or assertion. Teacher-marked and board-moderated according to five criteria plus spelling, punctuation and grammar. Coursework common to both tiers but to be appropriate to student's ability.	Choice of three coursework submissions. Either: 1 One full investigation involving fieldwork and secondary data, or 2 a main fieldwork investigation and a smaller secondary-source investigation, or 3 a main secondary-source investigation and a smaller teacher-led field investigation, stemming from any part of syllabus. Total length of 2000–2400 words expected for 20% of total marks. Teacher-assessed and moderated by the council on the basis of six criteria. Coursework is common to all students though the work needs to be suited to the student.

▷ **Place knowledge**

Knowing case studies and examples of places, which illustrate where the key ideas and issues around which your syllabus and the examination papers are written, is at the very core of your GCSE Geography. Only NEAB syllabus B is place-specific and sets the places and areas which you must study; all the other syllabuses allow you and your teacher to choose your own areas to illustrate the ideas and issues. NEAB syllabus B papers will have questions set on the Lake District, East Anglia, the M4 corridor of the UK, Southern Italy, the Ruhr, Mediterranean Spain, Rotterdam, the Rhine, Amazonia, Japan and the Ganges Delta of India. Studies within these areas will be included throughout this book. All syllabuses insist that your studies of places should be at a range of scales from local to global, within the UK and European Union, and within LEDCs (less economically developed countries) and other MEDCs (more economically developed countries).

Local area to global scale studies

One thing all the syllabuses have in common is that the content must be spread over five **scales** from the **small** or **local** scale throughout the **regional**, **national** and **international** scales, to the **world** scale. All syllabuses state in their introduction that work at a variety of scales is essential, ranging from local to global. Your course will have included studies of a range of different environments and studies of areas of varying size (i.e. a variety of scales), from a small area, perhaps your local home area, to studies of distributions on a world map. These are the two extremes of scale.

Fig.2.4

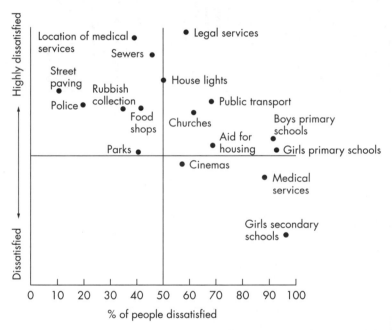

Your coursework should have provided first-hand experience of a local environment, perhaps either the immediate environment of your school or home, or a small area visited on a field course. Everyone must have conducted a first-hand study of a small (local) area.

The written examination will use material from all five scales. Fig. 2.4 which refers to a shanty town around Lima, Peru, is an example of the small or local scale in geography. Fig. 2.5 on the other hand, which shows the earthquake and volcano belts of the world, is an example of the **global** scale.

Examples of the three scales between these two extremes might be:

▶   **Regional** scale the development of high-tech industries in the so-called M4 corridor in England
▶   **National** scale government influence on the location of industry in Britain
▶   **International** scale trading patterns between MEDCs and LEDCs.

Remember the five scales in geography, and try to bring these into your work.

In the written papers you will need to be able to draw on examples at each scale. Candidates tend not to do this well, especially at scales beyond the local. Make sure you know *actual* case studies at a *variety of scales*. Work through this book and your notes,

'Remember the five scales in geography, and try to bring these into your work'

Fig.2.5

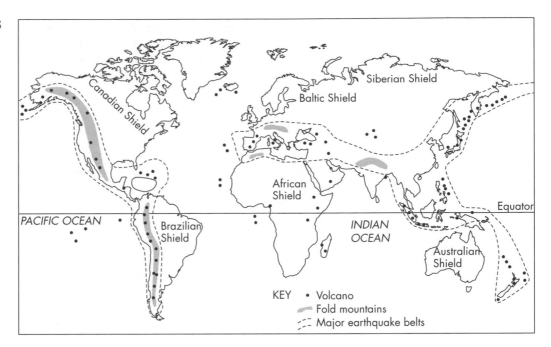

making a list of those case studies and maps which are at each of the five scales. The factors which influence people's activities can actually change from one scale to another: for example, at larger scales, such as the global, international and national, **farming** is strongly influenced by **climate**. However at the small, local scale, how farmers use their land is determined by **relief** of the land, e.g. its slope, or the **location** of the land, how near the land is to a large city or port. Make sure you can identify instances where you have studied a topic at *more than one* scale, and that you can pinpoint how various factors can *change* with scale.

Studies within the United Kingdom and European Union

All the syllabuses include studies set in the context of the UK and European Union. Studies will be of both the **physical environment** (e.g. climate) and **human geography** (e.g. population, agriculture, industry, communications, etc). Make sure though that your geography is not too 'Eurocentric' (not too European) and that you *do* have some knowledge of developments and places *outside* Britain and Western Europe.

Some of the examples and case studies in your geography course, and some of the resource material presented to you on the examination papers, will come from a variety of locations within the UK. GCSE expects you to have a reasonable working knowledge of your home country. For example:

▶ the location of its main regions, cites and relief areas (hills and low lands);
▶ the pattern of population, industry and transport facilities (i.e. the places where population and industry are more, or less, concentrated);
▶ specific examples throughout your course (e.g. differences in the environment and quality of life for residents of inner city and outer city suburban areas, etc.).

Ensure that you both 'know your way around Britain' and can give the examiner specific examples within Britain of aspects of geography such as settlement, population, etc. Being able to do this will benefit your performance enormously; it is a weak point with many candidates. Working through maps of Britain in an atlas, an AA book, etc., would be a good use of your time. It would also be a good idea to use some of the revision techniques mentioned in Chapter 1, such as making summaries, on the examples and case studies from Britain in your notes. Remember that these studies should be of a contrasting nature. For example, you only need one case study of a new industrial area with its high-tech industries and one study of an arable farming area in Britain. Repeating the same geographical thinking is a waste of your time.

Your course of geography will also need to have considered the United Kingdom's relationships with the wider world. Our trading relationships with the other member countries of the EU (European Union), and the development of the Common Agricultural Policy within the EU, are examples. They are also examples of geography on the international scale. Studying the British Isles provides examples of geography on the regional and national scales. Equally, if you have studied Britain's foreign aid to LEDCs or our trade with a country like India, the central themes of geography listed earlier in this chapter are being dealt with. These themes are clearly linked.

LEDCs and MEDCs

The terms LEDC (less developed) and MEDC (more economically developed country) will occur regularly throughout all GCSE Geography papers.

GCSE aims to encourage an understanding of different cultures and environments. It wants you to have a *balanced* view of the world, which means you should have studied the geography of the more economically developed world (the Western world) and the less economically developed world (countries in Africa, Asia and South America, some in the British Commonwealth and others having little direct contact with Britain). You will need to know and understand the differences, similarities and relationships between these two blocks of the world, and be prepared to answer questions testing this knowledge and understanding. Your work on Britain provides geography from the 'developed' world.

There are important *relationships* between the MEDCs and the LEDCs, and you must appreciate this. MEDCs provide financial aid for the development programmes of LEDCs. MEDCs and LEDCs trade with each other, and some geographers believe that these trading relationships, both now and in the past, are a *cause* of some countries being LEDCs. You must know something abut LEDCs, such as what makes them less economically developed, and the ways in which you can measure this (e.g. GNP per head; quality of life; see Chapter 9). You need to know something about their transport facilities, their population and their agriculture, and how particular industries compare with those in MEDCs, and perhaps with those in other LEDCs. You must know about the problems of development, such as population growth and rural to urban migration. Chapters 10 to 15 will help cover many of these aspects. *Detailed* knowledge of one LEDC, e.g. Brazil, will help. You can then take many of your *examples* of the various aspects of geography from that country (population, towns and cities, agriculture, etc.) and use them in the examination. Going into more detail on one country may be a useful piece of homework for you to do, with the help of library books, and other sources recommended by your teacher. Build up some good geographical case studies for the less economically developed world.

'Detailed knowledge of a particular country will give you lots of examples for illustration'

Clearly, the significant differences that can be observed in the level of economic and technological development *between* countries and *within* countries, are vital issues in the modern world. There are 'pockets of poverty' in MEDCs and 'pockets of prosperity' in LEDCs. Do not think that life for *everyone* in LEDCs is materially poor and primitive. Again, do not think that people living in these countries are always unhappy and culturally poor! Much of this book will look at the various contrasts and comparisons that can be made between countries in various states of economic development.

▷ **The interrelationship of physical and human geography**

All GCSE syllabuses must contain **physical** and **human** elements, as Fig. 2.6 shows, and study the interaction between the two. Topics which focus attention on people's relationship with the environment occur in all syllabuses and occupy chapters in this book, e.g. Chapter 7 on Natural Hazards and People. Agriculture too (Chapter 10) is partly about people–environment relationships. GCSE syllabuses take this theme as one of their most essential ones. Their approach to geography emphasises the relationship between people and their whole environment. Human and physical geography are therefore viewed as integrated components and not as separate parts within the syllabus. The reference to *whole* environment suggests that there are important people-human environment relationships to study, e.g. those between people and the people-made environment of inner city areas.

One of the important things about geography is that it *does* study these links between people and their environment. The idea of a relationship often involves a cause and an effect. In geography these relationships or links are two-way affairs. For example, the environment affects people (e.g. the environment around volcanoes strongly influences the lifestyle of those living close by); and people affect the environment (e.g. in city areas people have some control over their environment). Many students have difficulty in grasping the many relationships between factors which are part of geography. Relationships or links, with one factor affecting another, are at the very core of geography. Most of the physical geography that does occur in GCSE is studied in the context of people–physical environment relationships. As Chapter 5 shows, rivers are not studied solely for their own sake but because they have uses and applications for people, e.g. water supply. Take the topics covered in Chapters 3–15 and try to appreciate how people–environment relationships will be involved in each.

Natural physical environments, such as river flood plains and deltas, present both hazards and difficulties, and offer opportunities and advantages for human activities. They can be used and misused, may be fragile and vulnerable, and may need protecting and managing. Such environmental issues are matters of great concern around the world and are addressed by GCSE Geography. Geography deals with both the natural (physical) and the human world and the interrelationships between them. Environmental geography, a key theme in all GCSE syllabuses, comes from this interrelationship, as Fig. 2.6 shows.

▷ Map, graphical and enquiry skills

These skills are one of the central themes of GCSE Geography. GCSE prizes highly the development and the assessment of skills, with at least 30%, and often nearer to 40% of the final marks being allocated to them. The ability:

1   to *extract and use* geographical information from maps, graphs, diagrams and pictorial material; and
2   to *communicate* geographical information using maps, graphs, diagrams and pictorial material

is essential if you are to get a good result. Maps, graphs, diagrams, photographs and handling of data are the *tools* of the geographer's trade. They will appear in every longer GCSE examination question.

To learn *how* to do something is to learn a skill. Skills have to be *acquired* and then *practised*, but not in isolation from the rest of your geography course. Skills have to be *combined* with factual knowledge and with an understanding of ideas and values. The examination will test your ability to *use* these skills by asking you both to *draw* your own maps and diagrams, and to *interpret and analyse* other people's.

Maps, diagrams and photographs are tools used by geographers as part of the sequence of geographical enquiry. They enquire into geographical questions and issues by collecting evidence, including from maps, graphs and photographs; recording and presenting it in other maps and diagrams; describing, analysing and interpreting the evidence before drawing conclusions and communicating findings.

Some of the map and graphical skills shown in the second column of Table 2.2 involve the ability to present information clearly and concisely in appropriate graphical form. You may decide which form to use and then construct the relevant map, diagram or graph. You may also have to incorporate data into existing graphs by completing them. Other skills involve the ability to translate maps, graphs and tables of statistics into words. Extracting relevant information from a map or photograph, providing evidence of change, identifying patterns and relationships, is a skill that is required.

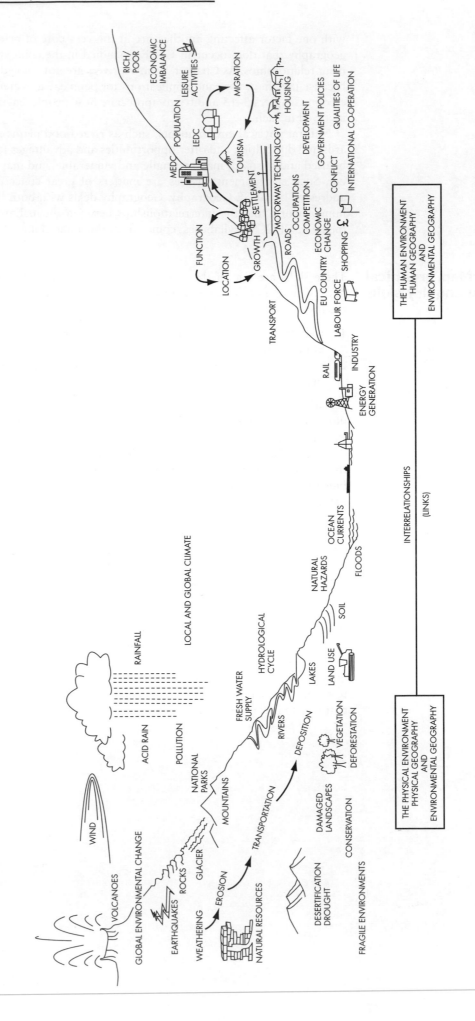

Fig.2.6

Table 2.2 Map, graphical and enquiry skills

Enquiry Skills	Associated Techniques and Map and Graphical Skills

Investigative skills – ability to make use of a variety of sources for obtaining information	▶ Data Collection:
	
	  1 through fieldwork (primary data)
	  2 from film, video, photographs, journals, reports, maps, at various scales, statistical data and graphs (secondary sources).

Communication skills – ability to present information in a clear and appropriate way to describe geographical distributions	▶ Transformation of data into:
	
	  1 graphs (line, simple and divided bar, pie, star, radials, triangular, scatter)
	  2 maps (sketch; choropleth; isopleth; flowline; topological) of various scales and annotate accordingly.
	▶ Communicating through speech and writing
	▶ Communicating landscape sketching (sketching skills)
	▶ Audio-visual materials (film, video, photographs, computers).

Interpretative skills – ability to give meaning to data	▶ Interpretation of data from:
	  1 graphs (line, simple and divided bar, pie, radial, triangular, scatter, star)
	  2 maps at a variety of scales:
	    (a) OS (especially 1:50 000 scale) using map symbols, compass directions, grid references, distance measurement, area estimations, cross-sections and landform recognition from contour patterns;
	    (b) simple weather maps, e.g. depressions and contour patterns, anticyclones from simple isobaric patterns;
	    (c) media maps, e.g. those found in newspapers;
	    (d) location maps, e.g. zones in a city;
	    (e) route maps and plans, e.g. road maps;
	    (f) publicity maps, e.g. those produced by an Enterprise Zone;
	    (g) simple geological maps and soil profile diagrams
	    (h) satellite images.
	The maps (b) and (h) above, might use a range of different techniques such as sketch maps, topological maps, choropleth maps, isopleth maps.
	  3 the analysis of documentary evidence, e.g. old maps, photographs (vertical and oblique, aerial and satellite), advertisements, questionnaires. Photograph skills used in association with OS maps.

Evaluative skills – ability to analyse critically and interpret evidence and to formulate valid conclusions Problem-solving skills – the ability to enquire, to think clearly, critically and constructively and make decisions based on evidence Conceptualising skills – the ability to organise information, to form a concept or generalisation Hypothesising skills – the ability to use hypotheses to predict, assess trends and evidence to make judgements.	These enquiry skills may be regarded as 'understanding' by the examiners. The practical skills above can only be 'skills'.

Graphs

Make sure that you can draw and interpret the following types of graph:

▶ line graphs
▶ pie graphs
▶ triangular graphs
▶ bar graphs (including divided ones)
▶ radial graphs
▶ scattergraphs

Practise your graph skills on the practice exercises numbered 1 to 9 later. Some involve translating graphs in the words when questions are asked about a completed graph. Here are examples of three of the less straightforward types of graph – triangular, radial and scatter – completed and ready for interpretation into words.

The **triangular** graph in Fig. 2.7 shows the percentage of workers in each of the main sectors of industry in selected countries in 1995.

Fig. 2.7

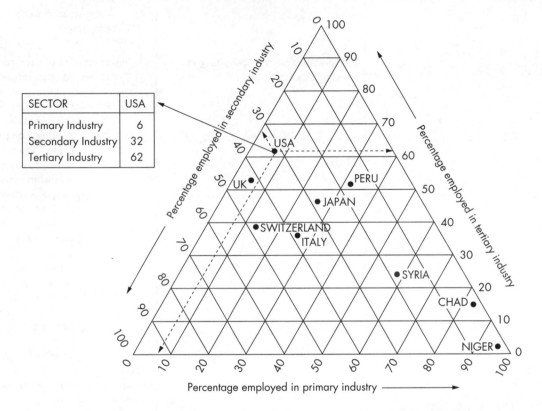

SECTOR	USA
Primary Industry	6
Secondary Industry	32
Tertiary Industry	62

The **radial** graphs in Fig. 2.8, each at a different scale, show the distances travelled by people to three leisure facilities: a sports centre, a Country Park and a National Park. Each line represents a journey made by one visitor.

Fig. 2.8

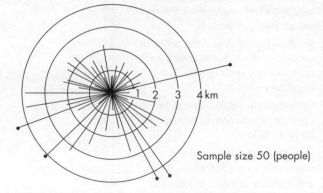

Distances travelled to a sports centre in town

Sample size 50 (people)

Fig. 2.8 *(cont)*

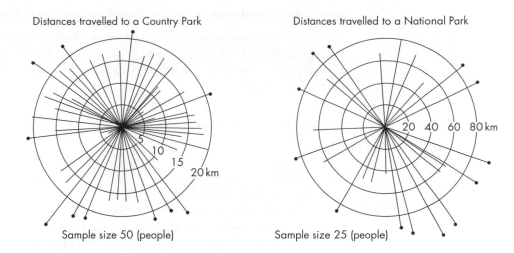

Distances travelled to a Country Park

Distances travelled to a National Park

Sample size 50 (people)

Sample size 25 (people)

The **scattergraph** in Fig. 2.9 shows the size of population and numbers of shops in each of eight villages.

Fig. 2.9

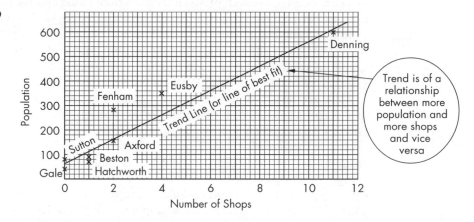

Drawing sketch maps

In the examination it is a good idea to draw sketch maps (Fig. 2.10) whenever possible and to try to stick to the following good habits: clear and simple; neatly drawn; clearly labelled; uses reasonably accurate scale and directions; uses a key; has a frame.

Fig. 2.10

'Checklist for your sketch map'

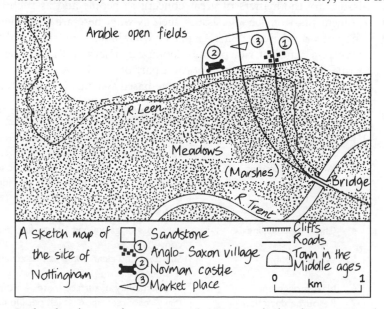

Is the sketch map shown in Fig. 2.10 a 'good' sketch map? Use the points mentioned above as a 'checklist' for assessing the sketch map.

Interpreting and analysing aerial and ground-level photographs

As with an Ordnance Survey map you may be asked to extract evidence from a photograph in order to answer a question the examiner has set. Try to obtain a past paper which used a photograph from your teacher. Have a go at looking for the photographic evidence to answer the question.

Ordnance Survey maps

Ensure that you:

▶ can use the scale of the map and calculate distances;
▶ can give accurate compass directions;
▶ can both give grid references for places and find a place from its grid reference;
▶ have a reasonable knowledge of the main symbols used on OS maps, understand how contours and other indications of the height of the land can be used to draw cross-sections;
▶ can tell the slope of the land and recognise landforms such as valleys and hills.

Patterns and relationships can also be seen on OS maps. GCSE might ask you for map evidence of a relationship between the pattern of roads and the pattern of settlements in an area, or between the farming use of an area and its physical features.

In the examination many of these skills will be linked together. For example, a question may ask you to *extract* some information from a table of statistics and then present it as a graph; or you might be asked to *combine* various sources of information (e.g. sketch map, OS map, photograph) to support an argument.

'Practice is a vital part of developing map and diagram skills'

Skills are best revised by frequent practice. Practise on as many different types of maps and diagrams as you can, doing all the tasks set on them. This is an area of geography in which many candidates do well, especially with the simpler skills such as graph drawing and with the different data-response questions, where you are asked to state something from the data. Most GCSE questions will contain map and diagram skill tasks somewhere. Longer structured questions will normally be *introduced* by maps and/or diagrams, with the opening parts of the question asking you to use your simple skills on this data. More complex skills, e.g. interpreting a photograph, drawing a sketch map, will be tested *later* in the structured question. Some of the short-answer papers will test little other than skills. Care and accuracy are important when you are answering *all* skill questions.

Turn to p.33 to practise these skills in the exercises provided.

▶ **Values, issues and decision-making**

Issues are the matters of great concern to people and as such attract opinions and value judgements from people. Issues such as why there are fewer hedges marked on the latest map of a rural area of East Anglia, or what impact transnational companies have in LEDCs, involve a range of viewpoints. Looking at issues and analysing the relevant attitudes and values behind them is an important part of GCSE Geography.

Table 2.3 based on the NEAB's issue-based syllabus C lists 22 current issues and concerns

Table 2.3

Issue	Illustration
1 Unstable plate margins	Despite the risks people continue to live at plate margins, i.e. earthquakes; volcanoes.
2 Weather extremes	Extremes of weather continue to pose challenges for people in many parts of the world, e.g. hurricanes; unreliable rainfall.
3 River floods	Despite drainage basin management, and sometimes because of it, rivers flood.
4 Changing coastlines	Land loss or gain along a shoreline brings significant local consequences.
5 Water supply	Sufficient and clean water is not always available when and where it is needed.
6 Mass movement	The instability of surface materials can create a local hazard.
7 Resource depletion	Many resources upon which people depend are in danger of running out and need efficiently managing, e.g. waste and recycling.
8 Power generation	Environmental pollution results from the generation of electricity, energy debate; acid rain.

Table 2.3 (*cont*)

Issue	Illustration
9 Climate change	A changing climate, whether natural or artificial, requires human adjustment to new conditions.
10 Disappearing forests	There are significant local and global consequences of large-scale deforestation.
11 Soil damage	Soil erosion and desertification are mainly the result of land mismanagement.
12 Threatened landscapes	Attractive natural landscapes are threatened by increasing tourist pressure, e.g. honeypots; National Parks.
13 Famine and starvation	Continued population growth threatens food supplies and living standards in LEDCs.
14 Ageing populations	New social and economic challenges confront nations as birth rates fall and life expectancy increases.
15 International migration	Despite some benefits, international migration can create serious economic and social problems for receiving countries. e.g. refugees.
16 Pressures at the urban fringe	The urban fringe is under increasing pressure as settlements continue to expand, e.g. urban drift and shanty towns; greenfield developments; housing on farmland, etc.
17 Inner city regeneration	There is no clear solution to the problems of decline in inner cities in MEDCs.
18 Urban transport	Traffic congestion threatens the survival of cities in MEDCs.
19 Unequal development	Inequalities of social and economic development exist on a global scale and within countries.
20 Development needs	Debt, trade, aid and tourism are both harmful and beneficial to LEDCs.
21 Swing to services	Major changes in industry and employment structures are taking place in the MEDCs.
22 New agricultural revolution	The environment and rural populations are threatened by increasingly intensive methods of food production.

in the world, which geographers can help with our knowledge and understanding of.

Geography is *not* free of people's values, motives, feelings, etc. For instance, these will affect how people use the land and therefore the appearance of the landscape. Attitudes will be involved in decisions for motorways, by-passes, rail networks, etc., and will therefore affect the transport system in the country. Issues arise because people have different beliefs and values. Issues that affect our lives today are as good a place as any to start your study in geography. Your local newspaper may provide a useful source of local geographical issues. Look out for articles on such things as by-pass proposals, the disposal of waste, requests to build superstores. Below is a typical article appearing in a local newspaper. Can you identify the issues involved?

COUNTRYSIDE AT RISK

More farmland at Walton looks set to be scrapped to make way for housing.

Two fields between Somersby Avenue and Somershall Park are next in line for residential development if council planners give the go-ahead.

An application to build on the land has been made by William Davis – based at Forest Field, Forest Road, Loughborough, Leicestershire.

The plans are on view at the Town Hall, Chesterfield.

▷ One issue is:
   Should planners allow new houses to be built on farmland at the edge of cities?
▷ Another is:
   Should industrial development in towns and cities, and associated housing needs, be given priority in terms of land use?

The various GCSE syllabuses call on you to appreciate the range of attitudes, values and beliefs, both individuals and groups of people (e.g. local residents, the World Wildlife fund, etc.) hold about these issues, and just how significant these are in influencing the decisions which are made in the world which affect the use and management of environments, places and space. Values are assessed in GCSE by asking you to clarify them, justify them and decision-make, and are included in the understanding assessment objective. MEG syllabus B goes further and states that it plans to enable you to develop your own attitudes and values on the issue of inequality and its elimination between races and sexes.

Conflicts of interest

'Conflicts are an inevitable part of decision-making. You need to be aware of various sides of an argument'

People's beliefs and values *conflict* and your GCSE course will raise your awareness of such conflicts. Building motorways, reservoirs and houses and quarrying/mining often cause disagreements/conflicts between different groups of people.

Here are some different points of view held by different interest groups over the issue of reservoir building:

> Easy navigation along rivers is important to us.
> We want to use inland waters for sailing.
> Sewage disposal should be made better.
> Our dangerous chemicals must be disposed of cheaply.
> Our inland fishing must be protected.
> Farmers want more water for irrigation.
> We want more cheap electricity.
> We will need more fresh water for our new houses.
> The flooding of our houses must be stopped.

Which groups might hold each of these views? You can quickly see how these views and interests conflict in just the same way as some people are for new motorways and others against them. The extension of the M40 from Oxford to Warwick caused such conflicts (Fig. 2.11).

Fig. 2.11

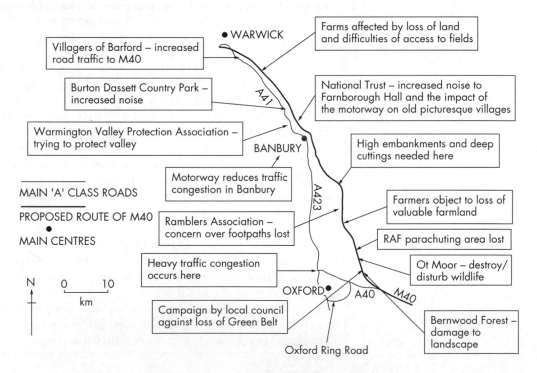

You will be asked to comment on the attitudes of both individual people and groups of people towards such geographical issues. You must be able to recognise conflicts of interest and to explain the alternative viewpoints. For example, see Table 2.4.

Table 2.4

The Development Puzzle: Which way ahead for LEDCs?	
Speaker	Point of view
Minister for Energy and Communications	How can we manage without communications and energy? The expense of development is tremendous: for every eight units invested you only get one unit of output – but in the long term you cannot be without roads, railways, electricity and ports.
Farmer cooperative manager	The best investment possible is agriculture. For every unit invested you get one back in return within a year. Food for a growing population is a must as is growing cash crops for export.
Owner of largest private company	We should invest in a *balanced* industrial programme. For every six units invested you get over one unit of output. Industry is vital in so many ways.
Child health expert in research hospital	These social welfare programmes are so very expensive. For every 10 units of investment you only get one unit of output – but think of the future – an investment in a healthy educated workforce.
Chairman of Workers' Party	It's all very well talking about investment but where's the money coming from? Let's not ruin our future with bank loans and investment by multi-national companies.

It is clear that the examiner is trying to get you to appreciate that there may be a variety of points of view, and more than one solution to a problem.

Look at one of the issues and try to put forward a balanced argument, taking into account other people's views. Historians call this trying to 'put yourself into other people's shoes', or 'empathy'. Seeing more than one side of an argument involves this.

After looking at these points of view, what do you think is the way forward for LEDCs? Biased, bigoted answers are not sought by the examiner. You must show that you appreciate a range of values. For example, the study of the development of a leisure complex within the suburbs of a town can be seen from a number of different viewpoints. If your house is sited next door to the complex, with increased traffic, noise and pollution, you may oppose the project. If you are a bored teenager you may welcome the project. You will be expected to appreciate *both* points of view, although naturally, you may have more sympathy with one than the other. On many issues you may have a *particular* point of view. By all means state it but you must be able to *justify* it with proper reasons.

'You can state an opinion; but you must be able to justify it'

Assessing values

Assessing values in an examination is relatively new, and GCSE does it. You will not be assessed according to the 'correctness' of your own values but according to:

▶ whether you show that you appreciate that there are a range of values and points of view which people hold, and look at all sides of a conflict;
▶ whether you support and justify opinions with convincing and valid reasons.

GCSE examinations include a number of types of question which assess your values:

Direct value-charged questions
Should quarrying be allowed in a National Park?

Here you could try to name the various groups of people who might be involved in the issue. You could then state their likely viewpoint and give reasons why they might hold such a view.

Open-ended questions which do not directly ask for values and opinions to be discussed
Here you may *choose* to introduce 'values' and yet still be answering the question, e.g.

What factors determine the location of industry?
or,
Give reasons for the rural-to-urban migration of population found in many 'developing' countries.

Both questions can be answered satisfactorily in an impersonal way without referring to ideas of personal choice and decision, or showing any real appreciation of people's ways and conditions of life. However, you would still be answering the question if you did make 'values' a part of your answer. Try to make your answer suitable for an examiner to give it some marks for values.

Here are some suggestions.

▶ In the location of industry question you could:
  (a) look at the 'work ethic' of employees in particular regions of the country, which might encourage *employers* to locate there;
  (b) look at the attitudes of the *employers*, who might want to stay in the South East because of *their* preference for living in and around the capital, etc.
▶ In the rural-to-urban migration question you could:
  (a) look at the hopes of young rural peasants who might see more 'attractive' ways of living in the towns/cities;
  (b) as above, but this time with the young rural peasants seeing little prospect for change in traditional ways of life that now seem too 'restrictive', etc.

There will usually be an opportunity in such questions to show 'empathy' with the thinking and ways of life of other people, while still answering the question set.

Decision-making questions and exercises

Some syllabuses will use decision-making exercises. They are a useful way of investigating values. Decision-making exercises will usually relate to a real issue. The following is a short exercise to find a suitable site for a new airport in Yorkshire.
   Try doing it!

Siting a New Airport in Yorkshire

1 A planning team has recommended that a new airport be sited in Yorkshire. Such an airport will need:
  (a) to be near/accessible to the centres of population (large towns and cities) it is intended to serve:
  (b) a large area of flat well-drained land at an economic price and capable of supporting concrete runways taking heavy aircraft, including jumbo jets;
  (c) an area as free as possible from weather hazards, particularly fog;
  (d) as few people as possible living along potential flight paths.
2 However, the planners will have to take the following points into consideration:
  (a) there will be resistance from resident's associations in some areas if they have to face the prospect of high noise levels;
  (b) there may be opposition from conservationists if the airport is a threat to wildlife or to an area of outstanding natural beauty such as a National Park.

Fig. 2.12

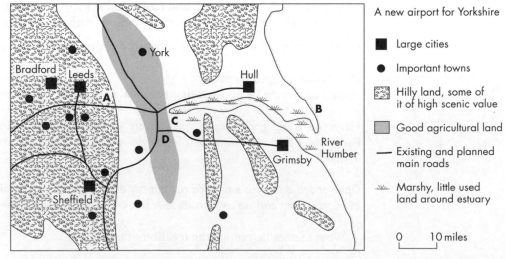

A new airport for Yorkshire

■ Large cities
● Important towns
▨ Hilly land, some of it of high scenic value
▦ Good agricultural land
— Existing and planned main roads
〰 Marshy, little used land around estuary

0   10 miles

▶ Study the map in Fig. 2.12 and compare the relative merits of the four possible sites for the airport – **A**, **B**, **C** and **D** marked on the map. You may find it helpful to use a table, such as the one given below, when comparing the four sites.

Factors	Near to large urban centres	Near to roads or railways	Near to valuable farmland	Other factors from 1 & 2 above
Site A				
Site B				
Site C				
Site D				

    write a report recommending one of the four sites for the new airport. Include your supporting arguments.

▶   It may be interesting to ask someone else to do the exercise. They may disagree with your choice. You can compare your choices together with the reasons for them.

Each of these three types of question expects you to think about situations and work out value positions, rather than to learn certain values, perhaps those of your teacher. Prejudice, that is prejudging or having a predetermined viewpoint, is *not* what GCSE is about! You can make your own opinions and values clear, provided you can justify them.

PRACTICE EXERCISES

▷ **Skills Exercise 1**   *Pie graph drawing*

(a)   Draw two circles, and on them illustrate the information provided below.

Percentage of workforce		Percentage of workforce	
Primary Industry	30%	Primary Industry	75%
Secondary Industry	40%	Secondary Industry	15%
Tertiary Industry	30%	Tertiary Industry	10%

(b)   Which graph is likely to represent an LEDC (less economically developed country)?

▷ **Skills Exercise 2**   *Bar graph drawing*

Complete the bar chart in Fig. 2.13, using the information about the Colorado River from the table below it.

Fig. 2.13

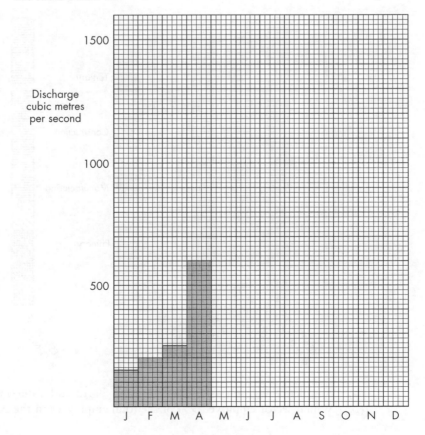

Months	J	F	M	A	M	J	J	A	S	O	N	D
Average discharge (cubic metres per second)	150	200	250	600	1000	1350	550	250	190	200	210	190

▷ **Skills Exercise 3** *Pie-chart drawing*

Bowland Kitchens Ltd of Lancaster produce complete kitchen units. In 1995 40% were sold locally, 40% were sold in the North West and the remainder throughout the rest of the UK. Complete the 'pie' (divided circle) in Fig. 2.14 to show where their markets were in 1995.

Fig. 2.14

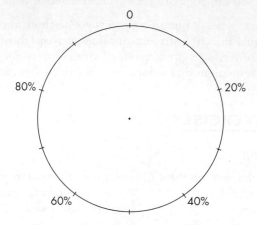

▷ **Skills Exercise 4** *Divided bar graph drawing and interpretation*

Study Fig. 2.15 parts (a) and (b), concerned with employment in the Western Isles of Scotland.

Fig. 2.15 PERCENTAGE OF EMPLOYEES IN EMPLOYMENT BY SECTOR, 1993

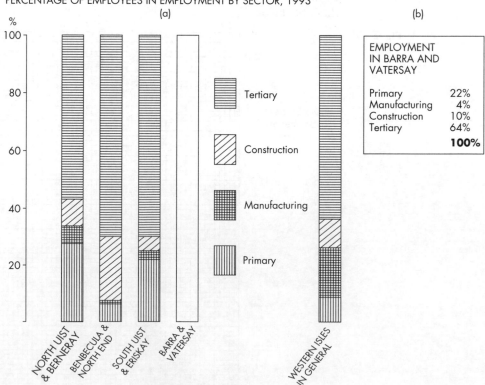

(a) complete the graph using the figures for Barra and Vatersay.

(b) Which sector employed 9% of the total employees in the North Uist and Berneray?

(c) What percentage is employed in the tertiary sector South Uist and Eriskay?

(d) State *one* way in which Bara and Vatersay's employment structure differs from that of the Western Isles in general.

▷ Skills Exercise 5   *Scattergraph drawing and interpretation*

The table below gives the percentage of people employed in agriculture and the percentage of people living in towns, in each of five countries.

Country	Italy	India	Japan	United Kingdom	Ghana
Percentage of people employed in agriculture	19	70	9	2	45
Percentage of people living in towns	52	20	72	76	29

1   Use the above table to complete the scattergraph in Fig. 2.16 below.

Fig. 2.16

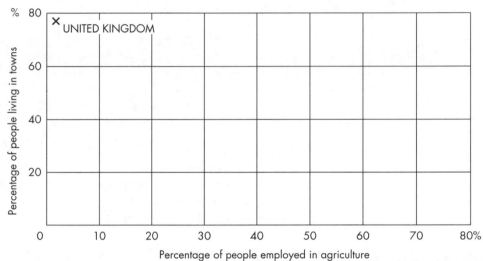

2   Study the scattergraph and describe how the percentage of people living in towns changes as the percentage of people employed in agriculture changes.

▷ Skills Exercise 6   *Radial graph construction and interpretation*

Fig. 2.17

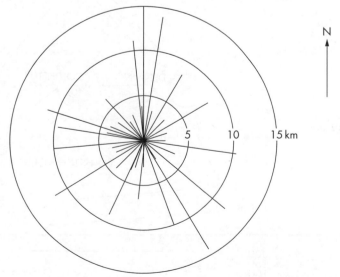

The radial graph in Fig. 2.17 shows the journey made by people during one day in order to shop in town. Each line or ray shows an actual journey made.

1   How far did the farthest shopper travel?
2   Using the graph, complete the following table:

Table 2.5

	From 0–5 km away	From 5–10 km away	From 10–15 km away	Total
Number of shoppers making the journey				

3   Mrs Garrett travelled 15 km from her home to the north east of the town in order to do the weekly shopping. Draw a line on to a copy of the graph to show her journey.

4   Outside the shopping centre she was asked by a GCSE student where she lived. The student is investigating for her GCSE coursework, where people using this shopping centre and two other local ones, come from. From the answers given, the student begins to draw the map in Fig. 2.18.
    (i)   Complete the sphere of influence of shopping centre Y.
    (ii) Suggest ONE reason why the sphere of influence of shopping centre Z stretches out to the east.

Fig. 2.18

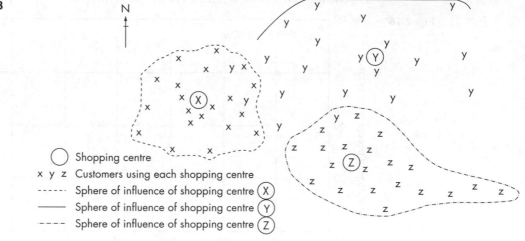

○ Shopping centre
x y z Customers using each shopping centre
- - - - Sphere of influence of shopping centre Ⓧ
——— Sphere of influence of shopping centre Ⓨ
-·-·- Sphere of influence of shopping centre Ⓩ

▷ **Skills Exercise 7**   *Flow line drawing*

The sketch map in Fig. 2.19 gives information about shopping patterns in a rural area.

Fig. 2.19

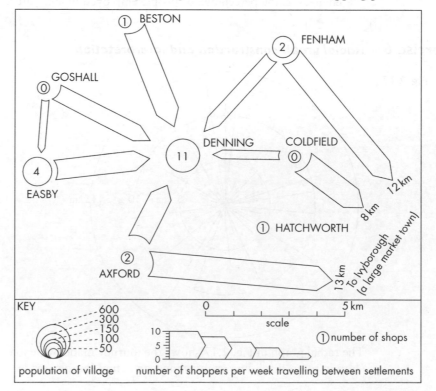

(a) (i) How many shoppers are there in Easby?
    (ii) How many people from Axford go shopping each week in Denning?
(b) On the map draw flow lines to show that
    (i) 6 people from Hatchworth go shopping in Denning each week.
    (ii) 15 people from Hatchworth go shopping in Ivyborough each week.

▷ **Skills Exercise 8** *Isopleth (isoline) drawing*

The sketch map of annual rainfall for part of West Africa in Fig. 2.20 below is incomplete.

Fig. 2.20

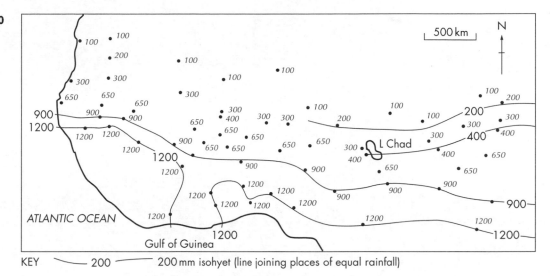

KEY ⎯⎯ 200 ⎯⎯ 200 mm isohyet (line joining places of equal rainfall)

(i) On the map complete the drawing of the 200 mm *and* the 400 mm isohyets (lines joining places of equal rainfall).
(ii) Using the information on the map, *print* the following labels on it in appropriate places: **desertification desert**
(iii) On your completed map, mark and name the likely direction of the rain-bearing winds.

▷ **Skills Exercise 9** *Chloropleth (shaded map) drawing and interpretation*

Study the map in Fig. 2.21 which shows the total precipitation in a part of Northern England, between 13 December 1992 and 6 January 1993.

Fig. 2.21

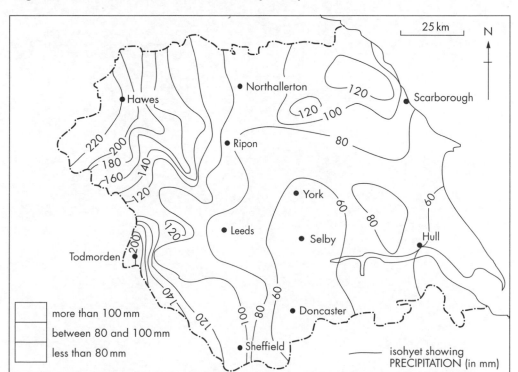

(a)   What was the total precipitation recorded at York during this period?
(b)   Shade the map and complete the key to show the areas experiencing:
         (i) less than 80 mm
         (ii) 80–100 mm
         (iii) more than 100 mm
(c)   With the aid of an atlas describe the pattern of precipitation shown on the map.

Weather processes and climate

▷ **GETTING STARTED**

This topic, as the chart below shows, appears in all but one of the thirteen syllabuses that this book helps you to prepare for. The chart also shows the combination of ideas, issues and places you should know and/or understand about, depending upon which of the syllabuses you are following. Most syllabuses require you to be able to answer questions about the factors affecting weather and climate; for example, latitude and distance from the sea, anticyclones, depressions, air masses and rainfall. With regard to climatic types and regions, the British climate is the main place for study; some syllabuses ask for a contrasting type, perhaps tropical, to be studied. The links between people and weather and climate are dealt with in some syllabuses; links can be two-way – people affect weather and climate, say in large urban areas, as well as being affected by weather and climate conditions.

All geographical topics have their own list of vocabulary and language. The geographical terms which you will find helpful to learn for this topic at GCSE are given on page 47. This is not a particularly ideal topic area for coursework/fieldwork at GCSE. It may be feasible to undertake investigations into an urban climate compared with conditions in the surrounding countryside, or to try to prove, for instance, that your garden has a micro-climate. Because it is not a strongly recommended topic area for such study, there is no 'suggestions for coursework' section in this chapter.

LONDON A	LONDON B	MEG A	MEG B	MEG C	NEAB A	NEAB B	NEAB C	NICCEA	SEG A	SEG B	WJEC	IGCSE	TOPIC	STUDY	REVISION 1	REVISION 2
✓			✓								✓	✓	Weather measurement			
✓			✓						✓				Climatic region and climatographs			
	✓			✓		✓			✓	✓			British climate			
	✓		✓	✓				✓	✓	✓	✓		Anticyclones, depressions and air masses			
✓						✓				✓	✓	✓	Contrasting climatic type to Britain: Equatorial (Amazonia); Tropical Monsoon (India); Mediterranean; Tropical Desert; Continental Interior			
✓		✓		✓					✓	✓	✓		Rainfall			
✓			✓					✓	✓	✓	✓		Factors affecting weather and climate			
	✓				✓		✓			✓			Hurricanes and weather hazards			
			✓					✓	✓				Links between weather and climate, and people			
				✓		✓							Climatic change			

WHAT YOU NEED TO KNOW

Weather refers to the conditions of the lower atmosphere at a particular time and place. These conditions result from the way in which the various elements that make up the weather – air temperature, pressure, precipitation, wind direction and speed, and sunshine – behave. These weather elements and conditions can be measured and recorded, for example:

Table 3.1

Element	Measured by
Air temperature	Maximum/minimum thermometer
Rainfall	Rain gauge
Air pressure	Barometer
Wind speed	Anemometer
Wind direction	Wind vane

This weather information can be:
1. presented as synoptic charts
2. used to derive the climate

▷ **Synoptic charts**   Synoptic charts are weather maps which summarise the weather conditions over a large area, and may enable some weather predictions to be made. Below is an example of a weather map and associated symbols (Figs 3.1 and 3.2).

Fig. 3.1

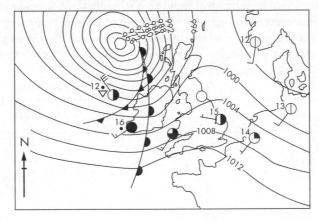

Fig. 3.2

Weather map symbols

CLOUD		WEATHER		WIND	
Symbol	Cloud amount (oktas)	Symbol	Weather	Symbol	Wind speed knots
○	0	=	Mist	◎	Calm
◔	1 or fewer	≡	Fog		
◑	2	,	Drizzle	╲	1–2
◕	3	⦂	Rain and drizzle		
◐	4	•	Rain	╲—	3–7
◓	5	⦙	Rain and snow		
◑	6	*	Snow	╲=	8–12
◗	7 or more	▽•	Rain shower		
●	8	▽⁚	Rain and snow shower	╲≡	13–17
⊗	Sky obscured	▽*	Snow shower		For each additional half-feather add 5 knots
⊗	Missing or doubtful data	△	Hail shower		
		⊼	Thunderstorm		

Station model	**Pressure**
Temperature —̶ ₋4 ◔ ← Cloud cover Precipitation ↗ , ↘ Wind speed and direction	1012 Isobars are drawn at intervals of 4 mb

▷ **Climate** Climate refers to the average expected pattern of weather for a place, derived from measuring and recording weather over a long period of time (usually 30 years). Weather and climate are different; the first is real and usually changing, the latter is the general pattern of weather.

There are various types of climate around the world, some very different from the UK's. Each climatic region, for example equatorial or continental interior, has its own distinct type of climate which can be described in the form of a climatograph.

Fig. 3.3

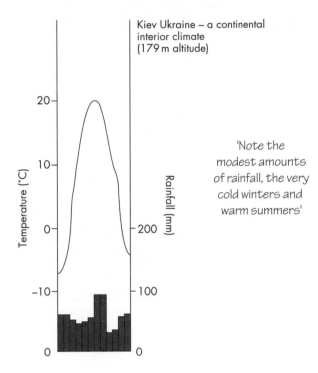

Kiev Ukraine – a continental interior climate (179 m altitude)

'Note the modest amounts of rainfall, the very cold winters and warm summers'

The distribution of these climatic regions can be mapped on a world map, each type tending to occur in various locations around the world because the factors causing that climate occur in more than one place.

Factors such as latitude, altitude and aspect, continentality (distance from the sea), ocean currents and wind direction affect weather and climate. They operate to influence both micro-climate and local weather, and the global pattern of climate.

▷ **British Climate** Use these notes alongside the maps in the Case Study section of this chapter.

Factors affecting temperatures in Britain

North Atlantic drift
This is a warm ocean current that starts in the Gulf of Mexico and moves across the North Atlantic towards north-west Europe. Any winds blowing over it will be warmed, and these in turn raise the temperature of the land they cross. This is especially true of coastal areas. As the commonest wind direction over Britain is from the south-west, these winds come from over the North Atlantic drift, and warm up the west coast more than the east. In winter, as the winds blow across Britain, they are cooled down by the cold land mass.

'Weather and climate are influenced by location'

Wind direction
Another reason why the east coast is colder than the west in winter is that on the rarer occasion when our winds come from the east they are very cold from their journey over the continent of Europe and Russia. Although they do cross the North Sea, the warmth from the North Atlantic drift is not felt very much here.

Land and sea (Continentality)
Do you notice those peculiar bends in the isotherms over the Irish Sea? These are explained by the heating and cooling properties of land and sea. Land heats up and cools down much

more rapidly than water. In winter, the sea is warmer than the land, and in summer the land is warmer (even if we ignore the effect of the North Atlantic drift). This means that the sea has a moderating effect on temperature in winter, and so Cornwall in January is warmer than London. In July, Cornwall near the sea is now cooler than London which is nearer the continent.

Latitude

Since the isotherms trend is roughly west–east in summer, and they decrease in value as you go north, one must suspect latitude as a major factor. Britain stretches through about 10 ° of latitude, and as the southern areas are nearer the equator, the sun's rays are more concentrated. In technical language one would say that the angle on incidence of the sun's rays is higher in the south.

Weather conditions, especially over Britain, also vary according to the nature and movement of different air masses and pressure systems (known as weather systems). Different air masses and weather systems lead to variations in weather and climate.

Air masses

These are large masses of air with uniform characteristics (temperature, humidity, etc.) carried with them from the place of origin. They are associated with the major winds. It is often said that 'winds bring the weather'; they certainly transport air from other places – places of origin and places on their route. For example, in winter cold air from polar regions (a polar continental air mass) can approach Britain as an easterly or north-easterly wind.

The importance of air masses in delivering 'Atlantic' or 'continental' weather to Britain is shown by Fig. 3.4. Westerly air flows from the Atlantic tend to bring rain. Southerly and easterly winds tend to bring dry, continental weather. Our warmest weather is usually brought by southerly winds from the Mediterranean (a tropical continental air mass). The flow of air masses and wind direction are determined by the atmospheric pressure pattern.

Fig. 3.4 The major air masses influencing the climate of the British Isles

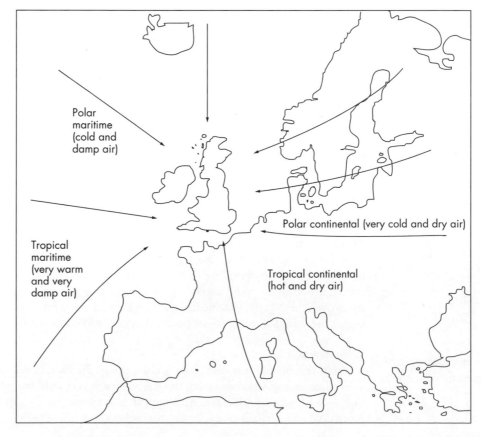

Weather systems

The isobars (equal pressure lines) are often arranged in particular patterns. There are four patterns which you should be able to recognise.

1. A closed area of low pressure is called a **depression**.
2. A closed area of high pressure is called an **anticyclone**.
3. An open-ended area of low pressure is called a **trough**.
4. An open-ended area of high pressure is called a **ridge**.

You should also understand the weather patterns and sequences associated with:
1. a depression
2. a summer anticyclone
3. a winter anticyclone

Fig. 3.5 A cross-section through a depression showing the weather experienced during its passage overhead

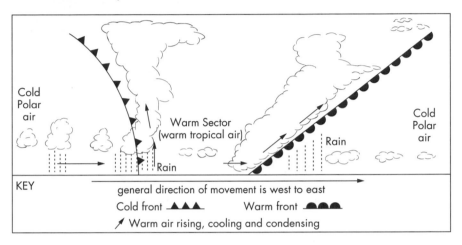

Depressions

Depressions bring cloud, rain and unsettled weather. One of the three types of rainfall – **cyclonic**, is that when air is forced to rise at the fronts in a depression or cyclone. The other two types are **relief** rain and **convectional** rain (Fig. 3.6).

Fig. 3.6 Two types of rainfall

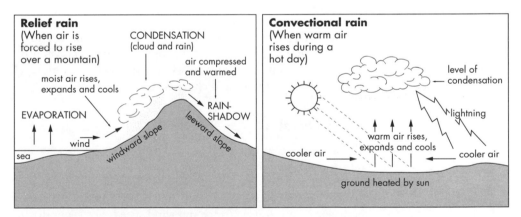

Anticyclones bring dry and settled weather, but the difference between summer and winter can be very marked.

Summer anticyclones

These bring the warmest and driest weather found in Britain. A permanent anticyclone centred in the mid North Atlantic (named after a group of islands there – the *Azores* anticyclone) occasionally moves much further north-east and affects Britain. This can draw air up from the north African deserts and lead to weeks of drought. Severe drought can be caused this way. However, early morning mist and fog can sometimes form as the lack of cloud cover allows night-time temperatures to drop enough. These are quickly dispersed by the high temperatures of the following morning.

Winter anticyclones

These commonly form over western Russia and direct very cold easterly winds over Britain.

Some of the heaviest winter snows can fall from these winds. Radiation fog and frost are common when cloud cover is small, as it often is in most anticyclones. 'Anticyclonic gloom' has been used to describe the lasting fog brought by a winter anticyclone.

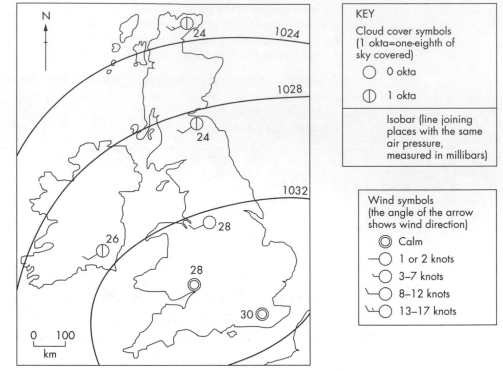

Fig. 3.7 A summer anticyclone over Britain

Anticyclones and depressions tend to bring distinct kinds of weather. A much milder version can be found as troughs of low pressure or ridges of high pressure pass over. As with depressions and anticyclones, these generally mean unsettled wet conditions and stable dry conditions respectively. However, the weather they do bring may last only a day at the most. Weather and climate influence human activity, and human activities, in turn, can have an impact on the atmosphere. Extreme weather conditions such as storms and droughts can become hazards for people living close by. The 'Issue' section of this chapter deals with this idea. Weather and climate affect people's activities constantly in a less dramatic way. Four studies in farming and tourism will provide many examples. Equally, human activity indirectly changes weather and climate.

Urban climates

Studies show that urban areas receive 15 per cent less sunshine, 10 per cent more **precipitation** (rain, hail and snow) and have lower visibility than rural areas. Fog is 30 per cent more frequent in summer and 100 per cent more frequent in winter, and cloudy days are 10 per cent more frequent over the year as a whole. However, urban areas are generally between 2° and 6 °C warmer and wind speeds are generally lower. Cities have climates that differ from those of the surrounding country areas. They tend to experience higher air temperatures (the **heat island** effect), lower wind speeds because of the greater friction and drag which buildings place on the wind, and have more air pollution, largely because of industrial emission and traffic exhausts. This is a major factor in the lower visibility and greater incidence of cloud and fog in cities.

Fig.3.8 shows the effect of buildings in a city on the wind, and how its speeds are generally reduced but can be greater in places because of turbulence, eddying and channelling.

Fig. 3.8 The effects of buildings on the wind

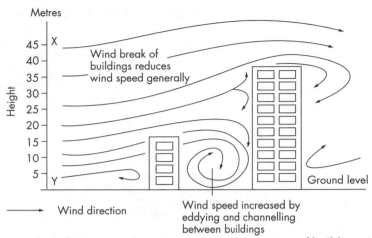

Urban climates are the unintentional consequence of building cities. Is global warming the unintentional consequence of creating an industrialised, wealthy world, at least in places?

Fig. 3.9 Global warming since 1950?

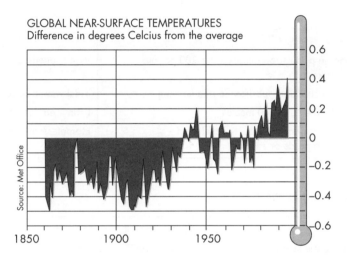

Any global warming is thought to be due to an enhanced **greenhouse effect** as pollution traps more heat in the lower atmosphere. Pollution puts more greenhouse gases in the atmosphere.

Fig. 3.10 Some consequences for Britain if global warming continues up to 2030

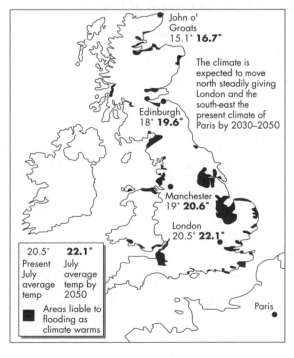

FORECAST 2030

There will be positive and negative impacts on the British Isles from climate change by 2030 to 2050, scientists said.

Weather and water supplies:
Temperatures will rise by about 0.2 °C a decade, reaching an average 1.6 °C hotter than now. There will be more rain but it will be mainly in the North with the North West wetter by 7 per cent. In the South, summer rainfall will fall 8 per cent, putting further pressure on supplies. More windy days are forecast and the frequency of gales across the whole country is expected to climb by a third.

Sea Levels:
A hotter world will raise sea levels as the oceans expand. Sea levels could rise 37 cm but the impact will be severest in the South and East, where the land is sinking, so the actual rise could be as high as 50 cm. Low-lying areas will be at increased risk of flooding and vulnerable to more storms. About 400,00 ha might be at risk in the Fens alone.

Agriculture and Forestry:
Timber production, mainly centred on introduced conifer species, is likely to increase 15 per cent by 2050. Some sensitive species, such as beeches, could die out. Urban trees, such as limes and planes, in the South will suffer from more pests and drought. Wetter warmer weather in the North should favour dairy herds. Sunflowers and maize could replace wheat and other crops in the South. Trout farming in the South is likely to be hit by rising temperatures and low-flow rivers.

▷ **Issue**   *Hurricanes – a weather event which can be a hazard*

Fig. 3.11 A cross-section through a hurricane (tropical storm/cyclone)

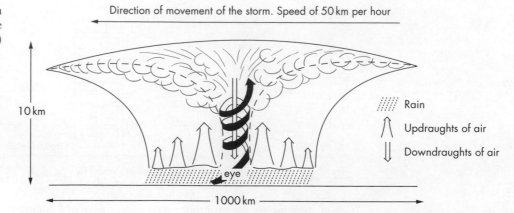

Bangladesh was hit by a hurricane in 1970. For more details, read the table below and look at the map on page 53 (Fig. 3.21).

Table 3.2

Characteristics of Ganges delta	Facts about the cyclone
Average population density: over 200 people per sq km	Wind speeds: up to 220 km/hour
Main occupation: subsistence rice farming	Tidal waves: up to 10 metres high
Relief: 90% below 10 metres	Estimated deaths: over 100,000
Transport network: poorly developed – few main roads or railways	Homeless: over 5 million

Managing the effects

Before the storm	Find a safe building e.g. storm shelter	Look for higher ground
During the storm	Stay indoors. Do NOT go outdoors when the eye of the storm arrives	Listen to the radio for advice

▷ **Case study**   *Temperature and rainfall pattern of Britain*

Remember to use these maps alongside the notes on the factors affecting British temperatures earlier. Fig. 3.12 (*below left*) shows the summer sea level isotherms and mean temperatures for July. Fig. 3.13 (*below right*) gives the corresponding isotherms and temperatures for January and Fig. 3.14 shows the direction of the prevailing winds and levels of rainfall.

Fig. 3.12 Summer sea level isotherms – mean temperatures for July

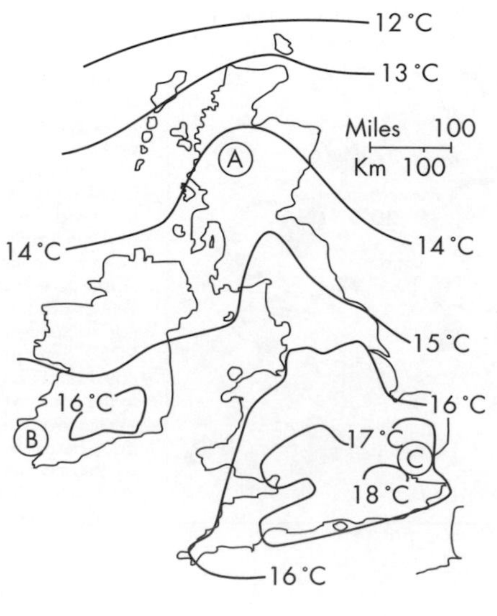

Fig. 3.13 Winter sea level isotherms – mean temperatures for January

Ⓐ Fort William, Scotland

Ⓑ Valentia Island, South West Ireland

Ⓒ Southend, Essex

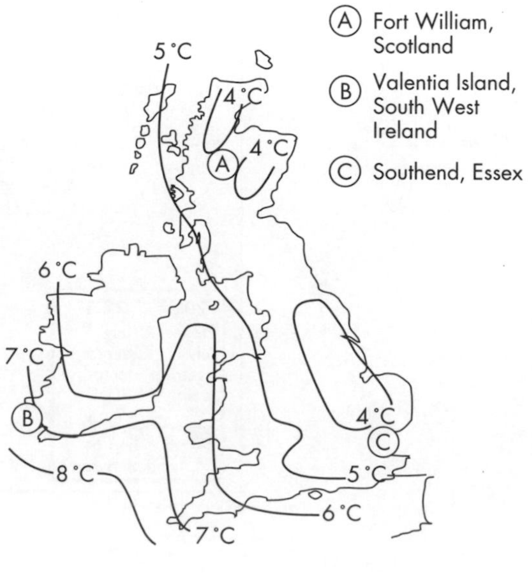

Fig. 3.14

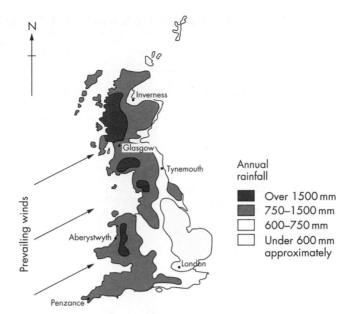

Annual rainfall

- ■ Over 1500 mm
- ▨ 750–1500 mm
- □ 600–750 mm
- □ Under 600 mm approximately

Prevailing winds

Inverness
Glasgow
Tynemouth
Aberystwyth
London
Penzance

▷ **Key terms**   *Make sure you understand and can apply these geographical terms*

Air mass	A large body of air in which temperature and moisture are more or less the same.
Altitude	Height of the land.
Anemometer	The instrument for measuring wind speed.
Anticyclone	An area of high pressure with light winds or calms and generally stable weather.
Aspect	The direction a slope faces.
Barometer	The instrument for measuring air pressure.
Continental(ity)	Air affected by land, so cold in winter and warm in summer.
Depression	A moving area of low pressure bringing cloud and rain.
Exposure	Refers to the openness or protection a place has with regard to weather elements like wind.
Front	The boundary between two air masses.
Isobar	A line joining places of equal pressure.
Isohyet	A line joining places of equal rainfall.
Isotherm	A line joining places of equal temperature.
Latitude	Measures the distance of a place from the equator.
Maritime (Oceanic)	Air affected by the seas/oceans, so cooler in summer and warmer in winter than that from land areas.
Maximum-minimum thermometer	An instrument used to measure the highest and lowest temperature within a period.
Micro-climate	The climate of a very small area.
Ocean current	A movement of surface water, warmer or colder than its surroundings in an ocean.
Precipitation	The various forms in which water falls from the atmosphere to the ground.
Prevailing wind	The most frequent wind direction at a place.
Rain gauge	An instrument used for measuring rainfall.
Relief	The differences in the shape of the earth's surface.
Synoptic chart	A chart of map showing weather details, including isobars.
Tropical	In or from the area between the two Tropics.
Wind vane	An instrument used to indicate wind direction.

STUDENT ANSWER WITH EXAMINER'S COMMENTS

Study Fig. 3.15 which shows selected July isotherms over Europe and North Africa

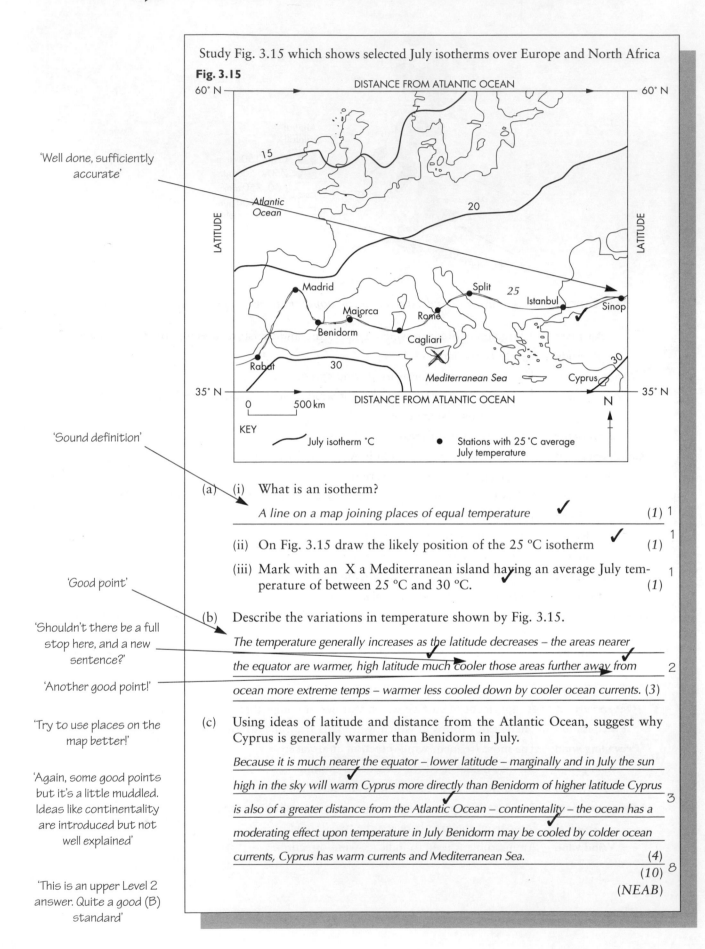

Fig. 3.15

'Well done, sufficiently accurate'

'Sound definition'

(a) (i) What is an isotherm?

A line on a map joining places of equal temperature ✓ (1) 1

(ii) On Fig. 3.15 draw the likely position of the 25 °C isotherm ✓ (1) 1

(iii) Mark with an X a Mediterranean island having an average July temperature of between 25 °C and 30 °C. ✓ (1) 1

'Good point'

(b) Describe the variations in temperature shown by Fig. 3.15.

The temperature generally increases as the latitude decreases – the areas nearer ✓ *the equator are warmer, high latitude much cooler those areas further away from* ✓ 2 *ocean more extreme temps – warmer less cooled down by cooler ocean currents.* (3)

'Shouldn't there be a full stop here, and a new sentence?'

'Another good point!'

'Try to use places on the map better!'

(c) Using ideas of latitude and distance from the Atlantic Ocean, suggest why Cyprus is generally warmer than Benidorm in July.

Because it is much nearer the equator – lower latitude – marginally and in July the sun *high in the sky will warm Cyprus more directly than Benidorm of higher latitude Cyprus* ✓ *is also of a greater distance from the Atlantic Ocean – continentality – the ocean has a* ✓ *moderating effect upon temperature in July Benidorm may be cooled by colder ocean* *currents, Cyprus has warm currents and Mediterranean Sea.* (4) 3

(10) 8

(NEAB)

'Again, some good points but it's a little muddled. Ideas like continentality are introduced but not well explained'

'This is an upper Level 2 answer. Quite a good (B) standard'

> ◢ **A TUTOR ANSWER**

Study Fig. 3.16, a west–east cross-section of part of north west England.

Fig. 3.16

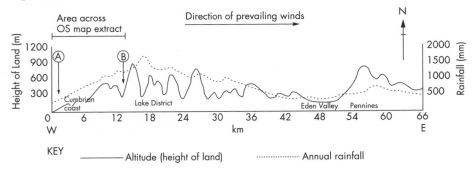

(a) (i) State the highest annual rainfall in the area shown.

1700 mm (1)

(ii) Which place receives the most rainfall? Tick the correct box below.

Cumbrian coast	
Lake District	✓
Eden Valley	
Pennines	

(1)

(b) (i) State the relationship between rainfall and altitude which is shown on Fig. 3.16. Give evidence from the figure to support your statement.

The basic relationship is that as altitude, or height above sea level, rises so

does rainfall and vice versa. For example, rainfall exceeds 1000 mm over the

Lake District where land often reaches 600 metres but is only about 300 mm

in the Eden Valley where altitude is down to around 100 metres. To be pre-

cise, the relationship is not always perfect. The wettest point is not at the

highest point. (3)

(ii) Explain this relationship. A diagram may help your answer.

Moist air from the west is forced to rise over the Lake District. This rising of

air leads to cooling and condensation to form cloud as the air's ability to carry

the moisture drops. Clouds often rain. As the air descends towards the Eden

Valley it warms and cloud and rain become less likely. This area of lower

rainfall on the leeward side of the Lake District is known as a rainshadow. (4)

'Diagram 1 of Fig. 3.6 is the one you need!'

(iii) What name is given to this type of rainfall?

Relief rainfall (1)

(c) Temperatures generally fall with altitude.
Explain why temperatures generally change with altitude in this way.

Air pressure falls with altitude under the influence of gravity. The lower the

pressure the lower the temperature and vice versa. There is less air to warm up at

altitude. Furthermore, the air is heated from below by the earth's surface; the fur-

ther from this source the colder it is. (4)

(d) Study Fig. 3.17 which shows the temperatures recorded during a winter's day in the Lake District.

Fig. 3.17 Times or recordings

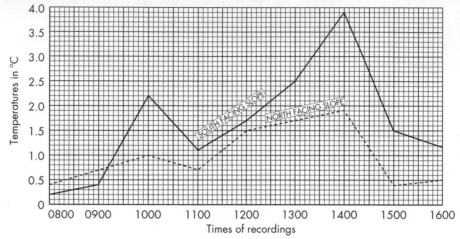

(i) At which time of day were temperatures highest on both slopes of the valley?

1400 hours (2pm) (1)

(ii) Which slope had the smaller temperature range? Give figures to support your answer.

South-facing slope has a temperature range of 3.7 °C (0.2 °C to 3.9 °C).

North-facing slope has a temperature range of 1.5 °C (0.4 °C to 1.9 °C),

hence, the lower. (1)

(iii) Explain why temperatures are generally higher on the south-facing slope. A diagram may help your answer.

The south-facing slope receives direct sunlight by virtue of the direction it

faces; a southerly aspect. The north-facing slope will be colder as it will be

the more shaded and receive less solar radiation. (3)

Fig. 3.18

(e) Study Figs 3.12 and 3.13 which show July and January isotherms over Britain.
Describe the pattern of temperatures for July and January. How do latitude and distance from the Atlantic Ocean help to explain these patterns?

(i) July pattern

Description *Temperatures generally rise from north to south with 13 °C on the north coast of Scotland to 18 °C on the south coast of England. The isotherms bend to show higher temperatures in eastern England than western England.*

Explanation *Latitude is mainly responsible for this pattern. The higher angle of the sun in the sky to the south explains the higher temperatures there. Also the Atlantic has a cooling effect on Britain in summer and this can be seen in the cooler temperatures in Cornwall than Essex.*

(ii) January pattern

Description *The pattern is a west–east one in winter. Temperatures fall from west to east with 7 °C in Cornwall and western Ireland and 4 °C on the east coast of both Scotland and England.*

Explanation *Latitude has a small effect on winter temperatures. The pattern is largely explained by distance from the Atlantic Ocean. The Ocean is warmer than the land in winter and warms the west of Britain. The further east you go and nearer the colder continent of Europe and further from the warmer Atlantic, the lower are temperatures.*

(6)

(25)

(NEAB)

▷ EXAMINATION QUESTION

(a) Study Figs. 3.19 and 3.20 showing weather in Britain during January.

Fig. 3.19 & Fig. 3.20

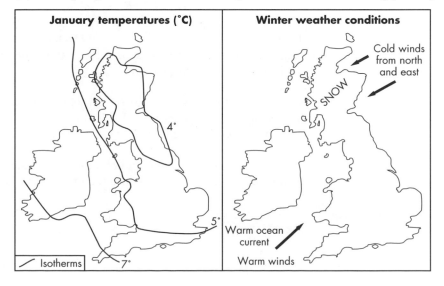

(i) On Fig. 3.19 shade the land area with a temperature above 5 °C.

(*1 mark – Tiers F and H*)

(ii) On Fig. 3.20 mark with an **X** the area with the lowest winter temperatures.

(*1 mark – Tier F only*)

(iii) Give one reason to explain why snow is most common in the area shown on the map. (2 lines provided here)   (*1 mark – Tier F only*)

(iv) State two reasons why the south-west of Britain is warmest in the winter. (2 lines provided here)   (*2 marks – Tier F only*)

(v) Describe and explain the pattern of temperatures across Britain in January. (11 lines provided here)   (*4 marks – Tier H only*)

(b) Study Fig. 3.21 showing some information about the Bangladesh Hurricane (Tropical Storm) in 1970.

Fig. 3.21

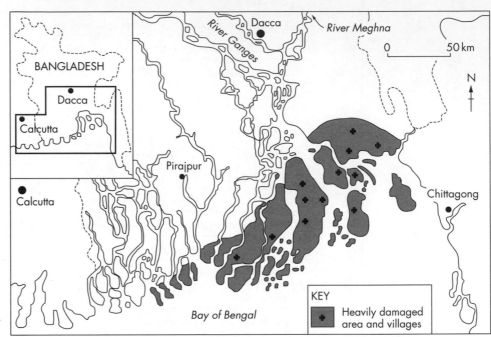

Source: adapted from Simon Ross, *Hazard Geography* (Longman) 1986

(i) How many villages were badly hit by the hurricane? (1 line provided here)

(*1 mark – Tier F only*)

(ii) Describe the location of the heavily damaged area. (6 lines provided here)

(*2 marks – Tier F only*)

(iii) State **two** effects on the weather a hurricane may bring. (6 lines provided here)

(*2 marks – Tier F only*)

(iv) Using an example from your studies, describe the effects of a tropical storm (hurricane) on the landscape and people. (12 lines provided here)

(*4 marks – Tier F only*)

(v) Name **one** way a government might try to reduce the impact of a hurricane. (1 line provided here)   (*1 mark – Tier F only*) (*Total 15 – Tier F*)

(c) Study Fig. 3.22 showing the main source areas and main paths taken by hurricanes (tropical storms).

On the map,

(i) name **two** continents severely affected by hurricanes and for each one name a likely source area. (5 lines provided here)   (*2 marks – Tier H only*)

(ii) Describe the world distribution of hurricanes. (5 lines provided here)

(*2 marks – Tier H only*)

(iii) Using an example from your studies, describe the impact of a tropical storm and the measures taken to try to reduce the impact. (17 lines provided here)

(*6 marks – Tier H only*)

(*Total 15 – Tier H*)

(*SEG syllabus A*)

Fig. 3.22

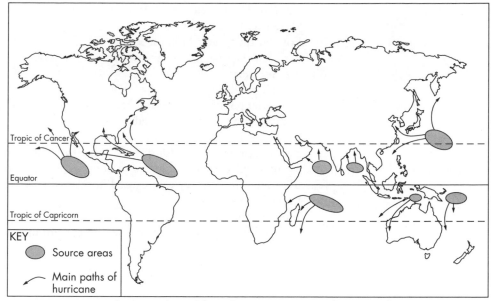

Source: adapted from Simon Ross, *Hazard Geography* (Longman) 1986

► EXAMINATION ANSWER

(a) (i) All areas correctly shaded, i.e. between 5 ° and 7 °C, and over 7 °C land areas only.

(1) (Tiers F and H)

(ii) **X** marked on NE of Scotland/NE England. *(1) (Tier F)*

(iii) *Any 1 mark*
An upland area – temperature decrease with altitude.
Cold temperatures, less than 4 °C in winter. *(1) (Tier F)*

(iv) *Any 1 for 1 mark. Up to 2 for 2 marks.*
Warm winds blow in from the south-west
North Atlantic Drift (warm ocean current)/Gulf stream. *(2) (Tier F)*

(v) Level 1 – 1–2 marks
Simple descriptive statements from the map, e.g. it is coldest in NE Scotland. It is warmest in SW England. Cold winds from the East. No explanation.
Level 2 – 3–4 marks
Describes trends and gives fuller explanation, e.g. temps decrease from NE to SW. The colder temperatures are a result of very cold winds coming from the continent, etc. *(4) (Tier H)*

(b) (i) 12 *(1) (Tier F)*

(ii) South part of Delta/next to sea *(2) (Tier F)*

(iii) Strong winds/Heavy rain *(2) (Tier F)*

(iv) Credit statistics, four points, e.g.
For example
Bangladesh in 1985
Level 1 – 1–2 marks
Simple statement, e.g. land flooded (26 000 km²), people killed, crops destroyed, cattle drowned, storm surge, 2000 people killed.
Level 2 – 3–4 marks
Clear depth of knowledge, linking of effects, e.g. the rice was destroyed so many people were starving, the lack of food and medical care led to starvation and disease so the death toll rose quickly. *(4) (Tier F)*

(v) (can be preventative *or* post-storm)
Radar tracking, early warning systems, evacuation, weather reporting, etc.

(1) (Tier F)

(Total 15) (Tier F)

(c)   (i)   e.g. North America – Mid Atlantic
               SE (Africa) – Indian Ocean   (2) (*Tier H*)
       (ii)   Low latitudes/near Equator = 1
               Between the Tropics except for around the Japanese coast = 2   (2) (*Tier H*)
       (iii) e.g. St Lucia
               Level 1 – 1–2 marks
               Two brief points on either impact and/or measures, e.g. strong winds caused trees
               to fall, people were evacuated.
               Level 2 – 3–4 marks
               Two developed points for 4 marks (one to be an impact/one a measure).
               More detailed answer with more knowledge, e.g. winds up to 200 km/hr,
               destroyed trees, heavy rain caused floods which washed houses away.
               Level 3 – 5–6 marks
               Three to four good points.
               Detailed description linking causes-effects and measures and proper case study.
                                                                                      (6) (*Tier H*)
                                                                              (*Total 15*) (*Tier H*)
                                                                                         (*SEG*)

SUMMARY

▷ Weather is made up of elements which can be measured and recorded.

▷ Weather and climate are different.

▷ Weather and climate are influenced by location.

▷ There are distinct climatic regions with types of climate very different from the UK's.

▷ These variations in climate result from a number of factors.

▷ Air masses and pressure systems, which have a major influence on weather, change but can be forecasted.

▷ Rainfall is caused in different ways.

▷ Human activities can indirectly affect weather and climate.

▷ Weather and climate inflence human activity.

Chapter 4

Natural environment system and landscape processes

▷ **GETTING STARTED**

This topic, as the chart below shows, is part of many of the syllabuses and quite important in some. It deals with rocks, processes like weathering and glaciation, landforms and natural landscapes, and how the three are linked. As in all good geography, people are not left out; they too modify landscapes and are offered possibilities for development by certain natural landscapes. Again, case studies are important; you are advised to know about a specific limestone and/or glaciated upland landscape in Britain. A list of the most common technical terms used in this topic is given along with their definitions.

This is not a particularly ideal topic area of coursework/fieldwork at GCSE. It may be feasible to investigate local weathering of buildings or gravestones or to pursue study of limestone or glaciated landforms in the field. However, because it is not a strongly recommended topic area for GCSE fieldwork investigation, no 'suggestions for coursework' section is included in this chapter.

LONDON A	LONDON B	MEG A	MEG B	MEG C	NEAB A	NEAB B	NEAB C	NICCEA	SEG A	SEG B	WJEC	IGCSE	TOPIC	STUDY	REVISION 1	REVISION 2
✓			✓	✓	✓			✓	✓		✓	✓	Systems approach of inputs, processes and product, to landscapes and landforms			
			✓	✓	✓			✓	✓				Inputs of rock type, rock structure, climate and people's activities			
													Different rock types			
			✓	✓	✓		✓	✓	✓			✓	Processes of weathering, mass movement, erosion, transport and deposition.			
✓			✓	✓	✓						✓	✓	Past processes and glaciation. Glaciated upland landscapes and valleys			
				✓				✓	✓				Limestone scenery			
												✓	Wind action in deserts			
✓			✓						✓				Landscape opportunities and quarrying			

WHAT YOU NEED TO KNOW

The form and shape of the land is ever changing, and changes naturally over time without any involvement from people. You will need to be able to start to explain some of these changes in GCSE Geography. Most syllabuses include some study of natural landforms and landscape-making. These can be explained by studying:

1   The **structure** i.e. the nature of the bedrock and surface materials of which the land is made. This includes how tough and resistant they are, whether they allow water to pass through them (permeable) or otherwise (impermeable), and whether they have lines of weakness in them like joints and bedding planes, and

2   The **processes** operating on it, i.e. agents which can destroy and construct landforms and landscapes such as running water, the wind, the sea, etc. These kinds of process continually modify landforms.

The idea is that landscapes are working systems involving structure and processes which interact with one another, and have landforms as products or output. A change in one part of the system, for example in the processes, will result in change elsewhere, for example in the landforms.

▷ A systems approach to studying coastlines

Fig. 4.1 shows the processes involved in this approach.

Fig. 4.1

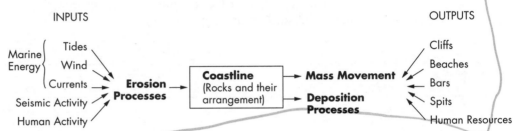

▷ Rock formation

Fig. 4.2 is a simple diagram showing the formation of rocks.

Fig. 4.2

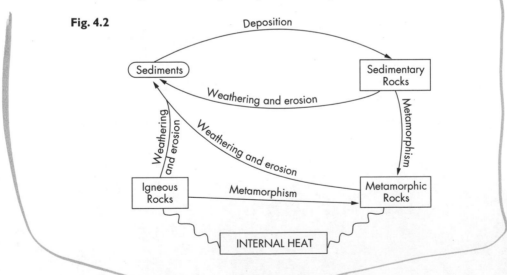

▷ Classification of rocks

All rocks can be put into one of three groups.

Sedimentary

Most of these were formed on the sea bed. Rivers bring eroded material from the land, and deposit it in the sea. Over millions of years these accumulating sea floor sediments are changed into rock by their great weight. Some rocks formed like this are made up of the accumulation of the shells of dead sea creatures. Later, uplift of the sea bed exposes these rocks for us to see today. Sedimentary rocks are thus formed in layers or **strata** and come in a great variety. For example, those composed of extremely fine particles are called **shales**; those of small but visible particles are called **sandstones**. Other well known sedimentary rocks include chalk, limestone and coal.

Igneous

These are rocks connected with volcanic activity.
The lava or magma may reach the surface before it cools and turns into rock, or it may become rock well underground. Most igneous rocks are made up of a complex mesh of crystals. Granite is the best know example, and is formed deep in the earth's crust.

Metamorphic

These are any sedimentary or igneous rocks which have been changed by great temperature and/or pressure. For example, shale is changed by pressure into **slate**, or **schist**, depending upon the amount of pressure. Limestone is changed into **marble**.

Fig. 4.3

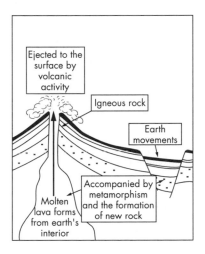

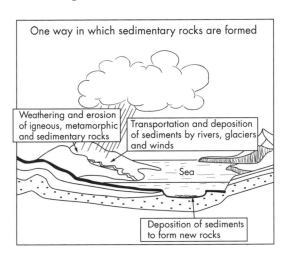

▷ **Weathering** The term **weathering** is used to describe the breakdown of rock through exposure to the atmosphere. Rain, wind, heat, frost, temperate change and organisms such as worms are responsible for rock decay and disintegration. The principal difference between erosion and weathering is that there is no movement of the broken-down material in the case of weathering. Weathering factors are not, unlike erosional agents, capable of transport. Rock is weathered to provide rock fragments from which soil is formed.

Weathering factors are generally classified into three groups of process: **mechanical** processes such as freeze-thaw, which shatters jointed rocks when water in the joints freezes and expands; **chemical** processes such as hydrolysis, when a chemical reaction between water and a rock mineral leads to the breakdown of the rock; and **biological** processes such as animal burrowing, tree roots embedding themselves in rocks, the decay of dead organisms producing acids, etc. Some of the principal ways in which rock is weathered are shown in Fig. 4.4.

Weathering is clearly influenced by climate as Fig. 4.5 shows. In tropical areas, with high temperature and heavy rainfall, chemical weathering is at its maximum. In temperate regions such as Britain both mechanical and chemical weathering are common as a result of frost action, heat expansion of rock and moderate rainfall. In arid areas weathering is mainly mechanical, due to heat during the day and frost at night. In polar regions there is very little weathering. Taken overall, chemical weathering is the dominant means of rock breakdown in the world today. **Hydrolysis** is the most important chemical weathering process, and takes place wherever rock and water are in contact.

Fig. 4.4

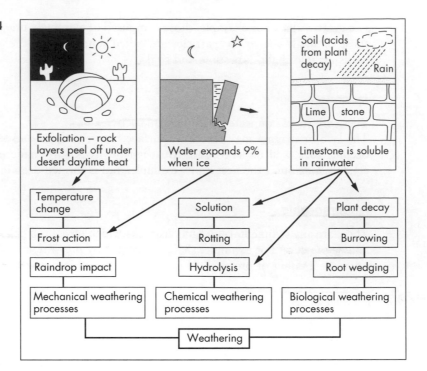

Fig. 4.5

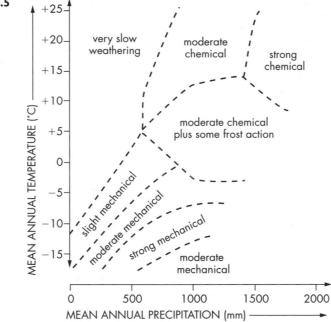

▷ **Mass movement**   The term mass movement refers to the movement downslope, under the influence of gravity, of loose materials produced by rock weathering. Movement is not due directly to moving forces like rivers, ice and the sea. It is believed that mass movement of some kind takes place on all slopes with an angle of more than 5° and that this is the most important process of landscape change in Britain today.

There are four types of assessment movement, some involving movement and landscape change at a very slow pace, often too slow to observe directly, and others with rapid movement. Material can move downslope by **creeping**, by **sliding**, by **flowing** and by **falling** (or by a combination of these). **Soil creep** leading to the formation of terracettes is one common type of mass movement (Fig. 4.6). The material involved in soil creep is generally fine and moist, and the process tends to be slow but fairly continuous.

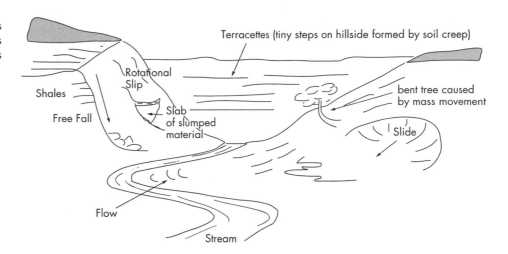

Fig. 4.6 Mass movement types in the Pennines

Terracettes (tiny steps on hillside formed by soil creep)

Rotational Slip

Shales

Free Fall

Slab of slumped material

bent tree caused by mass movement

Slide

Flow

Stream

▷ **Issue**   *Should quarrying of limestone scenery (especially in National Parks) be allowed?*

Aspects of this issue are shown below in Fig. 4.7.

Fig. 4.7

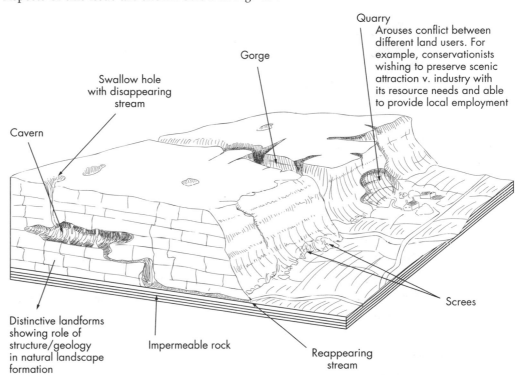

Quarry
Arouses conflict between different land users. For example, conservationists wishing to preserve scenic attraction v. industry with its resource needs and able to provide local employment

Gorge

Swallow hole with disappearing stream

Cavern

Distinctive landforms showing role of structure/geology in natural landscape formation

Impermeable rock

Reappearing stream

Screes

▷ **Case study**   *A glaciated upland landscape around Snowdon in North Wales*

Fig. 4.8   **Before glaciation**

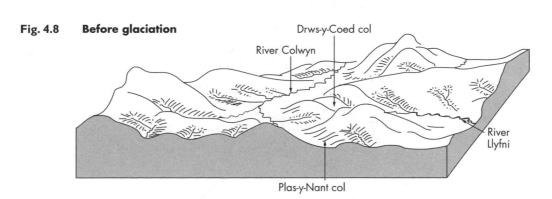

Drws-y-Coed col

River Colwyn

River Llyfni

Plas-y-Nant col

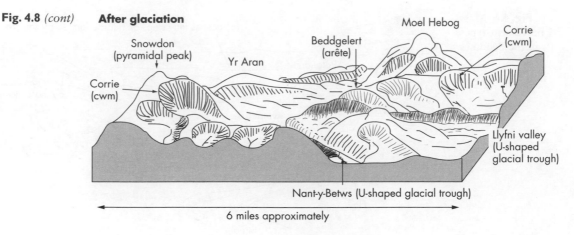

Fig. 4.8 *(cont)* **After glaciation**

6 miles approximately

(NB Arête and corrie are defined in the list of geographical terms that follows.)

▷ **Key terms** *Make sure you understand and can apply these geographical terms*

Abrasion	Erosion by water, ice or wind using moving debris, e.g. sand.
Arête	A sharp mountain ridge between two corries.
Corrie	A deep, rounded hollow with steep sides formed by glacial erosion.
Deposition	The laying down of material by water, ice or wind.
Erosion	The wearing away of the land surface by rivers, the sea.
Exfoliation	A weathering process, occurring in hot deserts and involving the peeling off of thin layers from a rock surface.
Freeze-thaw	A weathering process in which water freezes and expands in rock crevices, causing them to shatter.
Glaciation	The covering and action on an area by an ice sheet or glaciers.
Hanging valley	A tributary valley entering a main valley from a height above it so that streams have waterfalls.
Mass movement	The movement of weathered materials down a slope due to gravity.
Moraine	Debris or rock fragments deposited by a glacier.
Plucking	Erosion by a glacier when it freezes on to rock and pulls it away as it moves.
Ribbon lake	A long, narrow lake forming in a U-shaped glacial trough.
Scree	A mass of boulders and broken rocks accumulating at the foot of a slope after being weathered above.
Truncated spur	A former spur partly shoved off by a glacier.
U-shaped trough	A former river valley changed into a U-shaped cross-section with a level floor and steep sides by a glacier.
Weathering	The breakdown of rocks by exposure to the atmosphere.

[Handwritten annotations: "frost shatters", "molten by friction", "rising valley", "ARETE", "freeze-thaw", "Bergschrund crevasse.", "plucking on BACKWALL", "tarn", "abrasion", "Lip. (deposited material)", "valley glacier", "Tributary"]

> # STUDENT ANSWER WITH EXAMINER'S COMMENTS

Study Fig. 4.9 which shows some of the processes which shape the natural landscape.

Fig. 4.9

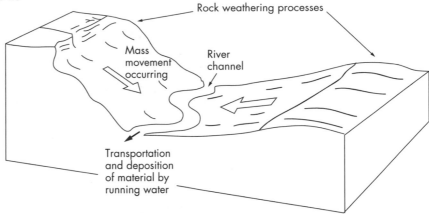

(a) (i) How do *weathering* and *erosion* differ?

Weathering is just the material being worn down and broken up. Erosion is ✓

the breaking down of material plus the transport of it. (Takes the weathered

material away)   L2   (2) 2

(ii) Name two weathering processes.

1 *Onion skin peeling (Exfoliation)*   ✓

2 *Frost shattering*   ✓   (2) 2

(iii) For a named type of rock, describe how it is weathered.

Name of rock type *Limestone.*

Limestone is permeable meaning water can pass through it. Its structure is not

a hard one. It is a soft rock and as water from streams running above the

limestone reaches the limestone the water starts to dissolve the limestone.

The same applies to rain water. Rain water is acidic enough to dissolve   3

limestone.   L2   (3)

(iv) What is meant by the term, mass movement?

Mass movement is a term used to describe the movement of a very large mass ✓
?
of rock, ice, mud. We use mass movement when describing glaciation as the   1

glaciers were huge.   (2)

                                                            L1 just!

(b) Study Fig. 4.10, a field sketch of an upland area.

Fig. 4.10

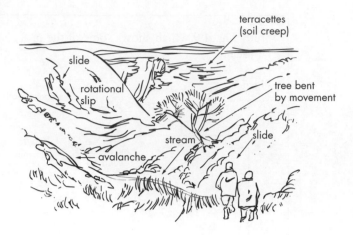

Various types of mass movement are shown on the field sketch. Suggest why mass movement occurs in such landscapes.

There are various types of mass movement occurring. Soil creep, slide, rotational slipping and avalanches etc. ✓ *This mass movement occurs because the land is very uneven. There are steep-sided hills and humps all over the landscape. As soon as it starts to rain, the rain infiltrates into all the surrounding* ✓ *area and on the steep slopes the soil becomes soggy and starts to slide down* ✓ *the hillside.*   L2   (5)   3

'No mechanism'

(c) Supporting your answer with evidence from the Buxton, Matlock and Dove Dale Ordnance Survey map suggest why:

(i) part of this area was chosen to be included within a National Park

The area chosen for the National Park was one of tourism. The National Park chose this because they didn't want quarriers digging all the land up (G.R. 7304) and spoiling the scenery. Plus they didn't want the residents of Buxton to be robbed of their landscape. There isn't much forest or coniferous wood also, so what they did was include this so it wasn't destroyed and protected the animals. (G.R. 7205) ✓ L1   (4)   1

(ii) conserving the natural landscape of this area can conflict with the interests of visitors, quarrying companies and water supply companies.

If they conserve the area, quarriers will get upset because they want to dig up limestone, but they can't because it is a conserved area. Water companies can't tap into the springs, e.g. Buxton mineral water, and they will lose their source and visitors aren't able to ramble where they want.   (4)   1

L1   ✓   (22)

(NEAB)13

'Not grade C standard.
No more than D/E
standard overall'

> **A TUTOR ANSWER**

(a)   Study Fig. 4.11 which shows a glaciated upland region.

Fig 4.11

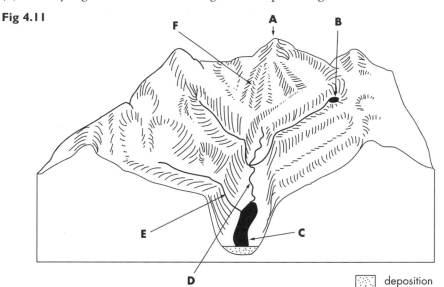

deposition

(i)   Letter **A** to **F** label six glacial features. Match each letter to the correct feature listed below. Place the correct letters in the appropriate boxes.

Feature	Letter
Arête	*F*
Corrie (with lake)	*B*
Hanging valley (with rainfall)	*E*
moraine-damned ribbon lake	*C*
Pyramidal peak	*A*
U-shaped valley	*D*

(5)

(ii)   Give three other pieces of evidence which suggest a glaciated landscape.

1. Screes (piles of broken rocks at the foot of a slope)

2. Boulder clay or till (unsorted deposits of stones and clay)

3. Very rounded or very angular landscape (depending on whether the ice

covered all or part of the landscape).   (3)

(b)   (i)   What is a glacier?

A mass of ice which moves slowly down a valley under gravity.   (1)

(ii)   What name is given to the past period when glaciers were common in Britain?

Ice Age   (1)

(iii)   Glaciers erode and deposit material. Name **one** feature produced by glacial erosion and **one** by glacial deposition.

Erosional: *Corrie*

Depositional: *Moraine*   (2)

(iv) For **one** of the features named in (b) (iii), explain how it was formed. A diagram may help your answer.

Corries are steep, horseshoe-shaped basins where glaciers once started. The

basin is deepened by the ice plucking on the back wall, steepening it, and

the movement of the ice erodes the basin floor (3)

Fig 4.12 Development of a corrie

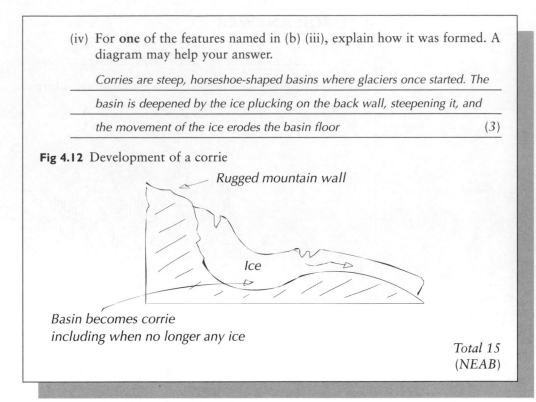

Basin becomes corrie
including when no longer any ice

Total 15
(NEAB)

EXAMINATION QUESTION

(a) Study the cross-section, Fig. 4.13, showing some of the features of limestone (karst) scenery near Gaping Gill in the Yorkshire Dales National Park.

Fig. 4.13

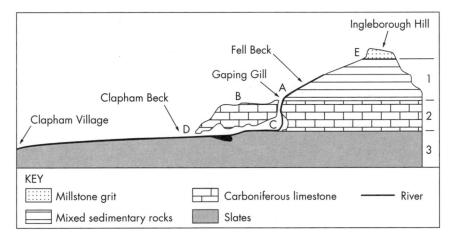

(i) Which of the rocks, **1**, **2** or **3** is limestone? (1 line provided here)

(*1 mark – Tier F only*)

(ii) Which of the letters **A**, **B**, **C**, **D** or **E** shows where you would find:

	Letter
A limestone pavemement?	
A swallow hole/sink hole?	
A cavern?	

(*3 marks – Tiers F and H*)

(iii) Describe the course of Fell Beck (9 lines provided here) (*3 marks – Tier F*)
(*4 marks – Tier H*)

(iv) Explain the formation of Gaping Gill and course of Fell Beck. (16 lines provided here) *(6 marks – Tiers F and H)*

(b) (i) Suggest **two** reasons why Gaping Gill may suffer from too many visitors. (2 lines provided here) *(2 marks – Tiers F and H)*

(ii) What might be done to stop the visitors causing any more damage? (2 lines provided here) *(1 mark – Tiers F and H)*

(c) State **two** uses of an area of limestone other than for tourism. (2 lines provided here) *(2 marks – Tiers F and H)*

(Total 18 marks)

(SEG)

▷ **EXAMINATION ANSWER**

(a) (i) 2 *(1)*

(ii) Limestone pavement = B
Swallow hole = A
Cavern = C *(3)*

(iii) Fell Beck flows across the impermeable (mixed sedimentary) rocks (1) and disappears down Gaping Gill (1), as a waterfall (1), until it reaches the impermeable slates (1) where it flows underground (1) until it re-emerges (1) at the surface as Clapham Beck (1). *(3 marks – Tier F) (4 marks – Tier H)*

(iv) Level 1 – 1–2 marks
Statements only use information on the diagrams, i.e. flows across this type of geology, flows down Gaping Gill, etc.
Level 2 – 3–4 marks
More explanation using impermeable and permeable; Gaping Gill explained as a swallow hole formed by limestone solution.
Level 3 – 5–6 marks
Full understanding shown including sound explanation of Limestone solution – rain is a weak acid – attacks the limestone, dissolving the calcium carbonate – weathers the limestone, particularly along joints. *(6)*

(b) (i) *(2 x 1)* Much bare ground suggesting trampling; people in foreground; well worn footpaths. *(2)*

(ii) For example, fence off some pathways down to the Gill, etc. *(1)*

(c) *Any two of*: Sheep grazing, quarrying, horse training (or any other suitable suggestion). *(2)*

(Total 18)

(SEG)

SUMMARY

▷ A landscape is the output of a system of inputs (e.g. rocks, etc.) and processes (e.g. weathering, etc.).

▷ The earth's crust is composed of different rock types.

▷ These rock types are associated with different landforms and landscapes (e.g. limestone scenery).

▷ The earth's crust is modified by weathering, erosion and deposition.

▷ Moving ice erodes and deposits material and produces distinctive landforms (e.g. corries, glacial troughs, etc.).

▷ Landscapes are influenced by people. Quarrying is an issue.

Chapter 5

Drainage basins and water supply

> ► **GETTING STARTED**

This topic is one of the core areas of GCSE Geography; it appears in all 13 syllabuses, as the chart below shows. This lists the key areas you must know and understand, some of which need studying in the context of one or more places. These places become case studies; specific knowledge of which can be used in the examination to illustrate key ideas. These ideas are summarised at the end of the chapter. You should be clear about the meaning of the geographical terms in this topic listed on page 74. Make sure that you are able to understand them when they are used in examination questions, and that you are able to bring them into your answers where appropriate.

LONDON A	LONDON B	MEG A	MEG B	MEG C	NEAB A	NEAB B	NEAB C	NICCEA	SEG A	SEG B	WJEC	IGCSE	TOPIC	REVISION STUDY	REVISION 1	REVISION 2
	✓	✓	✓	✓	✓	✓	✓						The hydrological (water) cycle			
✓	✓			✓	✓	✓	✓	✓					Drainage basins			
✓	✓	✓	✓			✓			✓	✓	✓	✓	River processes of erosion, transport and deposition			
✓	✓	✓	✓			✓			✓	✓	✓	✓	Upland and/or lowland river valley landforms and their processes of formation			
	✓		✓	✓			✓	✓					Human influences on drainage			
	✓		✓		✓	✓	✓		✓	✓			The cause, effect and management of river flooding			
✓			✓		✓	✓	✓	✓	✓	✓		✓	The importance of fresh water supplies and water management to avoid conflict			

> ► **WHAT YOU NEED TO KNOW**

> ► **The hydrological cycle**

All the waters of the surface of the earth and the atmosphere form one massive closed system known as the **hydrological** or water cycle. Water movement takes place within this cycle and changes from one form to another. For example, evaporation as vapour from the sea forms clouds, which are condensed to fall as rain, etc. Over 97% of the world's water is stored in the oceans (see Fig. 5.1).

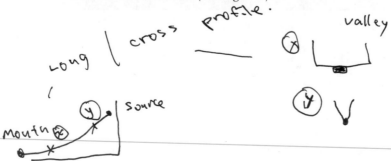

Fig. 5.1

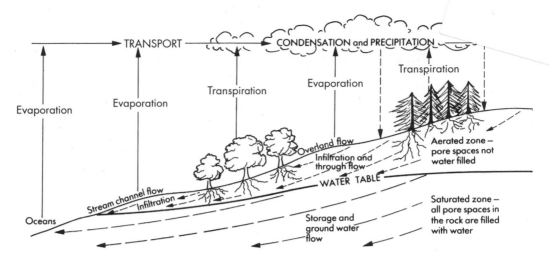

River systems

River systems are part of the hydrological cycle. Like the wider hydrological cycle, river basins can also be seen as a system with inputs of precipitation, stores of underground water, flows of water within streams and the river (discharge) and outputs into the ocean. If the inputs change, there are changes throughout the basin, e.g. flooding. The source of a river may be in an upland region, where precipitation is heaviest and where there is a slope down where the run of water can flow. The upland, therefore, forms a major part of the catchment area of the river.

Drainage basins

The river is included in the **drainage basin**, i.e. an area in which all the drainage water, particularly over the surface, is linked in one system. The **watershed** is the boundary or dividing line between the drainage basins. A watershed may be the crest of a mountain range, where the streams flow down the slopes on both sides (Fig. 5.2).

Fig. 5.2

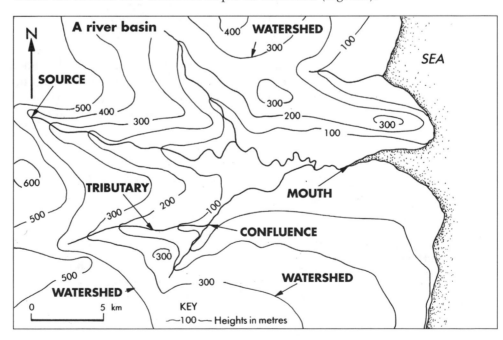

Drainage systems develop a **pattern**. Four patterns are shown in Fig. 5.3 below. **Dendritic** drainage has a tree-like appearance, with the tributaries appearing as roots of the tree. Streams flowing outwards and downhill from a dome give rise to a **radial** drainage pattern, just like the spokes of a bicycle wheel. When the tributaries join the main stream or river at right angles, so that the drainage pattern developed is rectangular in shape, it is described as **trellised**, like the popular type of garden fencing. **Parallel** drainage, as the name implies, shows a drainage pattern that is parallel in shape.

Fig. 5.3

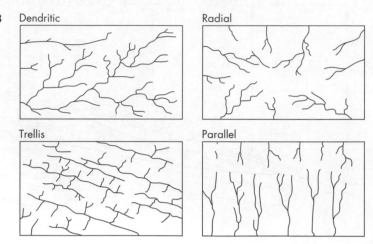

The idea of drainage basins as systems is well illustrated if you look at a hydrograph, as in Fig. 5.4 showing rainfall and run-off into a river channel. Discharge is the amount of water in the channel.

Fig. 5.4

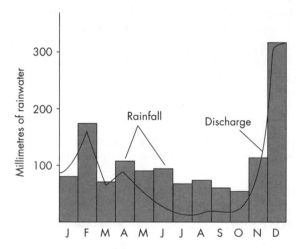

Rainfall clearly affects the amount of discharge in this drainage basin; discharge is highest in the winter when it is wettest. There may be time-lags between rainfall and discharge so it may take some time before high rainfall affects the amount of discharge. Discharge is also going to be affected by the nature of the soil and the type of land use. For instance, clay-based soil will retain water on the surface, tending to increase discharge. Deforestation of hillsides will also tend to increase discharge, and so on.

Running water is the most important process responsible for shaping the landscape. It erodes and deposits, and produces distinctive landforms, both in its stream channels and its wider valleys.

Processes of erosion, transport and deposition

Erosion

The process of erosion refers to the removal and breakoff of material. It should be distinguished from weathering which is the disintegration (but not the removal) of material. Rivers erode material in several ways.

Corrasion

Any material that the river is carrying rubs against the sides and bottom of the river and slowly wears them away.

Attrition

As well as wearing away the river bed and banks, rock fragments also grind against each other and are thus slowly reduced in size.

Solution or Corrosion

River water *dissolves* certain minerals in rocks as it moves along. This is like chemical weathering, but as material is moved as well, it is an erosional process.

Hydraulic Action

Erosion by the power of water alone.

Although rivers are eroding all the time, the greatest amount takes place when a river floods. It is then that the largest boulders are carried.

Transport

Solution

Dissolved material is carried along by the river.

Suspension

Very small rock particles are carried within the river water. Because the river is moving, they do not settle on its bed.

Rolling

Heavier pieces of rock remain on the bed until moved along, in time of flood for example.

All material transported by a river is called its **load**.

Deposition

Deposition occurs when the river can no longer carry its load. This happens when the river loses energy for one of several reasons:

(i)   The volume decreases, e.g. because of lack of rainfall, so the river slows down.
(ii) The river may slow down because of increased friction with the bed and banks of the river.
(iii) The river may slow down on flowing into a lake.

Variations in river characteristics are shown in Fig. 5.5.

Fig. 5.5 Typical variations in river characteristics from their source to the sea (mouth)

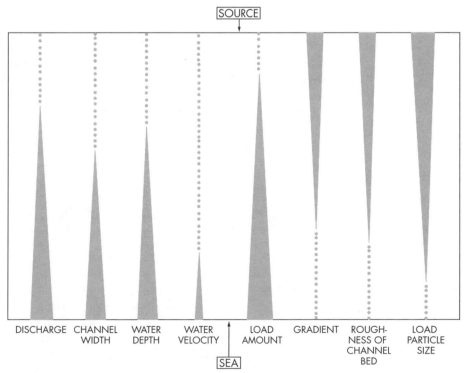

Two features and landforms found along channels in river valleys and formed by erosion and deposition are waterfalls and meanders.

Waterfalls

Erosion of the channel bed can lead to the formation of a **waterfall**. Waterfalls are commonly formed where rocks of different resistance meet. In Fig. 5.7 water plunges over a hard rock band, known as a **cap rock** into the plunge-pool below. Niagara Falls in the USA is an example.

Figs. 5.6 & 5.7

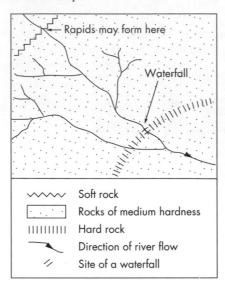
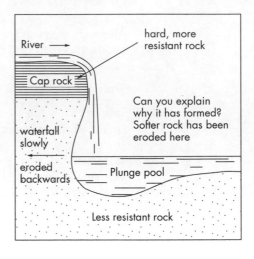

Meanders

Many rivers have channels which swing (**meander**) across the landscape. The extent to which a channel meanders can be measured by calculating its **sinuosity**. This is done by comparing the overall length from source to mouth as a straight line with the overall length of the actual channel (Fig. 5.8). The width across the valley floor which is occupied by a series of meanders is known as the **meander belt** (Fig. 5.9).

Fig. 5.8
How to calculate the sinuosity of a meander

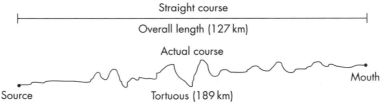

Why rivers meander, usually in their lower courses, is complicated and there is no clear and satisfactory explanation. It is not because of obstacles in their paths, nor because they are flowing more slowly (Fig. 5.10).

It is known that meanders migrate, moving both downstream and laterally (sideways). When they migrate, they leave behind evidence of their former position. For example, **swales** are hollows of fine sediment which were once in the river channel.

Fig. 5.9 The features of a meander

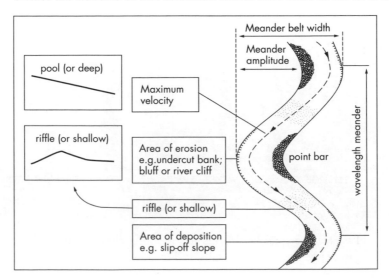

Fig 5.10 Block diagram of the lower course of a river valley

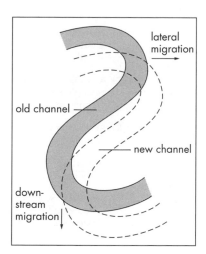

Conflicting uses of water resources and land in a river valley

The conflicts suggested by Fig. 5.11 need managing. Integrated river basin management is called for if all the various demands which people place on the resources of the drainage basin are to be met. Some of the management responsibilities of the River Authorities are listed below.

Fig. 5.11

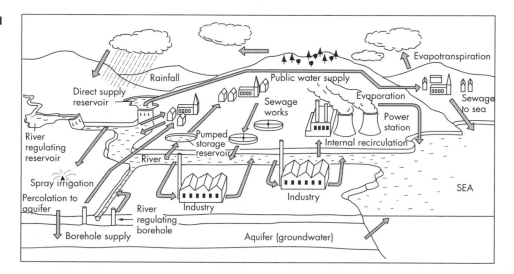

▶ Angling
▶ Birdwatching
▶ Conservation
▶ Water distribution to customers
▶ Running and upkeep of reservoir
▶ Land drainage
▶ Sewage treatment
▶ Water quality control
▶ Navigation
▶ Flood control
▶ Water treatment
▶ Underground drains and sewers

Fig. 5.12 illustrates an example of the effects of river management. Part (1) shows a stretch of the River Rhône and its valley *before* river management. Part (2) shows the same stretch *after* a period of management.

Fig. 5.12

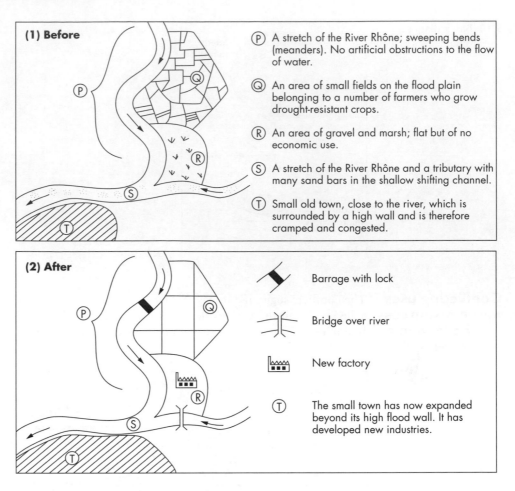

(1) Before

Ⓟ A stretch of the River Rhône; sweeping bends (meanders). No artificial obstructions to the flow of water.

Ⓠ An area of small fields on the flood plain belonging to a number of farmers who grow drought-resistant crops.

Ⓡ An area of gravel and marsh; flat but of no economic use.

Ⓢ A stretch of the River Rhône and a tributary with many sand bars in the shallow shifting channel.

Ⓣ Small old town, close to the river, which is surrounded by a high wall and is therefore cramped and congested.

(2) After

▬ Barrage with lock

╫ Bridge over river

▦ New factory

Ⓣ The small town has now expanded beyond its high flood wall. It has developed new industries.

▷ **Issue**   *Britain's unreliable water supply*

The world's supply of water for people's use does vary naturally from place to place. There can often be a mismatch between the supply and the demand for water. In Britain, as the maps show (Fig. 5.13), the areas of high water supply occur in the remote, thinly populated and mountainous areas of Wales, the North of England and Scotland. The largest areas of demand are, however, in the urbanised areas of the Midlands, North West, North East, and South East England. As far as people are concerned, the rainfall falls in the wrong place! This mismatch between supply and demand makes water collection and control necessary; especially the construction of dams and reservoirs. Any changes of climate and the droughts of the 1990s have made the situation worse.

Fig. 5.13

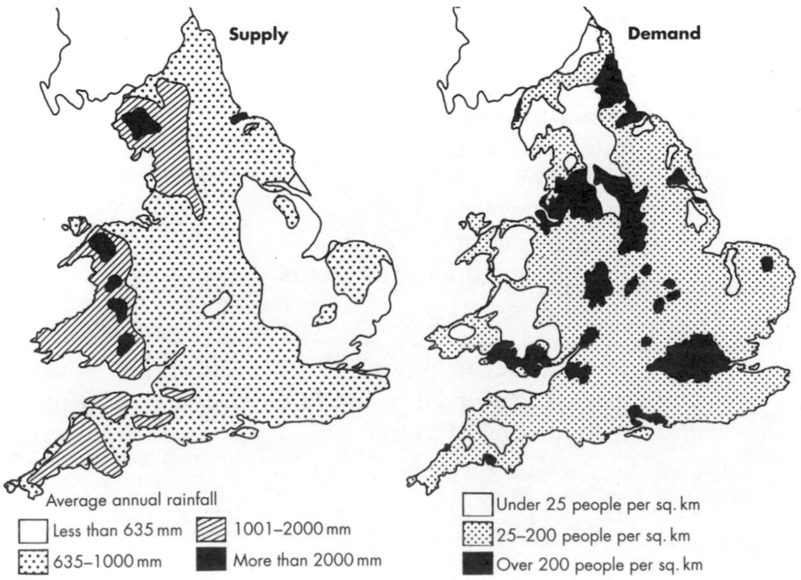

Supply   **Demand**

Average annual rainfall

☐ Less than 635 mm   ▨ 1001–2000 mm
▒ 635–1000 mm   ■ More than 2000 mm

☐ Under 25 people per sq. km
▒ 25–200 people per sq. km
■ Over 200 people per sq. km

Water demand continues to grow. Homes, industry and agriculture consume more water year on year. It is predicted that demand will have doubled in 30 years by the year 2000, and that water shortage, especially in the dry areas of South East England, will become a real problem. The general strategy in recent years has been:

1 The building of five new inland reservoirs, e.g. Brenig in North Wales, Kielder in Northumberland and Carsington in Derbyshire;
2 the enlargement of several existing reservoirs, e.g. Haweswater in the Lake District;
3 the use of river estuaries for water storage, e.g. the Welsh Dee;
4 more transfer of water from one part of the country to another, using rivers and aqueducts;
5 more use of underground water in, e.g., Shropshire and the Thames;
6 the unsuitability of large-scale sea water desalination.

▷ **Case study**   *The Lynmouth floods of August 1952*

Fig. 5.14 below shows five causes of flooding in the village of Lynmouth, Devon.

Fig. 5.14

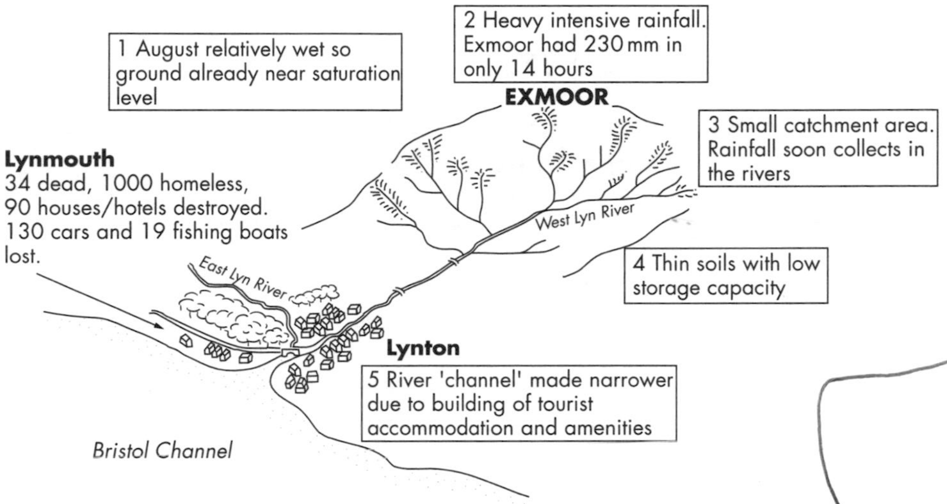

1 August relatively wet so ground already near saturation level

2 Heavy intensive rainfall. Exmoor had 230 mm in only 14 hours

EXMOOR

3 Small catchment area. Rainfall soon collects in the rivers

West Lyn River

4 Thin soils with low storage capacity

Lynmouth
34 dead, 1000 homeless, 90 houses/hotels destroyed. 130 cars and 19 fishing boats lost.

East Lyn River

Lynton
5 River 'channel' made narrower due to building of tourist accommodation and amenities

Bristol Channel

▷ **Key terms**   *Make sure you understand and can apply these geographical terms*

Acquifer	The area of saturated rock underground.
Abrasion (corrasion)	Defined and explained on page 68.
Attrition	Defined and explained on page 68.
Catchment area	The area of a drainage basin which feeds the rivers and streams.
Condensation	The change of water from vapour to liquid.
Confluence	The meeting of two rivers.
Corrosion	Defined and explained on page 69.
Delta	A large area of deposition where a river enters a lake/sea.
Deposition	The dumping of materials by natural processes.
Desalination	Removing the salt from sea water.
Drainage basin	An area in which all the drainage of water, particularly across the surface, is linked in one system.
Erosion	The breakdown and removal or materials/rocks.
Evapotranspiration	Water loss from the earth's surface by evaporation and by transpiration through plants.
Flood plain	Plain bordering a river formed from deposits carried by river.
Hydraulic action	Defined an explained on page 69.
Hydrological or water cycle	The system in which the world's water is contained, and flows from one type of water (e.g. liquid) to another (e.g. cloud).

Load	The material carried by a river/stream.
Meander	The swings of a winding river/stream.
Mouth	The end-point of a river where it enters the sea.
Permeable and impermeable	Rocks that allow water to pass through them and those that do not.
Precipitation	Includes rainfall, snow, dew, fog, etc.
Run-off or river discharge	Water which runs over the surface (i.e. run-off) and within channels (i.e. discharge).
Saturation or infiltration or percolation	Water which seeps underground off the surface.
Solution	Defined and explained on page 69.
Source	The start of a river/stream.
Suspension	Defined and explained on page 69.
Tributary	The branch of a river; streams which feed it.
Watershed	The boundary of a drainage basin.
Water table	The upper level of the aquifer.

Slip-off slope

Suggestions for further work

▷ The following titles are suitable for fieldwork investigation:
1 Do pebbles on the river get smaller downstream?
2 Does water speed in the stream vary?
3 To what extent can river valley X be viewed as a recreational resource?
4 How is stream discharge related to precipitation?
5 What would the impact on farming be of a proposal for the reservoir in valley X?

▷ It may be possible to undertake a study on the following lines, using Ordnance Survey maps in the classroom:
The size and the shape of the valley in river X varies from source to mouth.

▷ There are many possible enquiries that your teacher could plan for you as a classroom-based coursework unit, e.g. sources of water supply and its uses in your home area.

▶ **STUDENT ANSWER WITH EXAMINER'S COMMENTS**

▷ **Longer structured question**

This question is about a river in a drainage basin.
(a)   Look at the map in Fig. 5.15 below which shows part of Wales.

Fig. 5.15

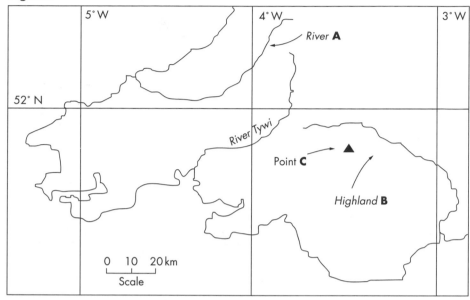

Use a map in the atlas to name the feature labelled on the map above.

(i)   Name of the river marked **A**.

Teifi   ✓

'Good accurate start'

(ii)   Name of the area of highland marked **B**.

Brecon Beacons   ✓

(iii)   Height of the land at point marked **C**.

886 m   ✓   3

(3 marks)

(b)   Look at the hydrograph (Fig. 5.16).
It shows the average rainfall and the average depth of the river for a place on the river Tywi.
(i)   What amount of rain fell in January?

175 mm   ✓

(ii)   What is the average depth of the river in October?

2 metres   ✓

(iii)   What is the relationship between the amount of rain that fell and the average depth of the river at this place?

'Basic relationship only stated. Expand/illustrate it'

The relationship is the average depth increases in proportion to the average

rainfall.   ✓

L1   3

(4 marks)

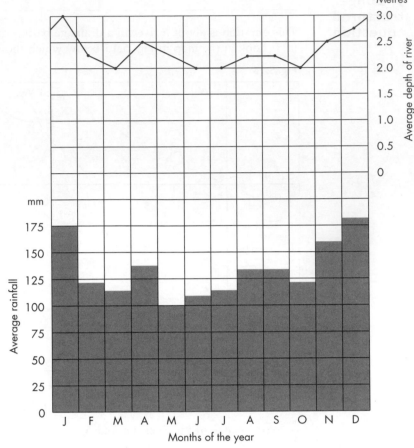

Fig. 5.16 Average rainfall and average depth of the river for a place on the river Tywi

Table 5.1

Month of the Year	September	October	November	December
Rainfall (mm)	135	125	165	180
Speed of river (metres per second)	1.25	1.25	1.50	1.60

(c)   A GCSE student wanted to find out if the speed of the river was linked to the amount of rain that fell at this place.
Some of the results obtained have been plotted on the scattergraph in Fig. 5.17 below; other results are shown in Table 5.1
(i)   Use these results from Table 5.1 to finish the scattergraph.

'Sufficiently accurate plotting'

Fig. 5.17

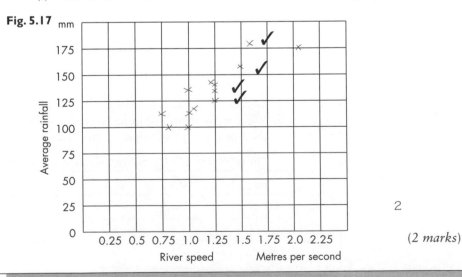

2

(2 marks)

(ii) What relationship does the graph show between the river speed and rainfall?

The more rainfall the faster is the speed of the river, for example 135 mm of

rain will produce 1.25 m/ps but 180 mm of rainfall will produce 1.6.

L2   *(2 marks)* 2

'Well done – relationship illustrated!'

(iii) The river erodes when it is travelling very quickly and deposits materials when it is travelling very slowly.
Explain why it does this.

It deposits material when travelling slowly because it finds the bedload too

heavy and it cannot carry or transport the heavy material when travelling

slowly. When the river is travelling quickly there is more water in the river

therefore the bedload can scour the surface. The speed is due to the depth so

the deeper the river the more erosion takes place but with lack of water the

materials are just too heavy.   L1+   2

(4 marks)

'Good geography'

'Why does it pick up more?'

(d) There is a meander at the place on the river Tywi.
The Wales Tourist Board want to put a picnic area here and have chosen three possible sites.
They are labelled **A**, **B** and **C** on the sketch of the meander in Fig. 5.18 below.

Fig. 5.18

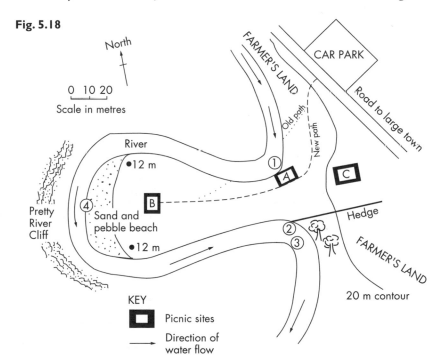

(i) Look at the points marked 1, 2, 3 and 4 on the sketch. Put the numbers in the right hand spaces on the table below to show whether erosion or deposition is happening at each point.   *(2 marks)*

| Erosion is happening at points | 1,2 ✓ | 2 |
| Deposition is happening at points | 3,4 ✓ | |

(ii) The Welsh Water Authority have told the Tourist Board that it would not be a good idea to put a picnic site at either **A** or **B**.
Explain why they said this. Use the following words in your answer:
erosion; undercutting, flood; cut-off; ox bow lake.

It would not be good because erosion is taking place at A and deposition at

B. A would become flooded because of the coming together of the convex

lanes of water. B would be surrounded by an Oxbow lake as that part of the

river is cut off from the rest. The picnic site would have to build a bridge to

cross the new channel. When the river is in flood the water would run

straight over A.   L1+   2

'Basic and broad answer. More detailed accuracy for full marks. No mention of undercutting'

(3 marks)

(iii) Imagine that you are the local farmer who owns the land around the meander. Write a letter to the Wales Tourist Board giving your views about the picnic area they want to make. You *must* mention *at least four* different points in your letter. You can include views for and against the picnic area.   *(4 marks)*

Wales Tourist Board,
Brunel House,
2 Fitzalan Road,
Cardiff,
CF2 1UY

Dear Sir or Madam

This area which holds the 3 sites is not suitable because it could be danger-

ous because if the river floods 'A' will be destroyed. If the picnic area is set

up the land owned by farmer will be trampled on by all the visitors ruining it.

The new path will cut across the land, that plus the old one is wasting the

land.

There will be a danger of the people being run over by cars when crossing

the main road from the car park. The road will be extremely busy in summer

as it leads to a large town.   L1+

'Objecting!'

'What type of land? How?'

'Objecting to it!'

'Not 4 points made!'

2

(6 marks)
(Total 30)
18   *(WJEC)*

'A grade C quality answer'

A TUTOR ANSWER

Short structured question

Study Fig. 5.19 below which is a field sketch showing part of the course of a river, and answer the questions which follow.
Fig. 5.19

(i) Complete Table A by stating another two types of sediment the river has probably deposited at point **A** on the sketch.

Table A

Deposited sediment
1 SILT
2 *Sand*
3 *Pebbles*

(2 marks)

(ii) State fully TWO ways materials such as these may have been transported by the river

ANSWER 1 *Sand is carried along suspended in the water as the river flows.*

(2 marks)

ANSWER 2 *Pebbles are rolled along the river bed. This process is known as traction.*

(2 marks)

(iii) At Point **B** on the sketch the river bank has collapsed. State ONE fluvial process of erosion and explain how it has caused this collapse.

FLUVIAL PROCESS   *Lateral corrasion*

(1 mark)

EXPLANATION *The river's load, especially its rock fragments, grind against the banks of the channel. This causes sideways erosion or wearing away of the banks.*

(3 marks)
(NICCEA)

▶ **EXAMINATION QUESTION**

Study Fig. 5.20 showing the upper courses of the River Wye and River Severn in Wales.

Fig. 5.20

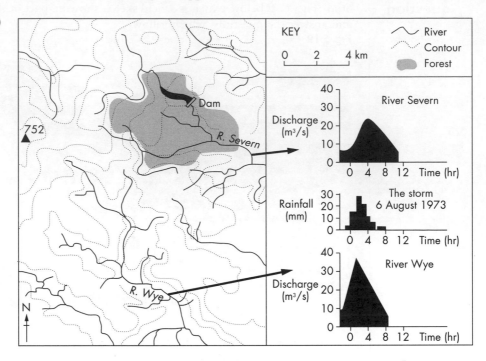

(a) (i) Which river had the higher discharge? (1 line provided here)
                                                                    (*1 mark – Tier F only*)
     (ii) Describe how the storm affected the discharge of the two rivers.
           (5 lines provided here)   (*2 marks – Tiers F and H*)
     (iii) From the map, name **one** feature which may have affected the discharge of the
           River Severn. Explain your choice.
           Name of feature (1 line provided here)
           Explanation (4 lines provided here)   (*2 marks – Tier F only*)
     (iv) Explain the different discharge patterns of the two rivers (4 lines provided here)
                                                                    (*3 marks – Tier H only*)

(b) (i) In the box below, draw a simple cross-section of the upper course of a river valley.
                                                                    (*1 mark – Tiers F and H*)
     (ii) Add **two** labels to show the features of the river and its valley.
           (Box of size equivalent to 9 lines provided here)   (*2 marks – Tiers F and H*)
     (iii) State and explain **one** disadvantage of the area in the map for human activity.
           (2 lines provided here)   (*2 marks – Tiers F and H*)

(c) Study Fig. 5.21 showing a section through the waterfall at High Force in Upper
     Teesdale.

Fig. 5.21

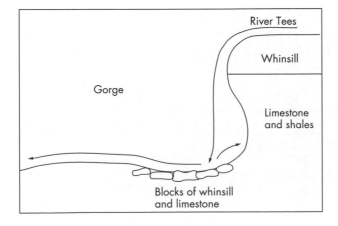

    (i) Describe the features of the waterfall as shown in Fig. 5.2. (6 lines provided h
(3 marks – Tiers F and H)

    (ii) Explain how the waterfall has been formed. (7 lines provided here)
(3 marks – Tiers F and H)
(Total 16) (Tier F and Tier H)
(SEG)

▶ EXAMINATION ANSWER

(a)   (i) Wye   *(1) (Tier F only)*

    (ii) Wye peaked sooner and higher (1 mark for timing).
          Severn peaked later and lower (1 mark for quantity).   *(2)*

    (iii) Reservoir (dam) or forested area (1 mark)
          Reservoir could hold back some of the flood water so reducing the peak, the woodland would absorb more of the moisture, (Any 1 mark) etc. *(2) (Tier F only)*

    (iv) Reservoir (dam) and forested area in Severn catchment
          Reservoir could hold back some of the flood water so reducing the peak, the woodland would absorb more of the moisture, etc. Absence of either on River Wye = faster run-off   *(3) (Tier H only)*

(b)   (i) Recognisable V-shape of valley with river.   *(1)*

    (ii) Two correctly labelled features, e.g. steep slopes, V-shaped valley, turbulent river, etc. *(2 x 1)*   *(2)*

    (iii) Steep slopes make it difficult to use farm machinery and to build settlement and roads, valleys difficult to bridge. (Any 1 mark). Must be explained for 2 marks.
                                                                     (2)

(c)   (i) *(3 x 1)*
          Three points, e.g. high head of water, steep cliff, plunge pool at base, cap rock of hard rock; steep sided gorge.   *(3)*

    (ii) Level 2 – 1 –2 marks
          The whinsill is a hard, resistant cap rock which erodes only slowly. The softer limestone and shales are eroded more quickly to form a plunge pool.
          Level 3 – 3 marks
          Specific reference to processes in formation, e.g. corrosion of limestone (chemical action); hydraulic action (force of water); creation of overhang waterfall retreats upstream, etc.   *(3)*
(Total 16)
(Tier F and Tier H)
(SEG)

SUMMARY

▷ The hydrological cycle and drainage basin are linked systems. The flow of water in a basin is part of the cycle.

▷ Processes of erosion and deposition (including weathering and mass movement) operate in basins to modify the landscape. This involves forming and modifying valleys.

▷ These processes create distinctive landforms in valleys and river channels.

▷ Human activities influence these processes and landforms.

▷ There are economic opportunities as well as environmental threats in river valleys for people who live and work in them. To avoid conflict between people and repercussions elsewhere, careful river management is necessary if they are to be used and altered for economic purposes.

Coastlines and their management

GETTING STARTED

As the chart below shows this topic figures in just over half of the GCSE syllabuses. These syllabuses mostly require you to know and understand the processes (mainly natural ones) which shape the coastline and the features (mainly landforms) which they produce. Coastlines differ significantly and change from time to time. Know about these differences and changes and be able to give examples. Coastal management by people is also called for at GCSE. Finally, check out the list of geographical terms important in this topic, which you will find towards the end of the chapter.

LONDON A	LONDON B	MEG A	MEG B	MEG C	NEAB A	NEAB B	NEAB C	NICCEA	SEG A	SEG B	WJEC	IGCSE	TOPIC	REVISION STUDY	REVISION 1	REVISION 2
✓	✓	✓	✓	✓					✓		✓	✓	Marine processes of erosion, transport and deposition and the coastal landforms/features produced			
✓	✓												Human causes of coastal change			
✓	✓				✓				✓	✓	✓		Opportunities along coastlines for people			
✓	✓	✓	✓		✓				✓				Coastal erosion, and management conflicts and issues			

WHAT YOU NEED TO KNOW

Marine energy   Coastlines can be studied as a natural system as in Fig. 4.1 on page 56.

Waves

Waves are the sea's agents of **erosion** and **deposition** which continuously alter coastlines. They are produced by the pressure of the wind making the surface of the sea undulate; the height and power of the waves depends on the strength of the wind and on their fetch, the distance they have been blown across the sea. The forward movement of a wave up a beach is called the swash, its backward or return flow the backwash (Fig. 6.1). Fig. 6.2 shows the parts of a wave.

The relative strengths of the swash and the backwash determine whether a wave is **constructive** (deposition exceeds erosion) or **destructive** (erosion exceeds deposition). Constructive waves will have a stronger swash, and this is more likely with a lower frequency of arrival (say, six to eight per minute), a longer wavelength and low height. Constructive waves which deposit material on a shoreline are generally shallower and are common on flatter, large beaches. Destructive waves, on the other hand, have a stronger backwash and a higher frequency of arrival (e.g., say, twelve to twenty per minute). They are steep waves and common on steeper beaches. The two types of wave are also known as **spilling** or **surging** breakers (constructive) and **plunging** or **surfing** breakers (destructive) Fig. 6.3).

Fig. 6.1 Swash and
backwash

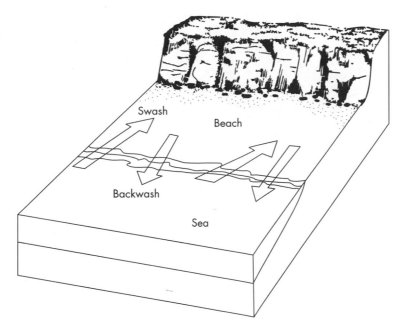

Fig. 6.2 Parts of a wave

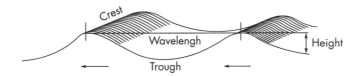

Fig. 6.3 Constructive and
destructive breakers

Wave refraction

Waves tend to break parallel to the shoreline, where their motion is checked by friction with
the sea bed, but at the points where headlands occur, the shallower water retards wave
advance. The rest of the wave moves on into the bay and is bent or refracted (Fig. 6.4). This
concentrates the energy of the advancing wave front against the side of the headlands.
Headland erosion is, therefore, increased by this wave refraction. Long-term, there is a tendency for a coastline of headlands and bays to be smoothed out with the help of wave
refraction.

Fig. 6.4 Refracted waves

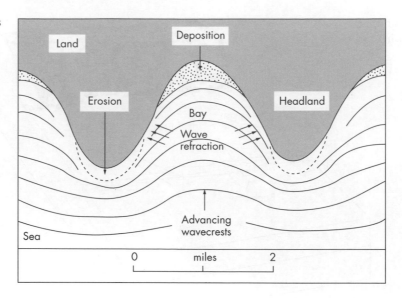

Processes of erosion

Corrasion
This is the same process as in rivers. The waves carry fragments which are thrown against the cliffs, particularly at the base.

Corrosion
Sea water dissolves rocks at the coast very slowly.

Hydraulic action
This is the action of the sea water itself striking the coast. Any air in the cracks and fissures in the coastal rocks gets compressed by the force of the water. When the wave retreats, this air expands and acts like a tiny explosion. After innumerable repetitions, a fragment of rock breaks off. Although this process is not the same, you might like to compare it with freeze-thaw in weathering.

Attrition
This is the wearing down of the sand by rubbing together, e.g. sand for beaches from boulders.

Landforms due to erosion

Cliffs
A cliff starts out as a small cleft cut into a sloping land surface. This cleft is enlarged, and the debris removed. After a lot of erosion the cliff will have moved back from its original position.

The shape of a cliff depends on the type of rock it is made of, the rock's jointing, layering and so on.

Wave-cut platform
This is an erosional feature cut by the waves as part of the general recession (backwards erosion) of a cliffed coastline. The cliff face recedes through undercutting by the sea at the base of the cliff, followed by collapse of the cliff face above. The retreat of the cliff face leaves the old base of the cliff as a platform (Fig. 6.5).

The waves eroding the coastline carry some of the small rock fragments back out to sea. In time deposition of these fragments may build up to form a terrace, referred to as a **wave-built terrace**.

groyne

Fig. 6.5 Wave-cut platform

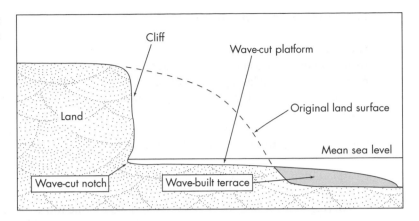

Features of headland erosion: cave, arch and stack

A **stack** is an isolated pillar of rock in the sea close to cliffs. It represents a short stage in the recession (erosion backwards) of a cliffed coastline.

In Fig. 6.6 the Old Harry Rocks are examples of stacks. They were previously part of the land and later were probably the outer wall of an arch, now collapsed. **Arches** are generally thought to have developed from sea **caves** (Fig. 6.7), formed at large joints or weaknesses in the rocks during the general undercutting, collapse and recession of the cliffs.

Fig. 6.6 The Dorset coast showing Old Harry Rocks

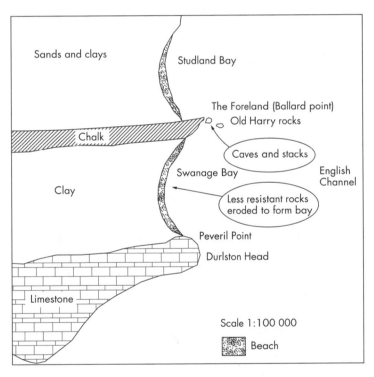

Fig. 6.7 The development of a stack from an arch and a cave

Landforms due to deposition

Beaches

Beach deposits are usually pebbly and sandy materials sorted by wave action. Beaches form best on gently shelving coasts or at the back of a bay protected from severe wave erosion. In a bay, waves are slowed down by friction, as in shallow water, so that deposition takes place.

Storm waves can move very large boulders, throwing them high on the beach – a **Storm beach** – beyond the action of ordinary waves.

Longshore drift

This is the name for the process by which beach material is moved along a coastline by the waves (Fig. 6.8). Along the south coast of England the most frequent winds are south-westerly. The result is a general movement of eroded material along the coast from Cornwall eastwards. When waves advance at an angle to the coastline, material is moved along the shore, because the backwash will be down the gradient of the beach at right angles to the shore.

Fig. 6.8 The process of longshore drift

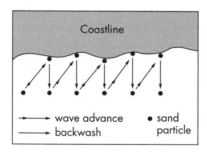

Fig. 6.9 How longshore drift forms a spit

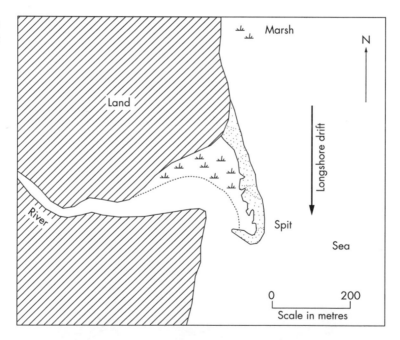

Fig. 6.10 What the coastline will look like

Groynes are constructed on beaches in an attempt to stop beaches being moved along the coastline by longshore drift. Where there is little or no attempt to halt this drift and where coastlines experiencing longshore drift change direction, various depositional features can form. **Spits** are an example (Figs 6.11 and 6.12). A spit is a long narrow ridge of sand or shingle projecting into the sea and connected to the land at one end. Fig. 6.11 shows the spit at Hurst Castle near Milford-on-Sea, Hampshire, which is a compound, recurved spit. You will see that its end has been curved or deflected more than once by waves and currents. At Orford Ness on the East Anglian coast a spit has grown parallel to the coast and diverted the mouth of the River Orford. Chesil Beach near Weymouth (Fig. 6.12) is a **tombolo**, that is, a shingle spit which has developed to join the mainland of Dorset to an offshore island, the Isle of Portland.

Fig. 6.11 Hurst Castle spit

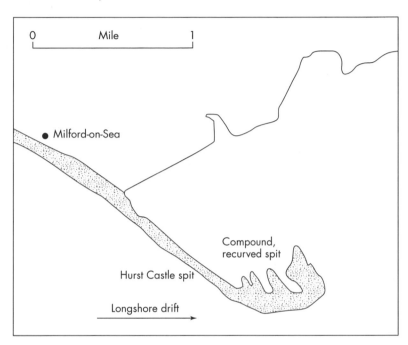

Fig. 6.12 Chesil Beach

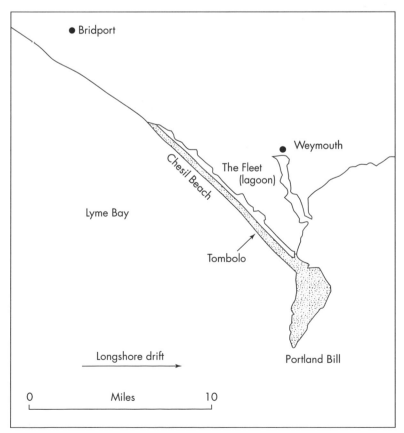

▷ **Issue** *Coast protection or 'managed retreat'?*

Examples of two different approaches are shown below.

SHERINGHAM COAST PROTECTION SCHEME
AN ACTION PLAN FOR RECOVERY
NORTH NORFOLK DISTRICT COUNCIL
TECHNICAL SERVICES

THE PROBLEM

Sheringham's sea walls were mostly constructed between 1900 and 1930. Many repairs have been made since then but now the walls have come to the end of their useful life. Time has also stripped away much of the sand from the east beach leaving it unattractive to visitors. Loss of the beach also leaves the walls open to attack by the sea at each high tide.

THE SOLUTION

Solving the problem requires a two stage approach.

Stage 1 involves the refurbishment of the sea walls and promenade. The whole length of wall is to be completely encased in high strength concrete. To protect the wall a rock armour revetment is to be placed at its toe. A total of 13 000 tonnes of concrete, 166 tonnes of steel and 28 000 tonnes of rock will be used.

Stage 2 will replace the beach that has been lost, covering the rocks over. They remain as an additional defence. A vital part of the work that must be carried out beforehand is to renew the present groyne system.

Sea wins land battle

On the Essex coast people are losing the battle against the sea.

Some 140 of one Essex farmer's 400 acres lie below sea level. Late last year, he learnt that the National Rivers Authority was considering demolishing the wall, three-quarters of a mile long, that keeps the North Sea at bay. He stands to lose 30 acres of summer grazing. A switch in government thinking on flood control might lead to replacing the old concrete sea defences with 'managed retreat' and 'working with nature'.

New hard sea walls can cost up to £8 million a mile.

Money will be spent on managing rather than trying to stop the retreat of the coastline.

(Adapted from *The Times*)

▷ **Case study**   *Conflicting uses of the coastline around Newbiggin-by-the-Sea, Northumberland*

Fig. 6.13

'Conflicts arise because people hold different values and attitudes, and have different interests. They need managing out!'

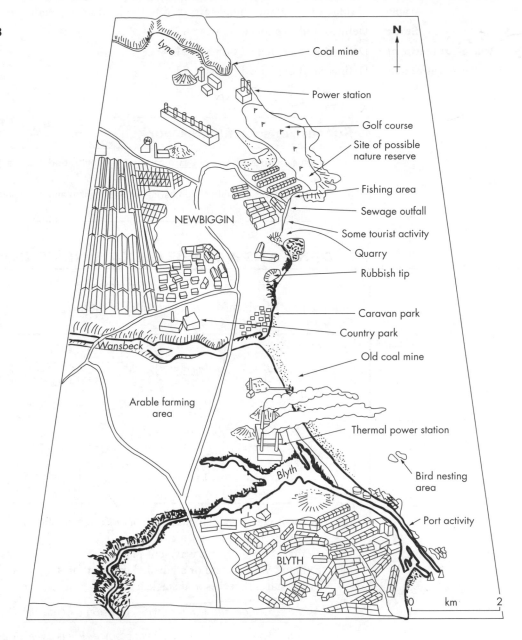

Coal mine

Power station

Golf course

Site of possible nature reserve

Fishing area

Sewage outfall

Some tourist activity

Quarry

Rubbish tip

Caravan park

Country park

Old coal mine

Thermal power station

Bird nesting area

Port activity

NEWBIGGIN

Wansbeck

Arable farming area

Blyth

BLYTH

Lyne

N

0   km   2

✕ **Key terms**   *Make sure you understand and can apply these geographical terms*

Arch	Defined and explained on page 85.
Attrition	Defined and explained on page 84.
Base level	Sea level.
Beach	An area of deposited material at the water's edge.
Cave	Defined and explained on page 85.
Cliff recession	Landward retreat of a cliff.
Constructive waves	Swash of wave stronger than backwash.
Corrasion (abrasion)	Defined and explained on page 84.
Destructive waves	Backwash of wave stronger than swash.
Gabions	Cages of boulders placed to protect coast from marine erosion.
Groynes	Wooden fences running from top of beach into sea to slow down longshore drift.
Hydraulic action	Defined and explained on page 84.

Headland·
Lagoon

Longshore drift	Defined and explained on page 86.
Spit	A ridge of sand and shingle attached to the land at one end.
Stack	Defined and explained on page 85.
Wave-cut platform	Defined and explained on page 84.
Wave refraction	Defined and explained on page 83.

solution (handwritten annotation next to Stack)

✱ — example of erosion (handwritten annotation)

Suggestions for further work

▶ Investigate how the size of beach particles and infiltration rates vary with distance from the sea.

▶ What effects is coastal erosion having on Sheringham and its people? What can be done?

▶ STUDENT ANSWER WITH EXAMINER'S COMMENTS

Study Fig. 6.14 which shows a stretch of coastline.
Fig. 6.14

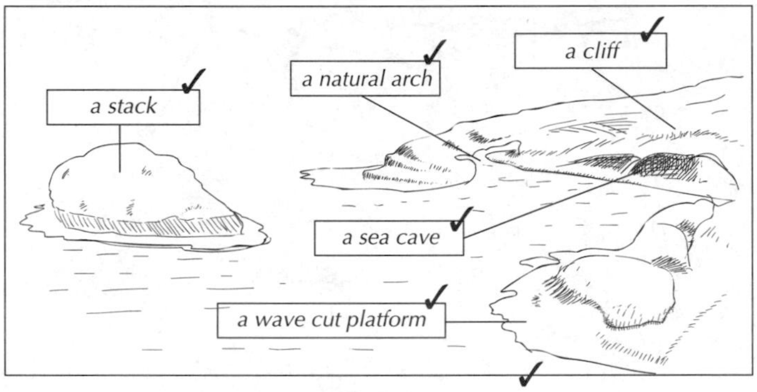

'Excellent start – knowing and identifying all 5 features'

(a) In the boxes provided, label the field sketch to show:
a natural arch   a sea cave
a cliff   a wave-cut platform   a stack   (5)

5

(b) Explain, with the aid of a labelled diagram or diagrams, the formation of sea caves, natural arches and stacks.

'Geographical vocabulary – good!'

As the sea erodes the cliff face with corrosion (chemicals), corrasion (boulders bashing away) erosion and pneumatic power joints, weaknesses in the rocks, form and break away. Over time this leaves a sea cave. As water continues to erode it

'Some process explained'

wears through the rocks leaving a natural arch. Eventually the joints allow the arch to collapse in the middle leaving a separate island of rock, a stack.

Fig. 6.15

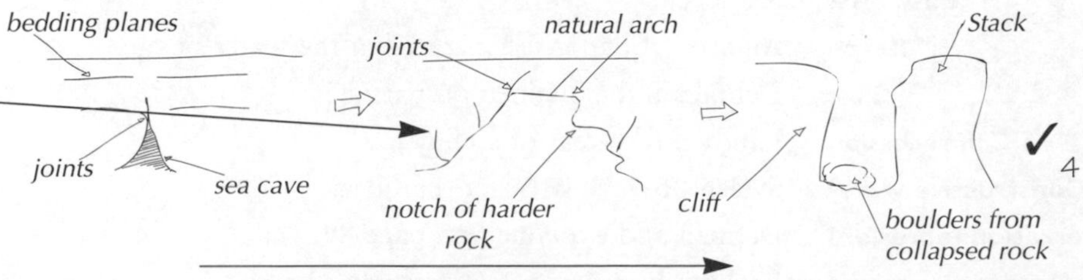

'This one not too clear!'

'The use of diagrams in exams is an excellent idea'

'Sequence of development correct – well done!'

(5)
(Total 10)
(NEAB)

9

'Grade A/B standard'

▷ **A TUTOR ANSWER**

Study Fig. 6.16 which shows the cross-section of a coastal area and Fig. 6.17 which shows a coastline of bays and a headland.

Fig. 6.16

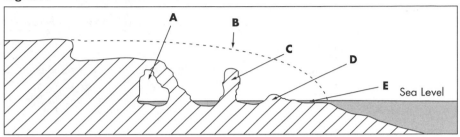

Fig. 6.17

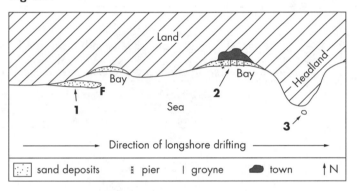

(a) (i) Name the five features labelled **A** to **E** on Fig. 6.16 by choosing from the following list:
arch   cave   cliff   original land surface   raised beach   stack
stump   wave-cut platform

A *Arch*	**B** *Original land surface*
C *Stack*	**D** *Stump*
E *Wave-cut platform*	

(5)

(ii) Which of the sites, **1**, **2** or **3** in Fig. 6.17 is the location of the cross-section in Fig. 6.16?

3

(1)

(b) (i) Name three uses which people may make of this coastline.

1. *Holidaymaking on beach*

2. *Birdwatching on headland*

3. *Fishing in bay*

(3)

(ii) What problems might these uses create?

Different land users can conflict, and newcomers and visitors can come into conflict with local residents. Birdwatching and lively holidaymakers do not match well, and decisions may have to be made about the most suitable location of caravan parks in the interests of the former. Equally, some local residents may be uneasy about mass tourism and the noise and crowds it brings.

(2)

(c) (i) Explain why headlands and bays have been formed on the coastline in Fig. 6.17.

Where the coastline is made up of alternate bands of harder and softer rock, particularly where they run at right angles to the coast, a series of headlands and bays will form. The harder and more resistant rock will form headlands.

(2)

(ii) Suggest why groynes have been built in the bay labelled 2 on Fig. 6.17.

Groynes are like wooden fences running from the top of the beach into the sea to counteract longshore drift. The sand deposits of the beach will otherwise be either lost from the bay or build up in a mound at the eastern end of the beach.

(2)

(iii) Name feature **F** shown on Fig. 6.17.

Name   *Spit*   (1)

By means of a labelled diagram ONLY, explain how such a feature was formed.

Fig. 6.18

Spits are ridges of sand or shingle attached to the land at one end. They are formed by longshore drift at places where the main coastline changes, e.g. at a river mouth or across a shallow bay.

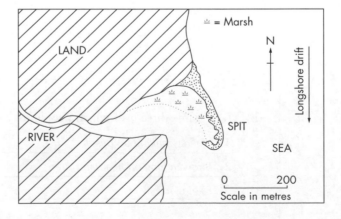

(4)

Total 20
(London)

> **EXAMINATION QUESTION**

(a) Study Fig. 6.19, a sketch of coastal scenery.

Fig. 6.19

(i) Complete Table 6.1 below to show the different landforms.

Table. 6.1

Letter on Fig. 6.19	Landform
	Beach
	Wave-cut Platform
	Cliff
	Headland

(4 marks – Tiers F and H)

(ii) Study Fig. 6.20, an incomplete sketch section from X to Y on Fig. 6.19. There is evidence of rapid erosion.

Fig. 6.20

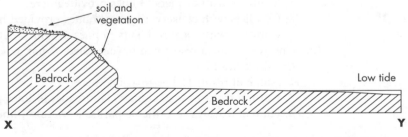

Describe the processes which cause this erosion. Add labels to Fig. 6.20 to help your answer (5 lines provided here) *(4 marks – Tiers F and H)*

(b) Study Fig. 6.21 which shows an area on the south west coast of Britain.

Fig. 6.21

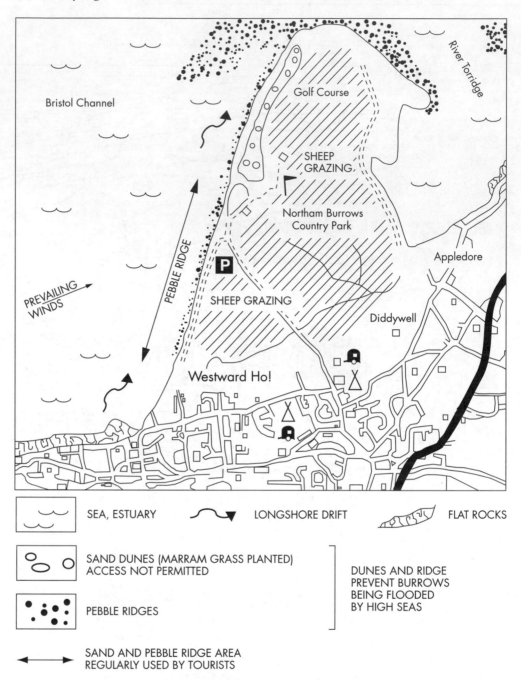

~~ SEA, ESTUARY	↷⃗ LONGSHORE DRIFT

⌒⌒⌒⌒ FLAT ROCKS

○ ○ ○ SAND DUNES (MARRAM GRASS PLANTED) ACCESS NOT PERMITTED

• • • PEBBLE RIDGES

DUNES AND RIDGE
PREVENT BURROWS
BEING FLOODED
BY HIGH SEAS

◄━━━► SAND AND PEBBLE RIDGE AREA
REGULARLY USED BY TOURISTS

  (i) State TWO attractions of the area for tourists. (2 lines provided here)

                                                                (2 marks – Tiers F and H)

EITHER (AT TIER F)
  (ii) Why might tourists cause problems when they visit this area? Use these headings:
      1. Conflicts with farmers (3 lines provided here)
      2. Conflicts with conservationists (3 lines provided here)
      3. Conflicts with local residents (3 lines provided here)   *(5 marks – Tier F only)*
  (iii) Choose a coastal resort you have studied. What makes it attractive to tourists?
       Use these headings:
      1. Name of resort (1 line provided here)
      2. Natural features (e.g. climate, landscape) (4 lines provided here)
      3. Human features (e.g. theme parks, services) (4 lines provided here)
                                                                  (5 marks – Tier F only)

OR (AT TIER H)
  (ii) Suggest how conflicts may arise with other land users and with conservationists
       when tourists use the area. (5 lines provided here)   *(4 marks – Tier H only)*

(iii) Choose a coastal resort you have studied. Describe the features that make it attractive to tourists. (7 lines provided here)   (*5 marks – Tier H only*)

EITHER (AT TIER F)

(c) **Global warming** will probably lead to a rise in sea levels over the next century.

   (i) Why should **global warming** cause a rise in sea level? (4 lines provided here)
   (*3 marks – Tier F only*)

   (ii) Describe how the coast can be protected from attack by the sea. Refer to places you have studied. (6 lines provided here)   (*4 marks – Tier F only*)

   (iii) Why do some people object to coastal defences being built? (4 lines provided here)   (*3 marks – Tier F only*)

OR (AT TIER H)

(c) Sea levels are expected to rise over the next century, perhaps by as much as one metre worldwide.

   (i) Explain why sea levels are rising. How could the coast be protected from this rise? Refer to a study you have made. (12 lines provided here)
   (*8 marks – Tier H only*)

   (ii) Some people say it is a waste of money trying to protect the coast. Do you agree? (6 lines provided here)   (*3 marks – Tier H only*)

   (*Total 30 marks*)
   (*Tier F and Tier H*)
   (*London*)

▶ EXAMINATION ANSWER

(a) (i) In order: B, C, A, D   (*4 x 1*) (*4*)

   (ii) Reserve 1 mark for annotations.
   Level 3 – Answer concentrates on process – describes what the sea is doing, but not necessarily with all correct terminology.   (*3–4*)
   Level 2 – Some parts of the process are there, but the sequence is incomplete.
   (*1½–2½*)

   Level 1 – Process becomes more simplistic and descriptive, talking about the waves breaking against the rock and washing it away.   (*½–1*) (*4*)

(b) (i) Several possibilities at 1 each – beaches; golf course; campsites; caravan sites; country park, etc.   (*1+1*) (*2*)

   TIER F ONLY

   (ii) Balance to be (*2+2+1*) (*2+1+2*)(*1+2+2*). Point mark.
   For each, an implied conflict is worth 1, and explicit conflict is worth 2, e.g. 'There are sheep where the golf course is' = 1; 'People using the golf course might leave gates open and let the sheep out' = 2.   (*5*)

   (iii) Read both parts together, and mark it to an overall level.
   Level 3 – There is some precise detail, perhaps the name of a theme park or local beauty spot, to tie the answer precisely to the chosen study.   (*3½–5*)
   Level 2 – Nothing is precise, but all is correct in general terms. Both parts have a decent answer.   (*2–3*)
   Level 1 – As above, but only 'natural' or 'human' features has answer of appropriate standard.   (*½–1½*) (*5*)

   TIER H ONLY

   (ii) Point mark, with 1 mark for idea and a further mark for development. The idea must clearly include **conflict** for a mark – 'tourists will want to visit the dunes, but conservationists want to protect them' = 1 mark. A comment on the instability of the dunes, could take this to a second mark.   (*4*)

   (iii) Level 3 – Answer could concentrate purely on human physical attractions, or be more balanced, it depends on the resort. At this level the answer will include precise recall of approximate climate data, perhaps, or named human attractions. As far as possible, within your knowledge of the chosen resort, look for the candidate having mentioned the main attractions.   (*3½–5*)
   Level 2 – Example well used, but not quite such precise recall.   (*2–3*)
   Level 1 – Answer is clearly about the resort chosen, but much of the detail could equally well refer to many other similar places.   (*½–1½*) (*5*)

(c)   TIER F ONLY

(i)   Point mark. 'Ice will melt'; appropriate names of ice caps = 1 each. Mark up any detail, like the fact that Antarctica is the biggest ice cap.   (3)

(ii)   Point mark. Credit mention of features like groynes, sea walls at 1 mark each. Any explanation of how they work is worth an extra mark. Reserve a mark for an appropriate coastal location.   (4)

(iii)   Point mark. Lots of possibilities, to do with cost, effect down coast, visual impact, etc. Stating a problem = 1, explanation of why it is a problem is worth an extra mark.   (3)

(Total 30) (Tier F)

(c)   TIER H ONLY

(i)   Level 3 – Both parts of the question must be clearly addressed. Rise in sea levels must be linked to global warming, which in turn leads to melting of ice caps and/or thermal expansion of water. Coastal defence must relate to the chosen example.   *(5½–8)*

Level 2 – Both parts of question are addressed, but perhaps not equally well. There is an awareness of global warming and its effects, but the answer lacks precision. Example is used for coastal protection, but is not well developed. *(3–5)*

Level 1 – Both parts must be considered, but answer is more descriptive than explanatory, or explanation is thin. There may be no link between global warming and melting of ice caps – only one of these might be mentioned. A coastal defence scheme is described, but how it copes with rising sea levels is not clear.   *(½–2½) (8)*

(ii)   Level 3 – Look for quality of the argument – the ideas are put across in a convincing manner with appropriate justification. Within the limitations of time, a rounded answer is achieved. *(3½–3)*

Level 2 – At least one well made point, but not quite the depth of level 3. *(1½–2)*

Level 1 – Some ideas are put forward, but none is well justified.   *(½–1) (3)*

(Total 30) (Tier H)

(London)

SUMMARY

▷ Coastlines are changing constantly and differ from place to place.

▷ Distinctive coastal landforms and features are shaped by marine processes of erosion and deposition, changes in sea level and human actions, and influenced by rock structure and length of time (how long they have been happening). Weathering and mass movement also occur along coastlines and play their part.

▷ Coastal landscapes affect human activities by offering opportunities and presenting problems for those living and working along the coastline.

▷ These opportunities and problems need careful coastline management because conflicts can arise. Attempts to control coastal erosion are an example.

Natural hazards and people

GETTING STARTED

This is a core area of GCSE Geography. It is studied by those following most of the 13 syllabuses. Earthquakes and volcanoes, the hazards chosen for this chapter, illustrate well the interaction between human, physical and environmental geography. They have a natural/physical mechanism causing them but they are a human hazard. Perhaps more of a hazard in LEDCs than MEDCs. Case studies from California or Japan and LEDCs such as India, show this with regard to earthquakes. As with other topics, places and specialist terms are as important as the ideas and skills. There is a list of geographical terms for the topic, and others are used and defined within the chapter.

Finally, remember there are natural hazards other than earthquakes and volcanoes.

LONDON A	LONDON B	MEG A	MEG B	MEG C	NEAB A	NEAB B	NEAB C	NICCEA	SEG A	SEG B	WJEC	IGCSE	TOPIC	STUDY	REVISION 1	REVISION 2
	✓	✓	✓	✓	✓		✓			✓	✓	✓	Kinds of natural/ environmental hazard			
	✓	✓		✓	✓		✓	✓	✓	✓		✓	Distribution and types of plate boundary			
	✓	✓		✓	✓		✓	✓	✓	✓		✓	Formation of volcanoes, and types and effects of volcanic eruptions			
	✓	✓		✓	✓		✓	✓	✓	✓		✓	Cause and effects of earthquakes			
	✓	✓		✓	✓		✓	✓	✓	✓		✓	Living in areas of crustal instability			
		✓		✓	✓	✓	✓		✓	✓		✓	Human response to earthquakes in California/Japan and LEDCs			
									✓			✓	Formation and distribution of fold mountains			
✓	✓	✓	✓	✓	✓	✓	✓		✓	✓	✓	✓	Cause, effect and management of non-tectonic natural hazards: pollution, extreme weather, flood, etc.			

WHAT YOU NEED TO KNOW

▶ **Natural hazards**   A natural hazard can be defined as 'an extreme natural event exceeding normal human expectations in terms of intensity of frequency, and causing major human hardship with significant physical damage and possible loss of life'. There are various different kinds of natural hazard; volcanoes and earthquakes, storms and hurricanes, floods and droughts, fog, global warming, etc. Some are both a natural and human hazard because people's activities have helped to cause them. This chapter deals only with volcanoes and earthquakes as natural hazards. There was some reference to extreme weather hazards in Chapter 3 and flooding as a hazard in Chapter 5.

▷ Plate tectonics

It is now accepted that the earth's crust is split into 14 giant slabs, or rigid 'plates' of crust, which move in relation to one another. Interesting tectonic activity takes place at the boundaries of these moving plates, or **plate margins**, as they are known. The term **tectonic** refers to the forces which sculpt the earth's surface from within the earth; they are internal forces (e.g. mountains built by rocks being folded upwards; volcanic eruptions creating new land) rather than external forces working on the surface itself.

Plate margins move in three ways – destructive, constructive and conservative (or transform).

Type 1 – Destructive

▷ They hit each other head on (**converge and collide**) which is sometimes called subduction.

▷ This is described as a **destructive** plate margin, because crust is likely to be lost as one of the plates is 'subducted' back into the earth's molten mantle below and melts.

▷ This will result in a fold mountain range or ocean trench.

▷ Some examples are the Nazca Plate under the Pacific Ocean and the American Plate forming the continent of South America meet and collide along the west coast of that continent (Fig. 7.1).

Fig. 7.1 A destructive plate margin

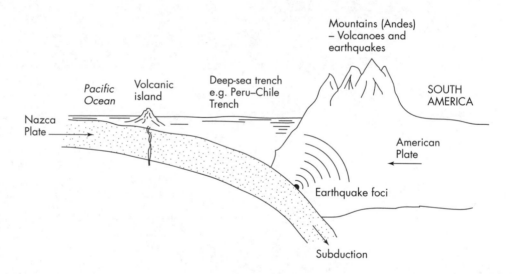

Type 2 – Constructive

▷ They pull apart (**diverge**) which is sometimes called spreading.

▷ This is referred to as a **constructive** plate margin because new crust is created as ridges and volcanic islands are built as a result of lava welling through from the molten mantle below.

▷ When plates diverge under the ocean, as they do beneath the mid-Atlantic Ocean around Iceland, where the North American–Greenland Plate and the Eurasian Plate move apart, sea-floor spreading is said to take place.

▷ This process will result in spreading ocean ridge or rift valley/ volcanoes.

▷ An example is the Mid-Atlantic Ridge, a 2500-metre-high mountain range rising from the bed of the Atlantic Ocean, has been built (see Fig. 7.2). Underwater volcanic eruptions, first noticed on 14 November 1963, had by February 1964 created the one-kilometre-square, 174-metre-high island of Surtsey, off the south coast of Iceland. It continued to grow at an equally rapid speed.

Fig. 7.2 A constructive
plate margin

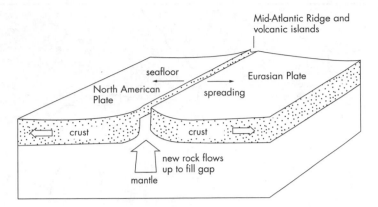

Type 3 – Conservative or transform

▶ They glide past each other sideways which is sometimes called a passive margin.

▶ The sideways sliding of plates is the principal cause of major earthquakes.

▶ A good example is the San Andreas Fault in California which provides a constant earthquake threat. The Pacific and North American Plates slide sideways past each other along this fault line (Fig. 7.3).

Fig. 7.3 Sliding plates

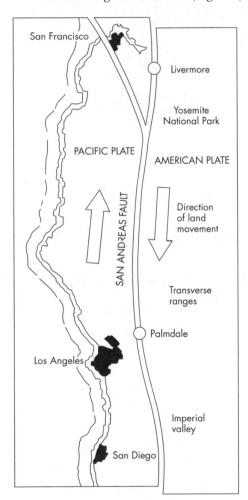

The major geological plates

Fig. 7.4 shows the major geological plates, their boundaries and their direction of movement and also the close association which exists between the location of these plate boundaries and the distribution of **earthquakes, fold mountains** and **volcanoes**.

Currently, Britain does not experience such tectonic activity and geological instability; it is safely located several hundred miles from the nearest plate edge.

Fig. 7.4 Location of plate boundaries and related features

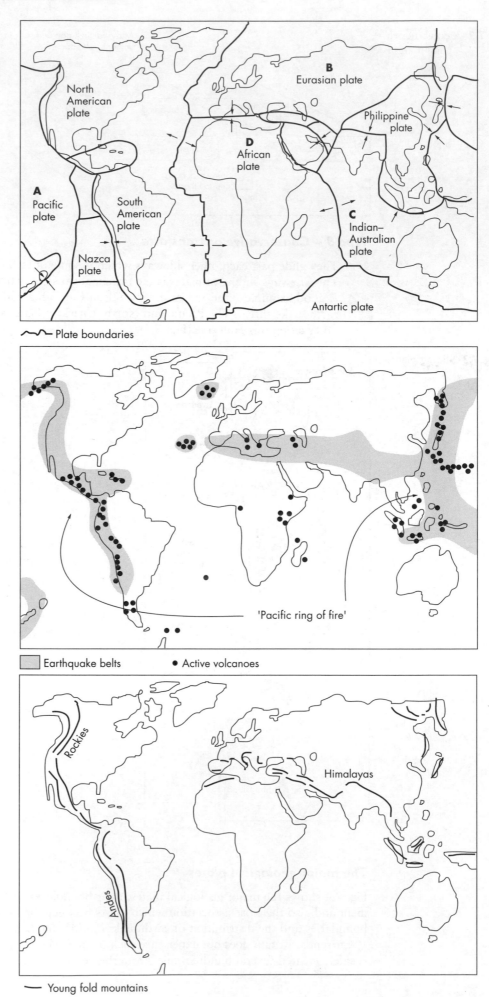

▷ Earthquakes

An earthquake is a shaking movement or tremor among the rocks in the earth's crust. Major earthquakes are the result of the geological plates which make up the earth's crust slipping and sliding against each other. This suddenly releases stresses and pressures which have been accumulating over the time they have been locked together. The energy released by an earthquake is measured on the open-ended Richter Scale. The world's greatest quakes have reached 8 and above: for example, the 1906 San Francisco quake measured 8.3. The world's most earthquake-prone regions are around the rim of the Pacific, in Indonesia, south-west Asia and the eastern Mediterranean. Major earthquakes can occur where plate margins are grinding past each other, colliding together or pulling apart. More modest earthquakes can and do occur in Britain, along small, local faults with intensities of around 5 on the Richter Scale. When an earthquake occurs waves vibrate swiftly in all directions from the focus deep in the earth's crust (Fig. 7.5). These can be recorded by a seismograph.

Fig. 7.5 Cross-section of an earthquake

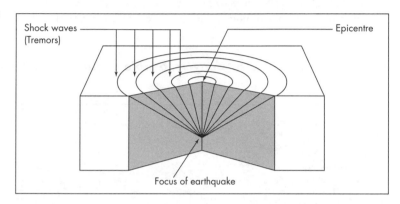

Major earthquakes are normally natural disasters, particularly when occurring in heavily populated areas. The Tangshan earthquake in China in 1976, which had a magnitude of 7.6, killed 250 000 people, although only 114 died in the 8.6 quake in Alaska in 1964. Damage falls off as you move away from the epicentre, but much depends on the construction of buildings and the preparations that have been made in an area. Fig. 7.6 shows why Mexico City was so vulnerable in 1985.

Why Mexico City was so vulnerable

Fig. 7.6 The 1985 Mexico City earthquake

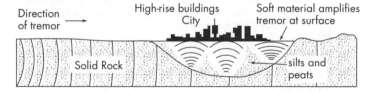

Mexico City was badly hit by this quake partly because the city is *not* built on solid rock, as shown in Fig. 7.6. It is built on soft deposits which were once a lake set in a bowl of mountains. The result being that the tremors shook the city like someone shaking a plate of jelly.

Many of the buildings of Mexico City, though high-rise, have been built to a high quake-resistant specification. Prediction of earthquakes along this Pacific belt is another way by which people have tried to reduce the risks and dangers of living near a plate boundary.

▷ Volcanoes

Molten lava ejected through a vent in the earth's crust can solidify close to the vent and build up a conical hill or mountain. Whether this happens, and the final shape of the cone built, depends largely on the nature of the ejected lava. **Viscous** or **acid lava**, which does not flow far from the vent before solidifying, develops a steep-sided cone. **Basic lava**, on the other hand, is 'runny' in texture and flows further before solidifying; a low cone or shield volcano results. Mauna Loa, Hawaii (Fig. 7.7), is an example.
Volcanoes are associated with both constructive and destructive plate boundaries.

Many different materials can be ejected during a volcanic eruption; gases, dust, ash, cinders, steam and 'bombs' (solid pieces of rock). Materials are also injected into the crust; known as **intrusive vulcanicity**.

Fig. 7.7 Mauna Loa, a
symmetrical
shield volcano

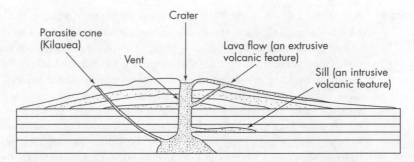

It is interesting that despite the hazards and dangers of such eruptions, people continue to live close to active volcanic cones. Soils are highly fertile in volcanic areas. Volcanic activity brings other benefits to people (e.g. geothermal energy). Iceland and New Zealand have plentiful supplies of cheap energy. Volcanic areas can also be tourist attractions.

▷ **Issue**   *Despite the risks and dangers, people continue to live close to volcanoes*

Fig. 7.8

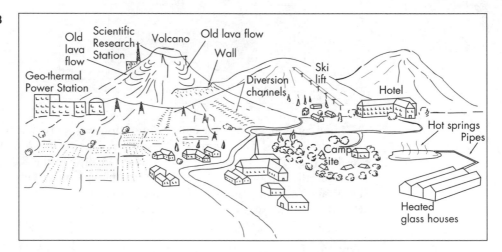

There are many kinds of natural hazard affecting populated areas:

▷   Earthquakes
▷   Volcanoes
▷   Floods
▷   Forest fires
▷   Blizzards
▷   Hurricanes
▷   Avalanches

▷ **Case study**   *Mt St Helens eruption in 1980*

During May 1980 Mount St Helens, a volcano in Washington State, USA, erupted violently after having been dormant since 1857. The once 3122-metre mountain lies roughly in the centre of a 300-kilometre-long chain of active volcanoes – the only ones in North America – running south from British Columbia, Canada, to the northern borders of California. The eruption gave little warning, killing some 100 people and leaving behind a trail of disaster (see Fig. 7.9).

Fig. 7.9

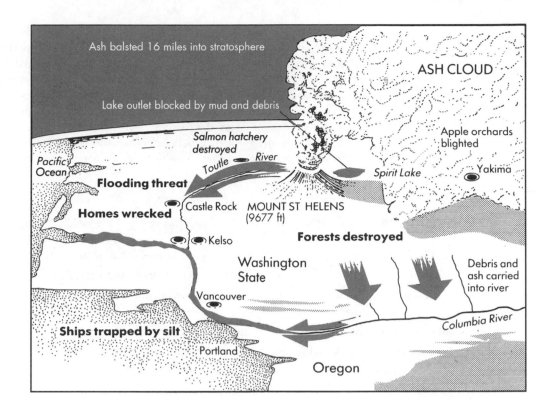

Fig. 7.10

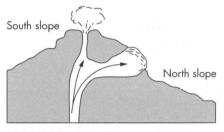

A 8.30 am

Small ash and steam eruptions were rising from the crater. There was a large bulge on the northern slope. It was growing bigger as new magma, rising in the volcano's vent was blocked by a thick crust of old magma.

B 8.32 am

An earthquake (Richter scale 5.0) caused a great landslide of rock, soil, snow and ice from the bulging north slope.

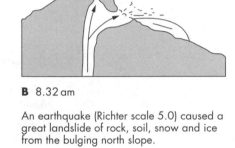

C 8.33 am

The landslide allowed the magma in the vent to escape. There was gigantic blast of gas, steam, dust and rock.

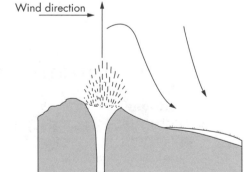

D later in the morning

Eruptions of gas and ash during the morning rose more than 20 km into the air before being deposited over a wide area.

Here is an account made by a geologist who witnessed the eruption (see Fig. 7.10).

Heavy, thick, white and blue clouds of pungent gas quickly built up so that the whole area went pitch black. Within seconds the crater's north wall collapsed as a six-cubic-kilometre mass of volcanic dust and rock was blasted up by an explosion 500 times more powerful than the atomic bomb dropped on Hiroshima by the Americans in 1945. Snow was instantly melted and avalanches of mud and rock hurtled down the volcano's slopes at up to 140 kph. Then the cloud of ash, sometimes as hot as 100 °C which had risen 15 kilometres began to fall over the whole US north west, even on areas over 140 kilometres away. The once-admired perfect symmetry of the cone was destroyed by the explosion which blew away the top 55 metres of the mountain to form a 4-kilometre-wide, 2000-metre-deep crater. One week after the eruption the fourth unpleasant expulsion from an erupting volcano – molten lava flowing down the mountain side – had not yet appeared.

▷ **Key terms**   *Make sure you understand and can apply these geographical terms*

Drought	A period of extreme dryness because of little or no rainfall.
Earthquake	A movement or tremor of the crust originating naturally and below the surface.
Flooding	Water above the ground surface which is normally below it. The water table is above rather than below the ground.
Fold mountain	Mountains thrown up into a massive fold by earth movements.
Igneous rock	Rocks which have solidified from molten magma.
Plate	The large 'slabs' of crust which make up the earth's surface.
Tectonic	Forces coming from within the earth to mould the surface.
Volcano	A mountain forming from a vent in the crust through which molten rock and other materials have passed.
Vulcanicity	The range of activity in which materials from the molten interior rise into the crust (intrusive) or are ejected on to the surface (extrusive).

Suggestions for further work

▶ This is a global topic which relates to areas remote from where most of you will live. It will therefore be difficult, if not impossible, to carry out **fieldwork**. However, classroom-based coursework, planned by your teachers, could be set on *specific* natural hazards. These might include the 'hole' in the ozone layer, or the 'greenhouse effect' i.e. the suggestion that the average world temperature is rising, as well as coursework based on the more obvious sources of natural hazard, e.g. volcanoes, earthquakes.

▶ **STUDENT ANSWER WITH EXAMINER'S COMMENTS**

▷ **Longer structured question**

'Clear, accurate definition'

1   Study the map in Fig. 7.11.
     (a)   Explain the meaning of the term 'Tectonic plate'.

     A term suggesting that the outer layer of the earth consists of several large
     plates which move relative to one another. L2   2
                                                          (2 marks)

     (b)   Name the Tectonic Plates **A, B, C** and **D**. Use the grid below.

Name of Tectonic plate			
A	PACIFIC ✓	**C**	INDO-AUSTRALIAN ✓
B	EURASIAN ✓	**D**	AFRICAN ✓

 2   *(2 marks)*

2   Study Table 7.1 below.

Table 7.1 Earthquakes 1981–1983

Major Region	Country	Date of earthquake
North America	USA USA	May 1983 October 1983
Central America	Mexico Cost Rica Honduras	October 1981, June 1982 April 1983, July 1983 July 1982
South America	Chile Colombia Peru	October 1981, October 1983 October 1981, March 1983 April 1981, April 1983
Pacific Asia	Japan Indonesia Philippines	March 1982, May 1983 January, February, December 1982 August 1983
Rest of Asia	Afghanistan India Iran Pakistan Turkey	January 1982 January 1982 June 1981, March 1983 September 1981 October 1983
Europe	Italy Greece Yugoslavia Romania	February 1981, March 1982, October 1982 February 1981, December 1981 August 1981, June 1982, July 1983 November 1981

Fig. 7.11

— Plate boundary
Some smaller plates have not been named

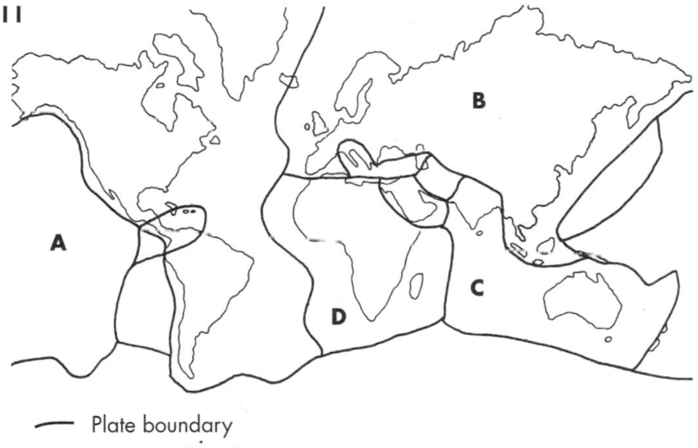

Table 7.2

Name of Tectonic plate		
North America	Antarctic	Eurasian
Caribbean	Philippine	Pacific
Nazca	Indo-Australian	Arabian
South America	African	

(a) Which major region received most earthquakes between 1981 and 1983?

South America   ✗   O

(1 mark)

(b) Describe the relationship between the information shown in Table 7.1 and that shown on the map (Fig. 7.11) used in part 1.   ✓   1

The countries where earthquakes occur are near to the plate boundaries.

(1 mark)

'When the plates slide against each other'

(c)   Explain why earthquakes occur.   L1 only
        Due to a build up of pressure at the earth's crust weakest point   ✓
                                                                        (2 marks)   1

3   Study the map in Fig. 7.12 below.
Fig. 7.12

The area around
Mt St Helens (USA)   N

▲ Mt St Helens volcano

⌐⌐ Boundary of national park
    (hundreds of camp-sites and
    tourist settlements)

── Inter-state highway

── Rivers (many farms
    along valleys)

⋔⋔ Coniferous forest (major
    logging region)

● Logging camp

① Spirit Lake (major tourist
    attraction for campers
    and fishermen)

② Swift reservoir (water supply,
    HEP, and flood control)

km
0   40

Dam

'Good use of map for evidence. Farms along valleys or river covered with volcanic ash. Same with Spirit Lake and Interstate Highway, etc.'

(a)   Describe the types of natural disaster which might be likely to occur in
        this area in the event of a volcanic eruption by Mt St Helens.   ✓

        The trees would be ripped up and large fires would occur. The reservoir is

        likely to be filled by a large mudflow and the water could be pushed

        downwards to cause a flood.   ✓   2
                                                                        (2 marks)

(b)   Name TWO groups of people in this area who might be reluctant to
        leave despite warnings of possible volcanic eruption.
        In each please give ONE reason why.

        Group 1   *The Elderly*

        Reason   *They may find it hard to adjust to a new area*

        Group 2   *Those on a low income*   ✓

        Reason   *Would find difficulty in finding a new home and coping with*

        general moving costs   1
                                                                        (2 marks)

'Imaginative answers but need to be more precise using evidence given or implied in the map. For example, lumberjacks stay with their jobs, farmers with their farms, engineers with the reservoir to regulate HEP, water supply and flood control, etc.'

4   Study the data below in Fig. 7.13.
Fig. 7.13

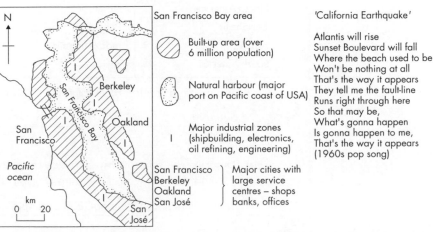

N

San Francisco Bay area

⌗ Built-up area (over
    6 million population)

⬭ Natural harbour (major
    port on Pacific coast of USA)

| Major industrial zones
    (shipbuilding, electronics,
    oil refining, engineering)

San Francisco
Berkeley   Major cities with
Oakland   large service
San José   centres – shops
                    banks, offices

Berkeley
Oakland
San Francisco
San Francisco Bay
Pacific ocean
km
0   20
San José

'California Earthquake'

Atlantis will rise
Sunset Boulevard will fall
Where the beach used to be
Won't be nothing at all
That's the way it appears
They tell me the fault-line
Runs right through here
So that may be,
What's gonna happen
Is gonna happen to me,
That's the way it appears
(1960s pop song)

(a) Describe the types of disaster which might follow an earthquake in this area. Give evidence from the map.

> *A large number of the population would be killed and many of the large buildings would come down.* ✓ *Electrical power lines would be destroyed and cause fire. Flooding of areas near harbour could occur.* ✓   2

(2 marks)

'Okay, but still more evidence could have been drawn from the map. High rise buildings in built up area and major industrial zones might collapse. Location of 6 million persons around Bay makes flooding a likely cause of loss of life, etc.'

(b) Name TWO groups of people living in this area who might be reluctant to leave despite warnings of possible earthquakes.
In each case give ONE reason why.

> Group 1 *People who have a job in shipbuilding.*
>
> Reason *Would find it hard to get a job elsewhere.* ✓
>
> Group 2 *Anyone involved in tourism.*
>
> Reason *San Francisco attracts many tourists.*   1

(2 marks)

'Rather vague. Try to be more specific'

'Rather vague. Try to be more specific'

5   Study the illustration in Fig. 7.14 below.

Fig. 7.14

COMO HACER
CASAS SEGURAS
en una
ZONA PROPENSA A TERREMOTOS

Using NAMED examples of areas subject to natural hazards, describe the responses taken by the inhabitants to reduce the effect of such hazards.
Types of area might include the following:
Slopes of volcanoes; plate boundaries (other than those areas in (c) and (d)), river flood plains; coastal deltas; areas in the path of hurricanes; areas subject to drought.

> *The Missouri river is subject to flooding. Ways to reduce the effects of such haz-* ✓ *ards includes levees and flood walls, reservoirs to store water. Some flood plain zoning is used. The Louisiana and Mississippi coastlines are areas subject to hurricanes.* ✓ *More effective detection and warning helps to better prepare people for evacuation. The Hawaiian islands are subject to coastal deltas.*   2

(4 marks)
L1+   (Total 20 marks)
14   (NEAB)

'Grade B/C standard'

'Not a response, a hazard'

'You named examples. That was good, but you have not really answered the questions. It's about what people do to reduce hazards. See the sketch!'

▶ **A TUTOR ANSWER**

(a)   Read the passage below.

When the Loma Prieta earthquake – as it is now called – hit San Francisco on 17 October 1989, with a force of 7.1 on the Richter scale, the clocks cracked, freezing the time at 5.04 p.m.

For 15 fateful seconds, the San Andreas fault – a 1040 km rip in the earth's surface running through California – came alive. Huge quantities of energy were released as the giant North American and Pacific tectonic plates, which make up part of the earth's floating crust, crunched against each other ...

... The death toll later turned out to be lower than feared – just 62 – but nearly 4000 people were injured and 12 000 made homeless. The total cost of the damage was estimated at $6 billion.   (*Geographical*, Dec. 1990)

(i)   Briefly explain what a 'tectonic plate' is. (It is also known as a crustal plate.)

One of the giant slabs of crust which make up the earth's surface, and

which move in relation to one another.   (2)

(ii)   Describe what the earth's crust 'floats' on.

The crust is said to 'float' on a sea of denser molten rock material called the

mantle.   (2)

(iii)   The death toll was fairly low because many buildings and roads had been designed to stand up to earthquakes.
Explain how buildings and roads can be designed to stand up to earthquakes.

There are several ways in which Californians minimise earthquake damage.

Large buildings are constructed with deep foundations on a thick bed of

concrete, a steel framework, flexible windows, as separate units and some-

times with rubber shock-absorbers, even on rollers at their base. Land use is

carefully planned so that key buildings and roads are rarely on the most

sensitive ground.   (3)

(iv)   Study the information in Table 7.3 below. It refers to two cities which recently suffered earthquake shocks.

Table 7.3

	City X	City Y
Population	Just over 1 million	Just over 1 million
GDP* for the country in which the city lies	$12 350 per head	$1845 per head
Strength of the earthquake shock on the Richter scale	6.8	6.8
Number of lives lost in the earthquake	12	3850

*Gross Domestic Product (GDP) is a way of measuring a country's wealth.

Suggest why the loss of life was much greater in City Y than in City X.

The greater wealth of the country in which city X lies as measured by its GDP

will be the key. MEDCs with their greater wealth and higher technology

levels are better able to adjust to and proof against great earthquake damage.

(3)

(b) There are three types of margin or boundary between tectonic plates. They are called:

constructive margins (e.g. the Mid-Atlantic Ridge)
destructive margins (e.g. the Pacific coast of Japan)
conservative margins (also called passive margins or transform faults).

(i) The Loma Prieta earthquake was at a conservative margin. Explain what a conservative margin is.

This is where plates slide past each other. Plates can lock; it is the jerking

effect when they suddenly unlock which is an earthquake. (2)

(ii) Volcanoes are often found at **constructive** and **destructive** plate margins. Choose either type of plate margin and explain why volcanoes happen there.
You may use diagrams to help your explanation.

Type of margin chosen *Constructive*

Explanation *The pulling apart of the plates allows magma/lava to plug the*

gap and solidify to form a volcanic feature such as Iceland – a volcanic island

on the mid-Atlantic Ridge where the Eurasian and North American plates pull

apart.

Space for diagrams

Fig. 7.15

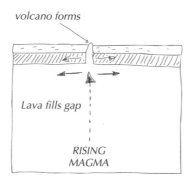

volcano forms

Lava fills gap

RISING
MAGMA

(6)

(c) If hazards like earthquakes and volcanic eruptions could be predicted then many lives might be saved.
Describe the methods that scientists are developing to try to predict when and where some of the following hazards might occur.

| earthquakes | *Choice* volcanic eruptions | tropical storms |
| desertification | floods | avalanches |

Close monitoring of the Hawaiian volcanoes by scientists has led them to believe

that they can predict volcanic eruptions there. Their observations and instruments

including satellite sensors, suggest that the volcanoes actually tilt and swell before

an eruption; subside after and during it. Earthquake activity around the volcano is

also believed to announce a coming eruption. Despite the constant monitoring of

volcanoes and these observations, accurate prediction of all volcanic activity in

the near future is unlikely. (6)

(*Total 24*)
(*NEAB*)

EXAMINATION QUESTION

Study Fig. 7.16 below. It shows how the city of San Francisco was affected by an earthquake in 1989 (San Francisco is located on the San Andreas fault line).

Fig. 7.16

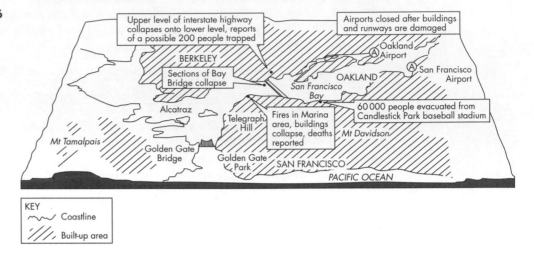

(a) *EITHER* (TIER F)
State TWO ways in which the people of San Francisco were directly affected by the 1989 earthquake. (4 lines provided here) *(2 marks – Tier F only)*
OR (TIER H)
Give TWO reasons why earthquakes are a special hazard to urban areas.
(4 lines provided here) *(2 marks – Tier H only)*
(b) Suggest TWO reasons why people continue to live in places where there is a risk of natural hazards such as earthquakes. (4 lines provided here) *(2 marks – Tiers F and H)*

Study Fig. 7.17 below. It is a map of plate margins and earthquake zones.

Fig. 7.17

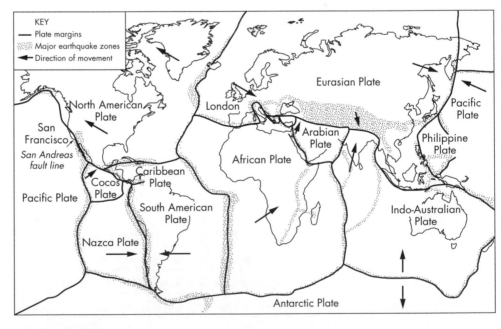

EITHER (TIER F)
(c) Explain why you would expect earthquakes to occur very often in San Francisco but not in London. (8 lines provided here) *(4 marks – Tier F only)*
OR (TIER H)
(c) Use evidence from Fig. 7.17 to explain why earthquakes and volcanic eruptions are common in western parts of South America but not in the British Isles.
(10 lines provided here) *(4 marks – Tier H only)*

EITHER (TIER F)

(d) Earthquakes which affect urban areas are usually more damaging than those which affect rural areas.
  (i) Explain why this is the case. (4 lines provided here)
  (ii) Suggest TWO ways of reducing the damage. (4 lines provided here)

(4 marks – Tier F only)

OR (TIER H)

(d) For two different kinds of natural hazard, explain how they can be made worse by human activities. (10 lines provided here)   *(4 marks – Tier H only)*

EITHER (TIER F)

(e) (i) Name a natural hazard, other than an earthquake, and one place where the hazard has been a problem. (1 line provided here)
  (ii) Explain why the hazard happens there. (6 lines provided here)
  (iii) Describe how it affects the people of the area. (6 lines provided here)

(8 marks – Tier F only)

OR (TIER H)

(e) Name a natural hazard, other than an earthquake or volcano, and locate an area where it occurs. Write a short account of the hazard using the following headings:
  (i) the reasons why it occurs there (6 lines provided here)
  (ii) the ways in which it affects people in the area (6 lines provided here)
  (iii) steps taken to reduce its effects on people (6 lines provided here)

(8 marks – Tier H only)
(Total 20 marks)
(MEG)

▶ **EXAMINATION ANSWER**

Tier F questions

(a) Two ways **people** were affected, one mark each. One mark for referring only to effects on infrastructure. (2)

(b) Two ways, one mark each, e.g. They do not happen very often. There may be other attractions, people forget, etc. (2)

(c) Level 1 (1) Gives one valid point, e.g. London is not at a plate margin.
Level 2 (2–3) and adds that San Francisco is at a margin where the plates are moving in relation to each other.
Level 3 (4) Explains the significance of the map evidence by describing how the movement at plate margins gives rise to earthquakes. (4)

(d) Level 1 (1) Gives one valid reason, e.g. tall/expensive buildings may be destroyed, greater density of population, etc.
Level 2 (2–3) and two ways or reducing damage, e.g. earthquake training in schools/flexible buildings.
Level 3 (4) Extends answer to part (i) by showing how urban system is disrupted by breakdown in services, etc. (4)

(e) Level 1 (1–2) Names a hazard and an appropriate place.
Level 2 (3–5) Provides basic explanation and gives one effect on people, e.g. in Bangladesh, flooding happens when the monsoon rains fall on the Himalayas where the country's rivers rise. The flat lands at the mouth of the River Ganges are easily flooded and people's farms and houses are soon under water.
Level 3 (6–8) Develops the explanation of the hazard, e.g. The floods are made worse by tree felling in the mountains/hurricanes can make the floods worse by causing high tides. Describes effect on the area as a whole and uses specific place information to support the answer. (8)
(Total 20)
(MEG)

Tier H questions

(a) Many people may be in a small area at the time of the earthquake leading to many deaths 1 mark.

The complex transport system may be damaged making it difficult for the emergency services 1 mark, etc. (2)

(b) Hazards are usually unpredictable in their timing and people 'risk' living there 1 mark.

Often settlements started when people were unaware of the hazard.

As a settlement is rarely completely destroyed it is easier to rebuild it than to move 1 mark, etc. (2)

(c) Level 1 (1) Explains that earthquakes and volcanoes occur where plates are moving in relation to each other as in South America but the British Isles are not near a plate margin.

Level 2 (2–3) Refers to place names and directions of movement shown on Fig. 7.17.

Level 3 (4) and gives brief explanation of why earthquakes and volcanoes occur at plate boundaries. (4)

(d) Level 1 (1) Links two hazards with a human activity, e.g. water extraction and drought, deforestation and flooding, atmospheric pollution and fog.

Level 2 (2–3) Gives explanation of one, e.g. 'Where rivers rise in forested uplands, felling the trees means that the rain is no longer intercepted or transpired back into the atmosphere. Instead it runs off rapidly causing more severe flooding'.

Level 3 (4) gives explanation of two. (4)

(NB The question is about how people affect the hazard not vice versa.)

(e) Level 1 (1–2) Names a hazard and its location, e.g. flooding around the mouth of the River Rhine in Holland and gives one valid point under one section, e.g. The floods occur because the land is at or below sea level and can flood if the Rhine rises to high levels when the Alpine snows melt/farmland is affected by salt from sea water/barrages have been built to stop sea water getting into the estuaries at very high tides.

Level 2 (3–5) Comments under all three sections and includes some specific information.

Level 3 (6–8) Develops each section in a balanced way showing a knowledge both of physical processes and links with human activity and includes specific information to support each section. (8)

(Total 20)

(MEG)

SUMMARY

▷ There are a range of natural/environmental hazards from hurricanes to earthquakes. Some such as pollution and flooding may be partly due to human activities and mismanagement of the environment.

▷ The earth's crust is unstable. Some areas though are more prone to tectonic activity (i.e. volcanic and seismic – earthquakes); these areas correspond to the crustal plate boundaries.

▷ Tectonic activity has varying effects on natural environments and people. Some of the human effects are opportunities, others threats. Despite the risk of these threats, people continue to live along plate boundaries. The effects of the threats and people's response to them tends to vary between MEDCs (e.g. California) and LEDCs (e.g. India).

Ecosystems, resource development and environmental management

> ## GETTING STARTED

This is a broad topic and a very popular one in GCSE syllabuses. It appears in most GCSE syllabuses in some form, and can be said to cross into other topic areas in the form of concern for the environment and the need to manage it. The ecosystem idea of everything being interlinked and balanced also applies across the whole of geography.

The topic is also very strong on values and attitudes: the need to enquire into those of your own and others in order to clarify and justify viewpoints and opinions. This is issues-based geography, much of which filters across the whole syllabus. The specialist geographical terms that are used at GCSE in this topic area are relatively few, and well-defined in the chapter so no separate list is included. However, case studies are important so these are included.

LONDON A	LONDON B	MEG A	MEG B	MEG C	NEAB A	NEAB B	NEAB C	NICCEA	SEG A	SEG B	WJEC	IGCSE	TOPIC	REVISION STUDY	REVISION 1	REVISION 2
✓			✓					✓	✓			✓	The nature and types of ecosystem			
✓								✓	✓				The features and types of soil			
✓		✓					✓		✓			✓	Tropical rainforests and vegetation communities			
✓		✓	✓	✓	✓			✓	✓		✓		Ecosystems as fragile environments and a human resource			
		✓	✓	✓							✓	✓	The types and provision of resources for development, even exploitation			
		✓		✓							✓	✓	Energy resources, production sites and environmental costs			
					✓		✓	✓			✓		Farming, soil erosion and desertification			
✓		✓	✓	✓				✓	✓		✓	✓	Resource management and conservation			

> ## WHAT YOU NEED TO KNOW

> **Ecosystem**

The term **ecosystem** refers to the interrelationships which exist between a set of living organisms in an area (plants and animals) and their non-living environmental surrounds (their habitat; e.g. climate, soil, slope, run-off, rock type, etc.). A pond can be seen as an ecosystem; each component of the pond environment, whether living or non-living, is linked together and interacts one with another to form a whole unit (a system). Ecosystems are open; each ecosystem is only a segment of the real world and is affected by and affects other parts of life.

Fig. 8.1 Model of an
        ecosystem

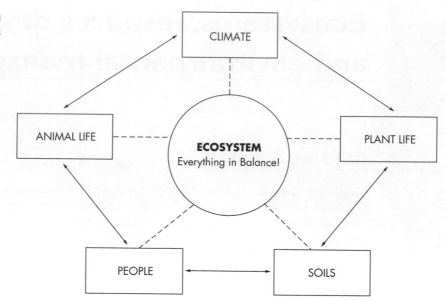

▷ **Soils**   As you can see, soil is a key component of a natural ecosystem. Fig. 8.2 shows what soil is
made of. Soil forms from various materials including weathered rock and vegetation.

Fig. 8.2

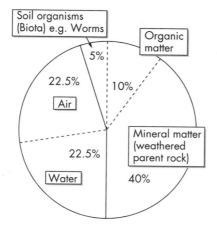

Soils develop a **vertical profile**, a series of layers called **horizons**. Climatic conditions play
a big part in the formation of the profile. Different soil types have different profiles. The
number of soil types in Britain is small because the country lies within one major climatic
region. In this region, rainfall is greater than evaporation, with the result that the movement of water in the soil is from the surface downwards. Minerals are washed out down
the profile, a process called **leaching**.

'Podsols' are the normal soils in Britain, except in the wettest parts with their '**moss-peat**'
soils; the drier forested lowlands of the South and Midlands with their '**brown earth**' soils;
and where the bedrock is of a special character e.g. chalk and limestone. Fig. 8.3 shows four
such soil types and the conditions in which they develop.

Fig. 8.3 Four soil types
and the conditions in
which they develop

Soil Type	Peat	Gley	Podsol	Brown Earth
Conditions	High rainfall and poor drainage	Low rainfall and poor drainage	High rainfall and good drainage	Low rainfall and good drainage

Fig 8.3 (*cont*)

Resulting Soil Water Balance

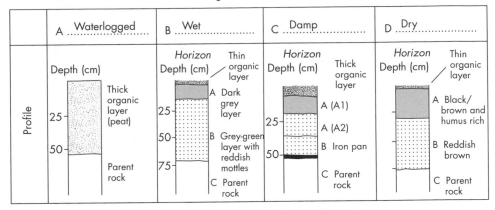

Misuse of the soil, especially by farming can lead to soil erosion.

Soil erosion

This is the removal of the soil by erosional agents, especially water and wind. Soil erosion is a consequence of **mass movement** and the processes responsible for soil erosion are mass-movement processes (e.g. **soil creep**). However, as soil erosion is principally a farming problem, it must be remembered that major soil erosion is often connected with poor agricultural practices; for example, the overgrazing of an area by farm animals, causing the destruction of the vegetation cover and a loss of protection and binding for the soil; the clearing of forest for farmland, which frequently has a similar effect; the wrong ploughing of sloping fields.

Fig. 8.4 suggests why **terracing** (cutting steps into a hillside with a small wall or bank to retain the soil and water on the farmed step), **contour ploughing** (ploughing around a slope, parallel to the contours, rather than up and down it) and **strip cropping** (the division of a field into strips so that the crops in each can be rotated, which means that as little of the field as possible is uncropped and unprotected from erosion at any time, and the demands on the soil are lessened, so reducing the risk of erosion through low soil quality) are commonly used methods of preventing soil erosion. Contour ploughing is the most effective method of soil conservation on slopes in temperate climates.

Weather elements, mainly wind and rain, keep soil constantly on the move, and at times strong wind can quickly remove good topsoil, blowing clouds of dust far afield. The natural grasslands of the western USA became known as the Dust Bowl in the 1930s after strong winds and drought were responsible for the erosion of dry, overploughed soil. These dust storms left the area an agricultural desert and led to large-scale migration of the farming population. The state of Oklahoma was particularly affected by such soil erosion, caused by a combination of human misuse of land and the natural results of physical geography.

Fig. 8.4 The advantages of terracing to combat soil erosion

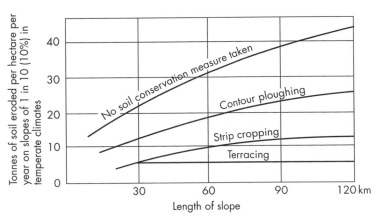

Desertification

Desertification (spreading deserts) can result from unwise agricultural development in non-desert ecosystems as a result of population increase, as Fig. 8.5 shows.

Fig. 8.5

```
Population Increase
        │
        ▼
Demand for more food crops
        │
        ▼
Trees are cut down
        │
        ▼
Protection of trees is lost
        │
        ▼
Ground exposed to seasonal
heavy rain and sun's rays
        │
        ▼
Soil becomes infertile or eroded
        │
        ▼
Desertification
```

```
Population Increase
        │
        ▼
Migration of animal farmers into areas
of low and unreliable rainfall
        │
        ▼
Overgrazing by animals
        │
        ▼
Decline in quality of pasture
        │
        ▼
Destruction of grassland vegetation
        │
        ▼
Bare soil exposed and eroded by wind
        │
        ▼
Desertification
```

Vegetation is a key component of an ecosystem; its nature reflects local soil, climate and people's activities. This can work the other way too. Fig. 8.6 shows how vegetation is influenced by the length of the period free from frost and the amount of moisture available (rainfall).

Vegetational change is a result of people's activities, because they see immediate benefit in extracting and using a resource at present part of an ecosystem, can have far-reaching consequences throughout the ecosystem and in wider environments. The demand for land resources for farming and building, and for timber resources has resulted in the changing distribution of forest in the USA between 1620 and 1990 shown by Fig. 8.7.

Fig. 8.6

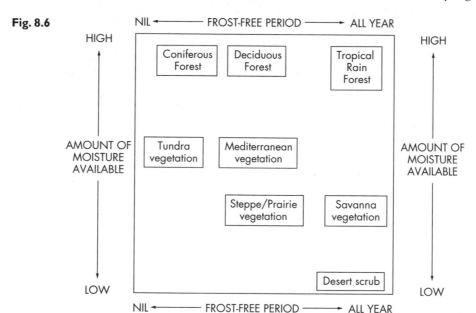

Fig. 8.7

Deforestation (forest clearance) and some **afforestation** (tree planting) in the USA are issues in geography about which there are conflicting views. What is certain is that deforestation can have effects throughout an environment and elsewhere, including putting people's lives at risk from flooding.

▷ **Energy**   Energy is a resource in high demand because of its importance in industry, economic development and an acceptable standard and quality of human life. The exploitation of scarce energy resources can lead to both environmental benefits and environmental degradation (loss).

Types of energy

Many of the world's resources are **finite**, their supply is fixed and cannot be renewed once used. There is thus a need for **resource conversation**. At the present rate of usage of some energy resources, there will be none left for future generations.

Table 8.1 World energy consumption

	Energy (Equivalent to thousand million barrels of oil)
World consumption in 1970	350
World consumption in 1980	500
Estimated world consumption in 2000	970
Estimated world oil reserves	40 000
Estimated world coal reserves	345 000

These figures suggest that oil might not be a major source of energy in a 100 years time. Sources of energy can be classified into two types – renewable and non-renewable.

> **Renewable** These are the sources which cannot be exhausted so that their use does not reduce their supply, e.g. hydroelectricity; wind; solar; tidal.
> **Non-renewable** These are exhaustible sources whose supply is fixed in quantity, e.g. oil, natural gas, and coal once burned are lost to people.

Table 8.2 shows six sources of energy and indicates whether they are renewable or non-renewable. Non-renewable sources may have to be replaced by renewable sources, or at least supplemented with them, to avoid eventual exhaustion of supplies.

Table 8.2 Renewable and non-renewable energy

Source of energy	Renewable	Non-renewable
Oil		✓
Natural gas		✓
Coal		✓
Hydroelectricity	✓	
Wind	✓	
Solar	✓	

The '**energy crisis**' which could face the world is partly a result of our dependence on fossil fuels, i.e. oil, coal, which are non-renewable. Study the bar chart in Fig. 8.8 which shows the main sources of energy used in the UK.

Any world energy shortage will also be due to rapidly increasing **energy consumption** resulting from growing population, increased industrialisation and rising prosperity. World energy consumption *doubled* between 1970 and 1990. Our whole way of life, especially in 'developed' countries like Britain, depends on plentiful supplies of energy.

Read the following newspaper extract about the importance of energy.

> A rise in a country's standard of living is closely accompanied by a rise in the amount of energy it uses. Hence, we find that the amount of energy used per person per year ranges from the equivalent of approximately 12 000 kilograms of coal in the USA to 20 kilograms in Ethiopia. A major reason for the economic backwardness and slow rate of development of countries like Ethiopia is that they do not have either the kind ('renewable' or 'exhaustible') or quantity of energy necessary to begin the progress out of poverty.

The single most important fuel in Kenya is wood, and in Bangladesh and China straw and crop stalks. About half of the world's population rely heavily on such materials, including dried dung for cooking and heating. Figs 8.9 and 8.10 show how energy resources are distributed unevenly and concentrated in MEDCs. The more economically developed a country, the greater is its consumption of energy. Energy was once the most effective of all the factors influencing the location chosen by manufacturing; it now has less influence. Energy-orientated manufacturing, such as riverside cotton mills using water power, is less common today.

Fig. 8.8

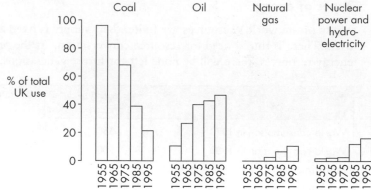

Fig. 8.9 Population and energy consumption in 1985

1985	More economically developed countries (MEDCs)	Less economically developed countries (LEDCs)
Population	👤	👤👤👤
Energy	🛢🛢🛢	🛢

Fig. 8.10 Expected population and energy consumption in 2020

2020	More economically developed countries (MEDCs)	Less economically developed countries (LEDCs)
Population	👤🧒	👤👤👤
Energy	🛢🛢🛢🛢🛢	🛢🛢🛢

There is often an imbalance between the location of energy resource supplies and energy consumption. Remote energy resources, with the help of modern technology, can now be extracted and transported over great distances. Fig. 8.11 shows how the Falkland Islands oil discoveries are to be exploited for economic benefit but need to be managed. Falkland Island ecosystems are worthy of conservation.

'Oil resources demanded by other countries'

'Resource to be exploited for economic gain'

'Potential for environmental gain and loss. To be managed properly for sustained development and ecosystem conservation'

New oil find in the Falklands will be bigger than the North Sea field

Massive oil reserves have been discovered under the stormy ocean around the Falkland Islands. These remote islands are 800 km from the mainland and over 8000 km from Britain but they could become one of the world's largest oil producers within ten years.

'It's very exciting,' said Ms Sakey Cameron, the Falklands' government representative in London. 'We are not a rich island, most of our people are sheep farmers and we have few other ways of earning money.'

Multinational oil companies will now be given the chance to buy licences to drill for oil under large areas of the sea floor surrounding the Falklands.

The Falkland Islands' government is looking for advice about the effects of the discovery on the largely unspoilt environment of the island and surrounding ocean.

Fig. 8.11

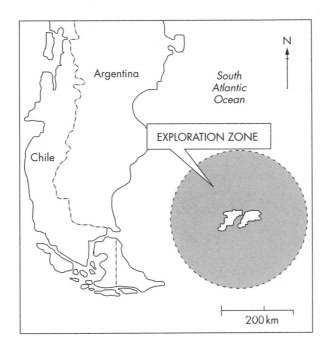

Managing resources

The extraction of limestone around Buxton, Derbyshire raises two issues:

1 There is a fixed supply of limestone.
2 The loss of National Park land and the appearance of scars and ugly blots on the landscape.

This area of the Peak District National Park is the largest source of limestone in Europe. It is accessible for quarrying, and limestone is demanded by the chemical, steel and road-making industries.

How should we control and manage its extraction? Or should we not bother and let things happen as they will? What do you think? See Fig. 8.12.

Fig. 8.12

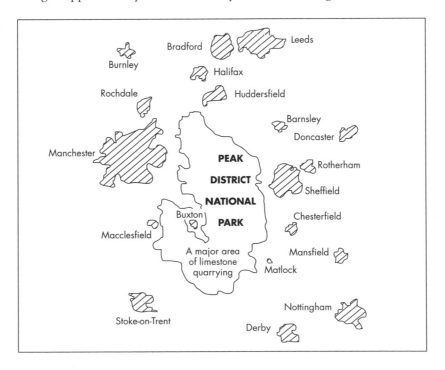

Environmentally sensitive areas

The UK government identifies the environmentally sensitive areas shown on Fig. 8.13. **Environmentally sensitive areas (ESAs)** are areas of particular ecological or environmental importance in terms of natural landscape, in which agricultural practices are to be compatible with conservation, while ensuring an adequate income for farmers. These ecosystems are considered worthy of conservation.

Fig. 8.13

Environmentally Sensitive Areas

Labels: Machair of the Uists, Benbecula, Barra and Vatersay; Glens of Antrim; Breadalbane; Loch Lomond; Whitlaw/Eildon; Stewarty; Pennine Dales; North Peak; Mournes and Slieve Croob; Shropshire Borders; Breckland; Broads; Lleyn Peninsula; Test Valley; Suffolk River Valleys; Cambrian Mountains; Somerset Levels and Moors; West Penwith; South Downs

▷ **Issue**   *Destruction of the Amazon rainforest*

Rainforests are one of the types of hostile environment in the world, but they contain a valuable resource, timber. The map in Fig. 8.14 shows all too clearly the pattern of destruction of the forest, partly for its timber but also as land clearance for agriculture. The presence of the Indians can protect the rainforest from timber companies and from agricultural concerns but once the Indians are forced out, the trees can soon be felled.

Fig. 8.14

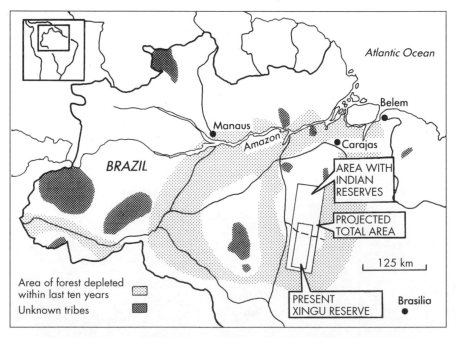

Labels: Atlantic Ocean; Belem; Manaus; Amazon; Carajas; AREA WITH INDIAN RESERVES; PROJECTED TOTAL AREA; BRAZIL; 125 km; Area of forest depleted within last ten years; Unknown tribes; PRESENT XINGU RESERVE; Brasilia

The ecological effects of deforestation are alarming, especially on the scale at which it is proceeding at present – an area the size of Wales felled each year. Fig. 8.15 shows what can happen to the rainforest area when the trees are cleared, and hence clearly shows how the forests must be viewed as one vital part of the ecological 'chain'. When deforestation occurs, events are set in motion which inevitably have impacts *elsewhere* in the chain. This is another example of how geographical issues must be looked at as part of a 'system'. Animals and plants are lost along with the trees, as Fig. 8.16 shows. Here is part of the case for rainforest protection and conservation.

Fig. 8.15

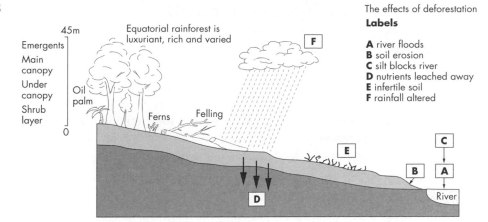

The effects of deforestation
Labels

A river floods
B soil erosion
C silt blocks river
D nutrients leached away
E infertile soil
F rainfall altered

▷ **Case study**   *Protecting the Mount Teide National Park, Tenerife, Spain*

The management of the National Park requires that the more delicate and fragile areas are protected. The area is divided into different areas of use and control. Tenerife is a holiday island attracting lots of visitors all year round.

Fig. 8.16

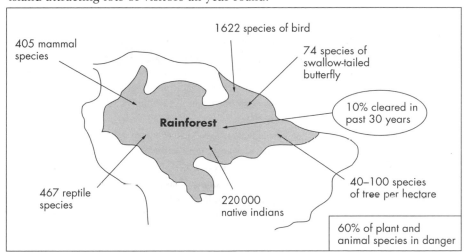

Fig. 8.17 shows how their access to Mount Teide National Park is controlled.

Fig. 8.17

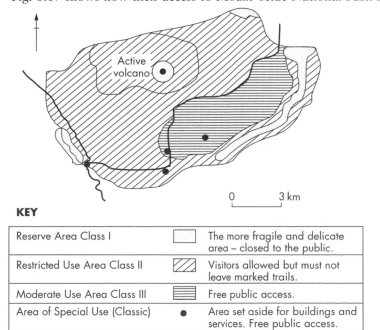

▷ **Key terms**   *Make sure you understand and can apply these geographical terms*

Deforestation	Defined and explained on page 116.
Desertification	Defined and explained on page 115.
Ecosystem	Defined and explained on page 113.
Fossil Fuel	Fuel which is based on fossil remains from the geological past, e.g. coal is the remains of decayed forest.
Fragile environment	An environment (e.g. on a sand dune) whose balance can be easily disturbed and the environment threatened.
Management	People's actions in order to have some influence and control of, in geography, the environment. Conserving and reducing exploitation is environmental management.
National Park	Defined in the list of Geographical terms in Chapter 11.
Primary energy	The sources of energy (ability to do work) e.g. coal, oil, etc.
Renewable/non-renewable	Defined and explained on page 117.
Resource	Any means used by people for their benefit, e.g. water, knowledge, oil, etc.
Soil erosion	The wearing away and loss of topsoil, mainly by the action of wind and rain.
Thermal energy	That produced by heat, through burning fossil fuels.
Vegetation community	The plant element of an ecosystem. Plants affect each other and share a common environment.

Suggestions for further work

▷   This is an appropriate area of geography for investigating values and attitudes and considering conflicts though this is quite difficult GCSE fieldwork, e.g.
  – The effects of extensive public use of parts of the Pennines.
  – The effects of new quarrying on a rural area.
  – What have been the results of the growth of the Trent Valley as a major area for electricity generation?

▷   Teacher-planned classroom-based enquiries could be appropriate, e.g. an investigation into the changing role of coal in the pattern of energy supplies in Britain or the current position of British nuclear power generation, including national political policy and the environmental arguments.

▶ STUDENT ANSWER WITH EXAMINER'S COMMENTS

▷ **Longer structured question**

1   One way of classifying energy resources distinguishes between renewable and non-renewable sources of energy.
Study Fig. 8.18 (below), which shows eight sources of energy:

Fig. 8.18

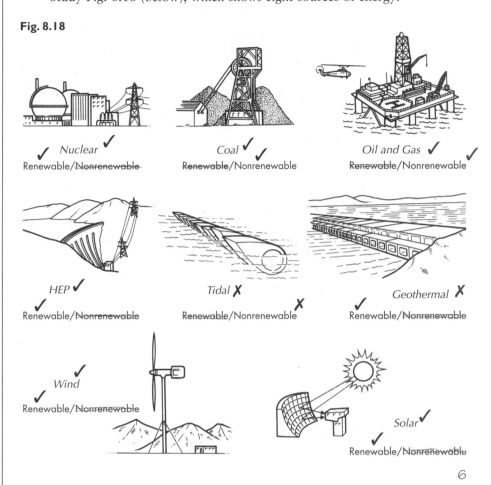

✔   ✔ Nuclear ✔
Renewable/~~Nonrenewable~~

Coal ✔ ✔
~~Renewable~~/Nonrenewable

Oil and Gas ✔ ✔
~~Renewable~~/Nonrenewable

HEP ✔
✔ Renewable/~~Nonrenewable~~

Tidal ✘ ✘
~~Renewable~~/Nonrenewable

Geothermal ✘
✔ Renewable/~~Nonrenewable~~

Wind ✔
✔ Renewable/~~Nonrenewable~~

Solar ✔
Renewable/~~Nonrenewable~~

6

'The tides won't run out! The correct energy resource is wave, which is renewable.'

(a)   Choose from the list below and insert the correct type of energy resource beneath each sketch:
wood   solar   wind   coal   HEP   tidal   oil and gas
nuclear   geothermal   wave

(b)   Cross out the *incorrect* description (renewable or non-renewable) beneath each type of energy.

(c)   Explain the difference between the terms **Renewable** and **Non-renewable** sources of energy.

Renewable is a resource which can be replaced. Non-renewable is a

resource which in time will run out.   ✔   1

(9 marks)

2   Study Fig 8.19 and 8.20 below, showing energy generation in the UK and India.

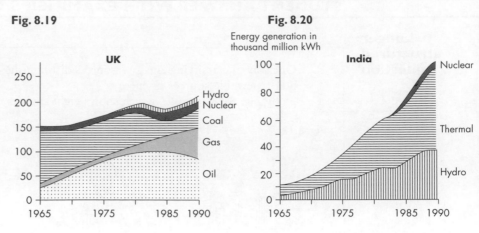

Fig. 8.19   **Fig. 8.20**

(a) Which country has most rapidly increased its energy generation?

India ✓ 1

(b) State the most important source of energy in the United Kingdom in

1965 *Coal* ✓   1990 *Oil* ✓   2

(c) Explain the word 'thermal' used in Fig. 8.20.

Energy produced by burning, e.g. coal ✓   1

(d) Describe the changes in energy generation in the UK.

Great Britain has become less dependent on coal due to more sources of ✓
energy now being available, e.g. natural gas, atomic energy and petroleum. A
surplus of coal has now built up.   1

(7 marks)

3   Study Fig. 8.21 below which shows the relationship between energy consumption and development.

Fig. 8.21

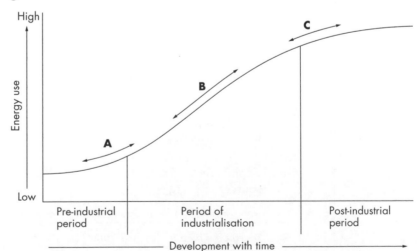

Complete the key to Fig. 8.21 using the following countries.

Great Britain ✗   India ✓   Ethiopia ✗

A = *Great Britain*   B = *India*   C = *Ethiopia*   1

(2 marks)

'A major point – good!'

*'How about the growth
of gas and the recent
fall of oil!!!'*

'What does this mean?'

*'Britain is the
post-industrial country,
and Ethiopia the
pre-industrial'*

4   Study the information provided in Fig. 8.22 below.
Fig. 8.22

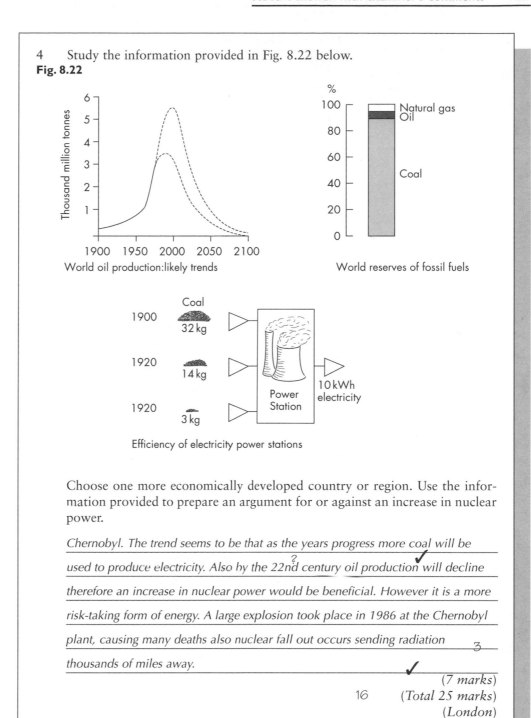

World oil production:likely trends

World reserves of fossil fuels

Efficiency of electricity power stations

Choose one more economically developed country or region. Use the information provided to prepare an argument for or against an increase in nuclear power.

Chernobyl. The trend seems to be that as the years progress more coal will be used to produce electricity. Also by the 22nd century oil production will decline therefore an increase in nuclear power would be beneficial. However it is a more risk-taking form of energy. A large explosion took place in 1986 at the Chernobyl plant, causing many deaths also nuclear fall out occurs sending radiation thousands of miles away.

3

(7 marks)
16   (Total 25 marks)
(London)

'Grade C standard'

'Okay, a basic point both for and against. But the question asks for one or other! Take one view and elaborate, using Fig. 8.22 as fully as possible. For instance you could take Britain as the developed country, and argue, say, against an increase in nuclear power. You could mention that Britain has good reserves of both oil and coal. Although world oil production is expected to fall after the year 2000 in Fig. 8.22, we can also see that coal is the much more important fossil fuel in the world, with over 90% of total reserves compared to only 5% from oil. Also between 1900 and 1960 the amount of coal needed per 10 kWh of electricity fell from 32 kg to 3 kg. Prospects for coal are encouraging'

A TUTOR ANSWER

▷ **Short structured question**

(a) Study the flow diagram below (Fig. 8.23) and complete the empty boxes from this list: bare soil   vegetation dies   overgrazing   (*3 marks*)

Fig. 8.23 The causes of desertification

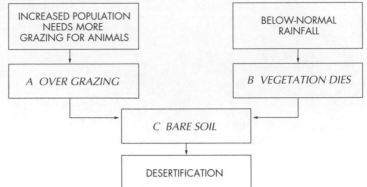

(b) Study the flow diagram (Fig. 8.24) which shows a sequence of events in the Sahel in the 1950s and 1960s.

Fig. 8.24 Sequence of events in the Sahel in the 1950s and 1960s

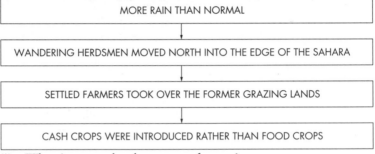

(i) What is meant by the term **cash crop**?

Crops grown for sale, perhaps in distant markets, even overseas.

(ii) The rainfall was much *lower* than normal from the 1970s. Suggest **two** reasons why this caused difficulties for the herdsmen.

1 *Confined to a smaller area so leading to overgrazing and loss of grass cover.*

2 *Search further afield for natural grass cover.*

(iii) Suggest **two** reasons why the settled farmers were also in difficulty from the 1970s.

1 *Growing the same cash crop (monoculture) used up soil nutrients and yields fell.*

2 *Lack of water for crop irrigation purposes.*

(*5 marks*)

(c) Suggest **two** ways in which the extension of the world's deserts may be prevented or lessened.

1 *Slower population growth and so lower food demand would not encourage farmers so much to cultivate marginal land with its easily eroded soil.*

2 *Less deforestation. Soil erosion follows the loss of trees as it becomes more exposed to the sun.*

(*2 marks*)
(*Total 10 marks*)
(*London*)

EXAMINATION QUESTION

Tier F only

(a)   Study Fig. 8.25 showing the conditions required for types of vegetation areas.

Fig. 8.25

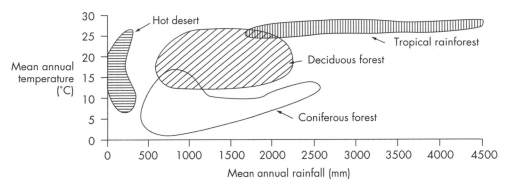

Source: adapted from Greg O'Hare, *Climate, Soils and Ecosystems*

   (i)   Which type of vegetation would be found where the mean annual rainfall is above 3000 mm? (1 line provided here)   *(1 mark)*

   (ii) What is the lowest and highest temperatures of an area where hot desert vegetation would be found?
Lowest mean annual temperature (1 line provided here)
Highest mean annual temperature (1 line provided here)   *(2 marks)*

   (iii) State **two** ways in which a coniferous tree is adapted to its climate. (6 lines provided here)   *(2 marks)*

(b)   Study Fig. 8.26 showing what happens to rain falling on an area of tropical rainforest.

Fig. 8.26

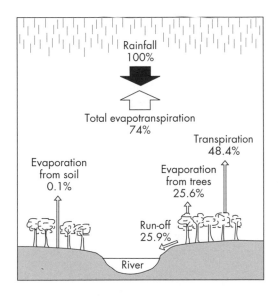

   (i)   What percentage (%) of the rainfall is lost through evapotranspiration? (1 line provided here)   *(1 mark)*

   (ii) What percentage (%) of the rainfall reaches the river shown? (1 line provided here)   *(1 mark)*

   (iii) Some of the rainfall never reaches the river. State **two** ways in which this happens. (4 lines provided here)   *(2 marks)*

(c)   If the area of tropical rain forest such as that shown in Fig. 8.26 was cleared, what would be the impact upon:

   (i)   The soil? (9 lines provided here)   *(3 marks)*

   (ii) The people living there? (8 lines provided here)   *(3 marks)*

(Total 15 marks)

(SEG)

Tier H only

(a) Study Fig. 8.25 (page 127) showing the conditions required for types of vegetation areas.
(i) State the features of the climate where the natural vegetation is coniferous forest.
(3 lines provided here) *(1 mark)*
(ii) What does Fig. 8.25 suggest about the global distribution of the world's forests?
(12 lines provided here) *(4 marks)*

(b) Explain how coniferous trees are adapted to the climate of the area in which they are found. (12 lines provided here) *(4 marks)*

(c) With reference to an area you have studied, explain the problems caused by the removal of tropical rainforest.
Name of area (1 line provided here)
Explanation (17 lines provided here) *(6 marks)*
(Total 15 marks)
(SEG)

EXAMINATION ANSWER

Tier F only

(a) (i) Tropical rain forest *(1)*
(ii) 6–7 °C – Lowest
26–27 °C – Highest *(2)*
(iii) *(2 x 1)*
Triangular shape to shed snow, evergreen to start photosynthesis quickly, seeds in cases to protect against cold, thick bark to protect against cold, etc. *(2)*

(b) (i) 74.1% *(1)*
(ii) 25.9% *(1)*
(iii) *(2 x 1)*
Evaporated from leaf, tree surfaces
Evaporated from the soil
Transpired from plants *(2)*

(c) (i) *(3 x 1)*
Soil – leaching and run-off would increase; removing trees means less roots to take up the water and bind the soil together. Topsoil washed away, nutrients reduced. *(3)*
(ii) *(3 x 1)*
People – local people may be removed from their lands. May have to be resettled in reserves, e.g. Amazonian Indians. Their way of life radically changed, subsistence culture is taken away. In the short/medium term the land produces less as soils eroded and cattle eat all vegetation. *(3)*
(Total 15 marks)
(SEG)

Tier H only

(a) (i) Attempts to give range, i.e. about 500–2500 mm rainfall and 0–16 °C (both needed) *(1)*
(ii) Level 1 – 1–2 marks
Candidate quotes temperature and rainfall ranges of the *forested* areas (not desert).
Level 2 – 3–4 marks
Distribution linked to latitudinal locations/overlaps noted. *(4)*

(b) Any four of:
triangular shape to shed snow, evergreen to start photosynthesis quickly, seeds in cases to protect against cold, thick bark to protect against cold, etc. *(4 x 1)* *(4)*

(c) Soil – leaching and erosion would increase
Run-off – increase – more flooding

Loss of vegetation and wildlife
Threat to indigenous people
Climatic change (local)
Level 1 – 1–2 marks
Simple statements of problems, unexplained (max 2).
Level 2 – 3–4 marks
More detail, greater understanding and explanation, e.g. removing the trees would mean less water was taken in by the roots so more would flow over the ground as run-off so increasing the likelihood of flooding and the silting of rivers, etc.
Level 3 – 5–6 marks
Level 2 but with specific reference to a detailed case study. (6)
(*Total 15*)
(*SEG*)

SUMMARY

▷ The components of an ecosystem – climate, soils, vegetation and animals – are interrelated.

▷ Different natural ecosystems exist. Each has distinctive vegetation adapted to the environment of the ecosystem.

▷ Soils can be classified (grouped) and their features linked to the other components of the ecosystem plus geology (rock).

▷ Ecosystems are a resource that can be used by people for their benefit. Human use includes farming and raw material extraction (e.g. timber, oil, etc.). Some resources are renewable, others non-renewable.

▷ Ecosystems are sensitive and fragile, and resource development, which can be large and exploiting, can result in environmental damage. People change ecosystems.

▷ Environmental damage can be due to mismanagement of a resource (e.g. soil) and/or to physical reasons (e.g. climate and desertification).

▷ The effect of people's activities on ecosystems needs careful management. Good management ensures ecosystem stewardship, resource conservation and sustainable economic development.

Economic development and human welfare

 GETTING STARTED

This is one of the core topic areas of GCSE Geography which is studied directly in almost all syllabuses, but which is studied indirectly in every syllabus quite regularly. It is a strand or theme which runs through our subject, that of variations between places in their standard of living and quality of life. There isn't a topic area in this book which does not have cause to refer to MEDCs (more economically developed countries) and LEDCs (less economically developed countries).

Development is closely linked to international trade and investment. Hence, Chapter 15 has something to offer in an understanding of this topic area. Tourism is also seen as an agent of economic growth by many LEDCs, so Chapter 11 also supports this chapter.

LONDON A	LONDON B	MEG A	MEG B	MEG C	NEAB A	NEAB B	NEAB C	NICCEA	SEG A	SEG B	WJEC	IGCSE	TOPIC	STUDY	REVISION 1	REVISION 2
✓	✓	✓	✓	✓	✓	✓	✓	✓	✓	✓	✓	✓	Unequal development at international/global scales: MEDCs v. LEDCs			
✓	✓		✓	✓	✓		✓				✓		Inequalities within countries and urban areas			
✓	✓	✓	✓	✓	✓		✓		✓	✓	✓		Development indicators and their strengths and shortcomings			
	✓	✓	✓				✓			✓	✓		Standard of living v. quality of life (i.e. economic v. social well-being)			
	✓		✓				✓						Relative v. absolute poverty/prosperity			
✓	✓	✓	✓	✓	✓		✓		✓	✓	✓		Reasons for contrasting levels of development			
	✓	✓	✓		✓		✓			✓			NICs (newly industrialising countries)			
	✓		✓	✓			✓	✓	✓	✓	✓		Agencies and measures to reduce inequality			

WHAT YOU NEED TO KNOW

▷ **Absolute and relative poverty**

Table 9.1

Needs	Examples	Types of poverty
Basic physical needs (essentials for life)	food clothing shelter	Absolute poverty when these needs not met
Other important needs	education contentment	
Wants: rising standards of living produce 'luxury' desires	annual holiday larger house 'named' trainers	Relative poverty when these wants/ needs lacking so people feel badly off compared with others

Most of the absolute poverty in the world exists in the LEDCs (less economically developed countries).

▷ **Unequal development: MEDCs v. LEDCs**

Table 9.2 LEDCs and MEDCs

MEDCs (The 'Haves')	LEDCs (The 'Have-Nots')
25 per cent world population	75 per cent world population
80 per cent consumption of energy	20 per cent consumption of energy
86 per cent of world industry	14 per cent of world industry
85 per cent of total world income	15 per cent of total world income

There is a wealth gap in the world, an ever-widening rift between the economically rich world and the economically poor world. Roughly 80 per cent of the world's population live in the so-called South (LED countries), with low incomes, malnutrition and illiteracy, and little hope of improvement since they have no more than 20 per cent of the world's wealth. The remaining 20 per cent of people live in a small group of wealthy, industrialised and highly armed countries (developed countries) in the so-called North (Fig. 9.1). This small group of industrialised countries is increasingly dependent on the other group for its industrial supplies. Some of the indicators of the gap between LED and MED countries are:

▷ Birth rates – higher in LED countries;
▷ Death rates – higher in LED countries;
▷ The percentage of the population living in urban areas – lower in LED countries:
▷ The size of the agricultural workforce – higher in LED countries;
▷ The infant mortality rate – higher in LED countries;
▷ Life expectancy – lower in LED countries;
▷ The percentage of the child population enrolled in primary schools – lower in LED countries;
▷ The energy consumption per person – lower in LED countries;
▷ The calorie intake of food per person per day and daily meat consumption – lower in LED countries;
▷ The number of newspapers sold per day per 1000 people – lower in LED countries;
▷ The average number of people per doctor – higher in LED countries;
▷ The road density per area – lower in LED countries;
▷ The percentage of adults who are literate – lower in LED countries;
▷ The number of television sets per 1000 people – this tends to be lower in LED countries;

The gap between these countries varies widely in terms of diet, wealth, health, education, literacy, housing, working and living patterns and shows little sign of narrowing. In fact, such gaps may be widening. Levels of wealth and economic development are spread unevenly across the world, as Table 9.2 and Fig. 9.1 show.

▷ Development indicators

Table 9.3

Indicator	Britain: an MEDC	Egypt: an LEDC
Birth rate	14	41
Death rate	12	14
Life expectancy	76	53
Adult literacy %	99	35
Urban population %	93	14
Gross domestic product US $	14 732	830
% of working population in Primary Industry	2	57
Secondary Industry	20	10
Tertiary Industry	78	34

The world map in Fig. 9.1 shows an economic division of the world, and the United Nations' **Human Development Index** for each country.

Fig. 9.1

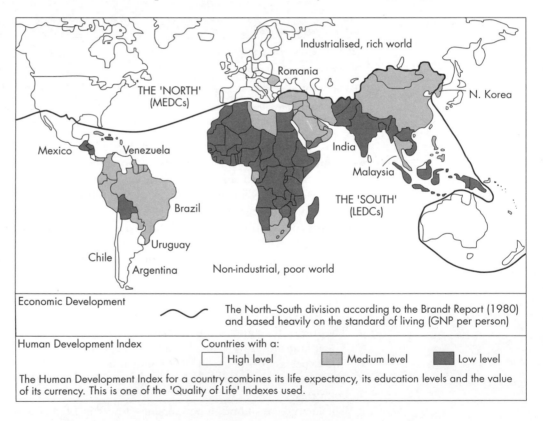

Economic Development — The North–South division according to the Brandt Report (1980) and based heavily on the standard of living (GNP per person)

Human Development Index — Countries with a: ☐ High level ▨ Medium level ■ Low level

The Human Development Index for a country combines its life expectancy, its education levels and the value of its currency. This is one of the 'Quality of Life' Indexes used.

GNP per person

Although each single indicator of development has its shortcomings and gives only a partial picture, **GNP per person** is the main single indicator.

Three important problems arise, however, when using it:

1   It does not measure human *happiness* and total well-being. People on low incomes in a 'developing' country may be as happy as those with higher incomes in 'developed' countries. It is only an indicator of *material* well-being.
2   It is only an *average* and does not show how wealth is distributed across the population of the country.

3 GNP per head may be difficult to use even when comparing average *material well-being* between countries. For instance, people living in cold climates will need more spending on heating, clothing, housing, etc. to keep as warm as people living in hotter climates. They therefore need a *higher* GNP per head to enjoy the *same* material well being.

As Fig. 9.2 shows, poverty also exists in MED countries and there are smaller numbers of people with higher incomes in LED countries. Inequality of income and wealth may be a particular problem in some countries, e.g. Brazil and much of Latin and South America as Table 9.4 shows.

Fig. 9.2

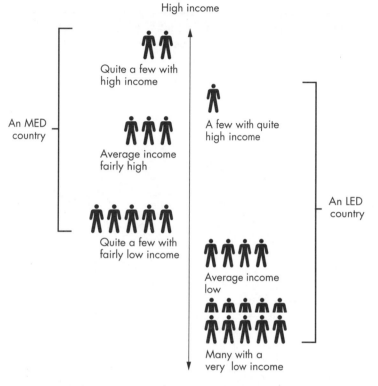

Table 9.4

	GNP per person (1996) US$	What the poorest 20% have of the country's wealth (%)	What the richest 10% have of the country's wealth (%)
Costa Rica	1790	3.3	39.5
Peru	1140	1.9	42.9
Chile	1970	4.4	34.8
Brazil	2080	2.0	50.6
Argentina	2330	4.4	35.2
Mexico	2840	2.9	40.6
Venezuela	4840	3.0	35.7

Because of the shortcomings of GNP per head figures and other single indicators of human welfare, a composite index made up of a number of indicators can be used. This is usually known as a 'quality of life' index because the indicators used tend to be about human welfare and social well-being rather than pure materialism.

▷ Quality of Life Index

The **Physical Quality of Life Index** (PQLI) tries to put a value upon the quality of people's lives. Table 9.5 shows the index for five countries in 1990. It is calculated using three indicators:

1 the infant mortality rate;
2 life expectancy;
3 the literacy rate.

'Using a range of indicators is likely to give you a more accurate picture of quality of life'

A *high* figure represents a *high quality of life*. The index can be used to give a clearer picture of how people's basic needs of life are being met. It shows where the developments in industry benefit ordinary people's lives. The figures in the table shows a gap in the quality of life between a number of countries. It must be remembered many quality of life indicators are closely related to GNP per person. Nevertheless, a country can have a higher GNP per person than another, but a lower PQLI. This is the case when comparing Nigeria with Sri Lanka. Although Nigeria has a higher GNP per head, its higher infant mortality rate, lower life expectancy and lower literacy rate all combine to depress its PQLI *below* that of Sri Lanka (Table 9.5. See also Fig. 9.3.

Table 9.5 The PQLI and GNP per head of five countries

Country	Physical Quality of Life Index (0–100)	GNP per person (US dollars) (1990)
UK	96	13 570
Sri Lanka	83	860
India	43	560
Nigeria	25	930
Ethiopia	16	210

Fig. 9.3 PQLI

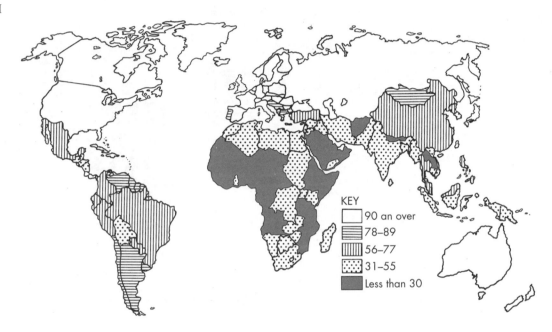

KEY
- 90 an over
- 78–89
- 56–77
- 31–55
- Less than 30

The **Human Development Index** (HDI), shown on Fig. 9.1, is a 'quality of life' index. Countries, especially LEDCs in which military spending takes priority, tend to have low, or lower than they could have, qualities of life; and where health and education spending takes priority quality of life will be higher. The ratio of soldiers to teachers in LEDCs and MEDCs is shown in Fig. 9.4.

Fig. 9.4

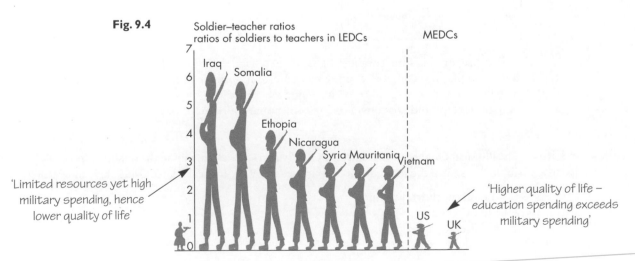

Soldier–teacher ratios
ratios of soldiers to teachers in LEDCs   MEDCs

Iraq Somalia Ethopia Nicaragua Syria Mauritania Vietnam US UK

'Limited resources yet high military spending, hence lower quality of life'

'Higher quality of life – education spending exceeds military spending'

Quality of life spending priority areas are shown in Fig. 9.5.

Fig. 9.5

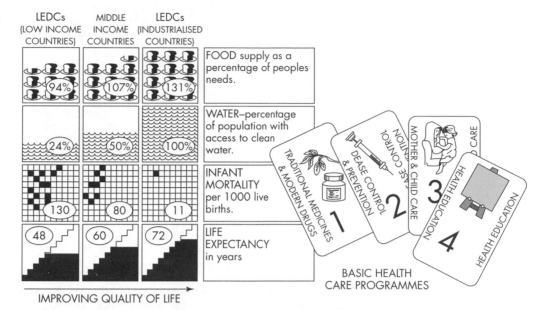

IMPROVING QUALITY OF LIFE

BASIC HEALTH CARE PROGRAMMES

There is evidence to suggest that these quality of life improvements might be directed into rural areas, where, at present, human welfare levels tend to be lowest, as Table 9.6 shows.

Table 9.6

	Access to safe water (percentage of population)		Infant mortality (per thousand live births)	
	Rural Areas	Urban Areas	Rural Areas	Urban Areas
Ivory Coast	10	30	121	70
Ghana	39	93	87	67
India	50	76	105	57
Indonesia	36	43	74	57
Mexico	51	79	79	29
Peru	17	73	101	54

There are many reasons which help to explain the variations in levels of development between countries for example,

▷ Some countries have hostile environments of uncomfortable climate, infertile soil or are relatively inaccessible to and from other places. They face **environmental constraints**.

▷ In some areas population growth has pushed **population densities** beyond the ability of other local resources to support them. On the other hand, some areas have too few people.

▷ MEDCs including Britain developed as the result of an industrial revolution using **raw materials** such as minerals which had often been taken from countries, then colonies but now LEDCs.

Other reasons to do with the types of economic activity in LEDCs, trade and the activities of multinational companies are also put forward as explanations for LEDCs.
United States investment of $8.8 billion in South America has produced profits of $31.5 billion for the United States. The USA does well out of its investment in South America, but does South America?

LEDCs can become trapped in a vicious cycle of poverty, as Fig. 9.6 shows, from which they find difficulty in breaking out. Table 2.4 on page 31 identifies some options, but there are various viewpoints which depend upon the values and attitudes of individual people.

Fig. 9.6 Vicious circle of poverty

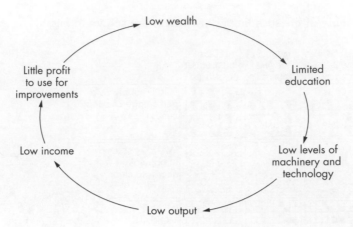

▷ Inequalities within countries

Variations in development and quality of life also exist between regions, within countries, e.g.

▷ The South-East region of Britain produces 36.1% of Britain's GDP (wealth)
▷ The Yorkshire–Humberside region produces 8.0%.

Merseyside, N. Ireland and the Highlands of Scotland generally have lower living standards than the rest of Britain, and certainly lower than the South-East of England. Geographers generally prefer to see Britain as a patchwork of wealthy and poorer areas/towns rather than as a rich 'South' region and a poor 'North' region. Areas of concentrated wealth exist within the North and pockets of poverty can be found in the South. Rich and poor areas/towns can be quite close to each other. Britain's wealthiest areas are: Aberdeen, Aldershot and Farnborough, Basingstoke, Bishops Stortford, Bracknell, Cambridge, Chelmsford, Didcot, Evesham, Guildford, Harrogate, Haywards Heath, Hemel Hempstead, Hexham, High Wycombe, Horsham, Macclesfield, Maidenhead, Maidstone, Malvern, Matlock, Newbury, Reading, Reigate and Redhill, St Albans, Stratford-on-Avon, Stroud, Tunbridge Wells, Watford, Winchester, Woking and Weybridge.

Most of these wealthiest areas are in the South, many are market towns which have attracted hi-tech industries in recent years. However, Harrogate, Hexham, Macclesfield and Matlock are not and are close to towns facing difficulties. Fig. 9.7 shows this patchwork pattern.

Variations can be discovered at an even smaller scale, particularly within a town or city. Fig. 9.8 reveals some of the differences in quality of life between two areas of Nottingham.

Similar patterns exist in all countries. In Brazil, a developing but LEDC, 40% of the population live in south-east Brazil which has 60% of the national wealth. North-east Brazil has 30% of the national population but 15% of the national wealth. Rio de Janeiro in wealthier south-east Brazil contains both highly prosperous areas *and* shanty communities.

Fig. 9.7

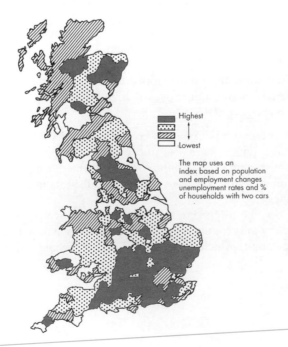

Highest
↑
↓ Lowest

The map uses an index based on population and employment changes unemployment rates and % of households with two cars

Fig. 9.8

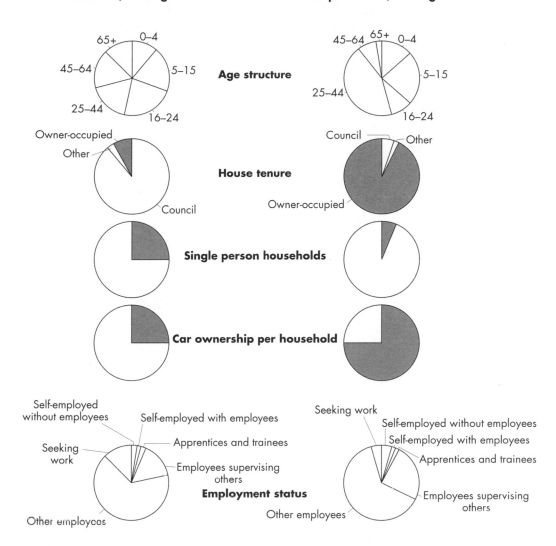

Crabtree, Nottingham   **Hempshill Vale, Nottingham**

Age structure

House tenure

Single person households

Car ownership per household

Employment status

Tourism in The Gambia, West Africa as an agent of economic growth

Fig. 9.9

The tourist season runs from November to April and visitors come mainly from Britain, Sweden, France and Germany. Since it began developing its tourism industry in the late 1960s, the numbers of visitors to the country has increased from just 20 in 1965 to 114 000 in 1990. This growth may partly be due to the American best-seller *Roots*, in which the writer Alex Haley claimed to have traced his ancestors back to the Gambian village of Juffure. The village is now a major tourist attraction.

Most of the country's 17 resort hotels are concentrated on the coastline around the town of Bakau; several of them are wholly- or partly-owned by the Gambian government. An estimated 7500 Gambians are directly employed in the tourism industry as cooks, receptionists, bookkeepers, drivers and guides. In 1990, tourism brought The Gambia $15 million (about £9m) in foreign exchange, or 10 per cent of Gross National Product.

The government also earns income from the sale of land, taxes paid by the companies which own the hotels and customs duties on foreign equipment such as construction machinery. Alongside the benefits tourism has brought to The Gambia's economy, many of the problems associated with it are also beginning to be felt. For example, creating social and political tensions by raising local expectations in life, encouraging crime and prostitution, killing local traditions and not benefiting the local area greatly. Too much reliance on tourism may be economically dangerous for a country; it offers little security.

▷ **Case study** *Taiwan, a NIC (newly industrialising country) of rapid economic growth*

Fig. 9.10

'A small, densely populated, mountainous island with no great mineral wealth and flat land only along the west coast'

'GDP per person was $2000 (US) in 1980 but had grown to $12 000 by 1996 – rapid growth!'

'Three reasons for Taiwan's recent industrial success are:
1. cheap labour
2. modern transport network under Japanese colonial rule up to 1945
3. aid from the USA, 1951–1965'

'An export boom esp. to the USA, has been behind much of the economic growth. See Fig. 9.11.'

'Tiger' economies (newly industrialising countries of South Korea, Taiwan, Hong Kong, Singapore and Malaysia)

Fig. 9.11

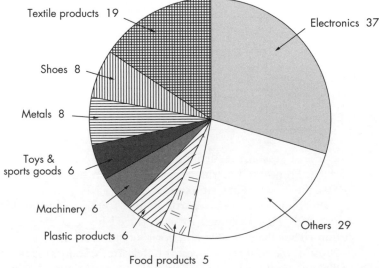

Textile products 19
Electronics 37
Shoes 8
Metals 8
Toys & sports goods 6
Machinery 6
Plastic products 6
Food products 5
Others 29

Total value of exports 124 $billion (1995)

▷ **Key terms**   *Make sure you understand and can apply these geographical terms*

GNP/GDP per head   Gross National Product/Gross Domestic Product per head. Sometimes referred to as average output per person or average income per person. GDP will be a *lower* figure because it ignores wealth generated by international trade.

Infant mortality rate   The number of babies per 1000 born not surviving their first year of life.

Infrastructure   Vital services that have to be provided before development can occur (e.g. transport).

Intermediate technology   Mechanisation which is not advanced technology, and which may, therefore, be more suitable to some 'developing' countries.

Life expectancy   The age at which you can expect to die.

'North' and 'South'   The more economically developed countries which generally lie North of the less economically developed countries of Africa, Asia and South America.

Quality of life   A wide measure of people's well-being which includes more than the standard of living.

Standard of living   Measures the material wealth of an area or country, e.g. GNP per head.

The terms used in the geography of population, settlement and industry (Chapters 11–14) may also be relevant to a sound understanding of this topic, e.g. population density; birth and death rate; and so on.

Suggestions for further work

▷   There are fieldwork investigations which you can undertake in this topic, e.g.

1   To what extent does the quality of environment and life vary in *your* town and why?
    Can environmental quality be related to the socio-economic characteristics of an area?
2   What factors influence the distribution of crimes and criminals in your town?

▷   These involve examining the 'quality of life' within Britain. Your teacher may be able to help you plan such an investigation, especially with regard to deciding which quality of life indicators you could examine.

▷   Coursework involving less economically developed countries would have to use secondary data, i.e. that collected by someone else. This would have to be a classroom-based enquiry, with perhaps your teacher guiding you towards sources of information and data.

▷ **STUDENT ANSWER WITH EXAMINER'S COMMENTS**

(a)   Study Fig. 9.12, showing development data for six countries.

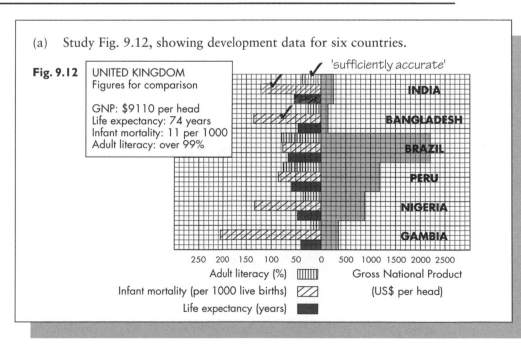

Fig. 9.12

UNITED KINGDOM
Figures for comparison

GNP: $9110 per head
Life expectancy: 74 years
Infant mortality: 11 per 1000
Adult literacy: over 99%

'sufficiently accurate'

INDIA
BANGLADESH
BRAZIL
PERU
NIGERIA
GAMBIA

Adult literacy (%)
Infant mortality (per 1000 live births)
Life expectancy (years)

Gross National Product
(US$ per head)

(i) What is the meaning of the term 'adult literacy?'

Adult literacy is the term given to how many adults can read and write per _____ 1

1000 ✓

(*1 mark*)

(ii) Complete the graph, Fig. 9.12, by plotting the following information for India:

Adult literacy: 34 per cent

Infant mortality rate: 121 per 1000 ✓ 3

Life expectancy: 52 years (*3 marks*)

(iii) Which TWO sets of data provide information on a country's health service?

The birth rate and death rate ✗ 0

(*1 mark*)

'No, infant mortality and life expectancy are what is wanted!'

(iv) What links are shown on Fig. 9.12 between Gross National Product per head and the other indicators of development?

Countries with a low GNP often have high infant mortality rates, as well as a ✓

low Adult literacy rate. Countries with a higher GNP per head often have a ✓

suitable life-expectancy, and lower infant mortality rates also an (average)

better adult literacy rate. 2

(*3 marks*)

'You've grasped the broad relationships between GNP per person, etc., and sound use of Fig. 9.12'

(v) Explain why the Gross National Product per head may not be a very good indicator of the level of development in a country.

Even countries with a high GNP have poor life expectancy and low adult ✓

literacy rates, compared to the world, e.g. Brazil. Brazil has a higher GNP per

head that most countries, but not very good adult literacy rates compared to

the world. Some countries with low GNP have a lower infant mortality rate

than countries with a higher GNP, e.g. India. 2

(*4 marks*)

'A bit repetitive from (iv) and too tied to the information in Fig. 9.12. You needed to introduce wealth v. welfare differences, and the idea of a "quality of life"'

(b) Study Fig. 9.13, showing the percentage causes of death in the LEDCs (less economically developed countries).

Fig. 9.13

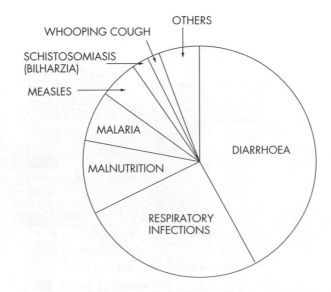

(i) Which is the most frequent cause of death in the **developing** world according to Fig. 9.13?

1

Diarrhoea ✔

(1 mark)

(ii) What is 'malnutrition'?

'A fair definition'

✔

Malnutrition is when people do not get enough nutrients in their body. They

are malnourished 1

(1 mark)

(iii) What can be done to reduce the number of deaths in LEDCs from EITHER malnutrition OR disease?

Choice: *Malnutrition*

✔

'A good general point'

Malnutrition can be stopped by giving poorer countries money and education

and technology to farm crops and animals for themselves. Developed

'Do you know any actual extremes or examples?'

countries can give money to developing countries to start farms and food

'I'm afraid it's all too vague and generalised. Try to be more specific'

reserves for the people. The food will give them nutrients. 1

(3 marks)

(c) In many LEDCs, tourism is being encouraged as a way of increasing the country's wealth.

(i) Name an example of a tourist development in a **developing** country that you have studied:

'No, a game park or tourist complex near Mombasa needed'

Country: *Kenya*   Location: *East Africa* 0

(1 mark)

(ii) What are the advantages and disadvantages of this tourist development?

✔   ✔

Advantages: *Tourism brings money, wealth, creates jobs into the area. Jobs are*

'Again, rather general though okay points'

created to take people to see animals, (go on safari). The money from tourism

can be used to build houses, buy food for the country. Tourism is a good way

of making money, tourists buy souvenirs to take home, etc, earning money for

the country.

✔

Disadvantages: *Tourists wreck the natural habitat of many animals. The*

'Good, both sides of issue dealt with'

tourists disturb normal Kenyan family life. The tourists bring noise and

pollution to the area. The rubbish left by the tourist poses a health risk to the

✔

natives. Natives normal way of life is broken by tourists. ✔ 5

(7 marks)

'Add some examples and detail from your geography course'

16/25 *(SEG)*

A TUTOR ANSWER

▷ **Short structured question**

Study Fig. 9.1 (page 132) which shows an economic division of the world, and the United Nations' Human Development Index for each country.

(a) Using map evidence, write one statement about the world distribution of **economic** development.

There is an unequal distribution of economic development in the world with a

'Rich North' and 'Poor South'.

(1 mark)

(b) Complete the map by showing the Human Development Index level for Brazil, India and South Africa. Use the information given in Table 9.7 below.

Table 9.7

Country	Human Development Index level (HDI)
Brazil	Medium
India	Low
South Africa	Medium

(3 marks)

(c) The Human Development Index (HDI) combines a country's life expectancy, educational level, and the value of its currency.

   (i) What is the meaning of the term 'life expectancy'?

   It is the average length of life expected for people at birth.

   (1 mark)

   (ii) Name one other indicator that could have been used in the HDI.

   Number of people per doctor.

   (1 mark)

(d) (i) Name **one** less economically developed country (LEDC) with a high HDI level.

   Mexico

   (ii) Name **one** more economically developed country (MEDC) with a medium HDI level.

   North Korea

   (2 marks)

(e) Suggest why the level of economic development alone is not necessarily a good indicator of the quality of life in a country.

A country can have a high level of economic development but not spend its

wealth on improving the life conditions for the bulk of its population. Money

could be spent as in Iraq on the military rather than on items to make ordinary

citizens happy.

(2 marks)
(Total 10 marks)
(NEAB)

> **EXAMINATION QUESTION**

Study Fig. 9.14, showing three different ways of measuring development and welfare in five areas of the less economically developed world.

Fig. 9.14

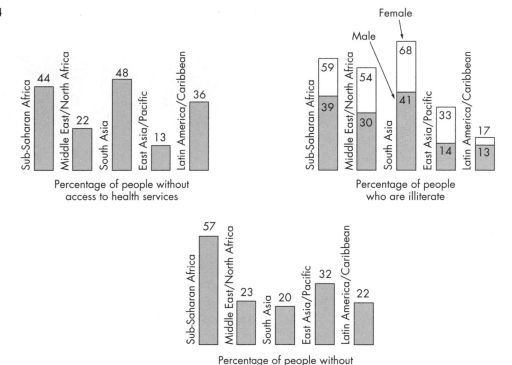

EITHER (TIER F)

(a) (i) Complete the phrases below.
1. access to health services means the number of
2. literacy rate means the percentage of population able to
3. access to safe water means the availability of

(3 marks – Tier F only)

   (ii) Which of the five geographical areas in Fig. 9.14 has the highest percentage of people living in poverty? Use information from Fig. 9.14 to support your answer. (3 lines provided here) *(2 marks – Tier F only)*

OR (TIER H)

(a) (i) 'Many people in LEDCs (Less Economically Developed Countries) are illiterate, unwell and have to drink filthy water'.
      Do you agree with this statement? Use information from Fig. 9.14 to give reasons for your answer. (5 lines provided here) *(3 marks – Tier H only)*

   (iii) (Tier F)
   (ii) (Tier H)
      Give **one** reason why female illiteracy is generally higher than male illiteracy in LEDCs (Less Economically Developed Countries). (3 lines provided here)
      (1 mark – Tier F) (2 marks – Tier H)

(b) Read the following headline from a recent newspaper.

Fig. 9.15

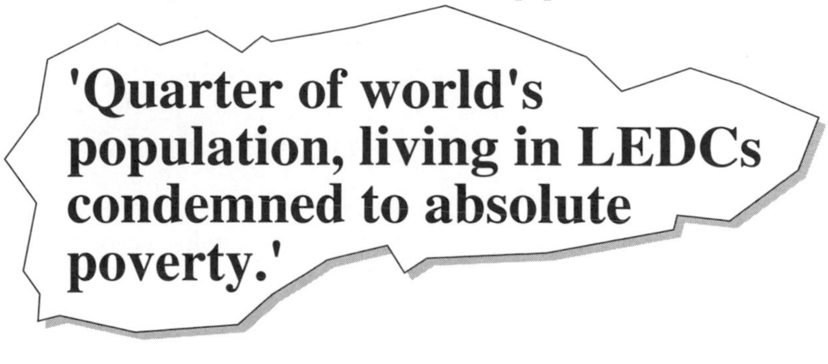

> **'Quarter of world's population, living in LEDCs condemned to absolute poverty.'**

(i) What does 'absolute poverty' mean? (4 lines provided here) (*2 – Tiers F and H*)

(ii) Give **two** other ways (not shown in Fig. 9.14) which show that people are living in absolute poverty. (4 lines provided here) (*2 marks – Tiers F and H*)

(iii) In some areas environmental conditions might help to explain the absolute poverty. Give an example of such an area and two reasons for these difficult conditions. (8 lines provided here) (*4 marks – Tiers F and H*)

(c) Study Fig. 9.16, showing the world distribution of wealth and trade in 1991.

Fig. 9.16

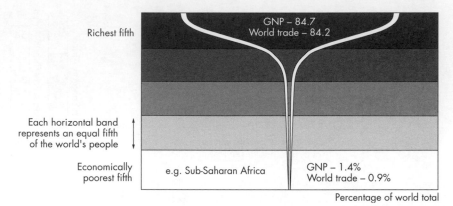

Richest fifth

GNP – 84.7
World trade – 84.2

Each horizontal band represents an equal fifth of the world's people

Economically poorest fifth

e.g. Sub-Saharan Africa

GNP – 1.4%
World trade – 0.9%

Percentage of world total

(i) What is the evidence that wealth and trade are not equally shared around the world? (6 lines provided here) (*3 marks – Tier H*) (*2 marks – Tier F*)

(ii) Suggest why absolute poverty in LEDCs might be caused by this uneven sharing of wealth and trade. (7 lines provided here)

(*4 marks – Tier H*) (*3 marks – Tier F*)

EITHER (TIER F)

(d) Study Fig. 9.17, showing how LEDCs can be trapped in an unending cycle of poverty.

Fig. 9.17

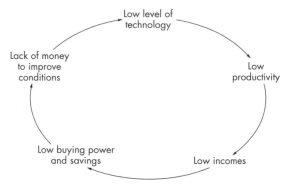

Low level of technology

Lack of money to improve conditions

Low productivity

Low buying power and savings

Low incomes

(i) The cycle of poverty in LEDCs can be broken. From examples you have studied, describe **two** ways in which this cycle can be broken. (8 lines provided here)

(*4 marks – Tier F only*)

(ii) For **one** of the ways to break the cycle of poverty you have used above, describe how the environment of the area has been affected. (4 lines provided here)

(*2 marks – Tier F only*) (*Total 25 marks – Tier F*)

OR (TIER H)

(d) Many LEDCs encourage either

tourism

the use of improved but appropriate technologies

or the arrival or multinational companies

as ways of increasing their national wealth.

(i) For a named country, describe the advantages of **one** of these approaches. Country (1 line provided here) Approach (7 lines provided here)

(*6 marks – Tier H only*)

(ii) For the approach you have identified in (i) above, describe how the environment of an area of the country has been affected by it. (9 lines provided here)

(*4 marks – Tier H only*)

(*Total 30 marks – Tier H*) (*NEAB*)

▶ **EXAMINATION ANSWER**

Tier F

(a) (i) 1 doctors or hospitals
   2 literacy; read and write
   3 clean, fresh water (3)

   (ii) Level 1 – 1 Accept sub-Saharan Africa or South Asia
   Level 2 – 2 Data-based reason depending on choice of area (2)

Tier H

(a) (i) Level 2 – 1–2 Expect agreement (though do not penalise if disagreement properly justified). Marks are for reasons supporting illiteracy (1 mark); ill health (1 mark) and filthy water (1 mark).
   Level 3 – 3 Extra justification (3)

Tiers F and H

   (ii)(iii)Level 1 – 1 Simply stated valid reason, e.g. differences in length of schooling, etc.
   2nd mark for full explanation (Level 2) (1)

(b) (i) Level 1 – 1 Expect focus on poverty
   Level 2 – 2 Accurate definition dealing with 'absolute' (2)

   (ii) Level 1 – 1–2 Accept any two valid points, e.g. hunger/malnutrition, etc. (2)

   (iii) (2+2) Level 1 – 2 Basic factors given, e.g. hilly, difficult farming, etc.
   Level 2 – 4 Offers an appropriate illustration of an actual area and some attempt to explain how poverty results (4)

(c) (i) Level 1 – 1 Expect 1–2 basic points from top and/or bottom of 'mushroom' diagram
   Level 2 – 2 or 3 Expect appreciation of entire skewedness of diagram and distribution it represents (2 or 3)

   (ii) Level 2 – 1–3 Expect appreciation that 80% of people live on 15–16% of GNP/world trade
   Level 3 – 4 Role of low and unfair trade in causing poverty (3 or 4)

Tier F

(d) (i) Level 1 – 1–2 Names a suitable attempt and provides some basic information
   Level 2 – 3–4 Adds a second or third development, and more specific information (4)

   (ii) Level 2 – 1–2 Expect responses to focus on phases of cycle and to stress lack of time, capital, scale of poverty, etc. (2) (*Tier F Total 25*)

Tier H

(d) (i) Level 2 – 1–3 Brief statement of valid example, e.g. Mexico and tourism with isolated but accurate points (1–3 marks)
   Level 3 – 4–6 Elaboration; full description offered/case study approach of at least 2 advantages (4–6 marks) (6)

   (ii) Level 2 – 1–2 Expect response to focus on 1–2 loose points about environmental impact, e.g. pollution, etc. (1–2 marks)
   Level 3 – 3–4 Full treatment of effects appropriate for the stated area (3–4 marks) (4)
   (*Tier H Total 30*) (*NEAB*)

SUMMARY

▷ Different indicators are used to judge development; both the standard of living (economic development) and the quality of life (human welfare).

▷ Variations in the levels of development (standard of living and quality of life) exist between countries.

▷ The gap between MEDCs and LEDCs is in many cases growing wider, though some countries are growing rapidly and becoming NICs (newly industrialising countries) from LEDCs.

▷ Contrasts in development are related to various factors, including environmental conditions, historical events and political and trading arrangements.

▷ Inequalities exist within countries and within urban areas.

▷ Governments and other agencies work to even out these inequalities with varying degrees of success.

10 Agriculture, food supply, and rural settlements and environments

▷ GETTING STARTED

This chapter looks at some of the geography of rural areas, especially farming and villages. Farming is the main source of food production and a key contributor to the welfare of villages and the countryside. There is a clear overlap between these studies and those concerned with environmental management in Chapter 8. Economic activities in rural areas, whether farming or reservoirs for water supply or quarrying for minerals, can put pressures on the environment and ecosystems, which sometimes can be of a fragile nature.

Again, it is important that you can illustrate your understanding of agricultural and rural settlement ideas by giving examples and case studies from both MEDCs (especially Britain) and LEDCs. There are also some pretty specific terms in this area of the syllabus, most of which include it. Work through the list of terms provided in the chapter, and make sure you can use them confidently on the examination papers.

LONDON A	LONDON B	MEG A	MEG B	MEG C	NEAB A	NEAB B	NEAB C	NICCEA	SEG A	SEG B	WJEC	IGCSE	TOPIC	STUDY	REVISION 1	REVISION 2
✓				✓	✓	✓			✓			✓	Farming as a system			
✓		✓	✓		✓	✓			✓		✓	✓	Rural land use patterns and farming types			
✓	✓			✓	✓	✓			✓				Factors affecting farming			
✓	✓	✓				✓	✓		✓		✓	✓	How farming is changing			
✓	✓		✓		✓	✓	✓		✓			✓	Farming and the environment			
✓				✓				✓	✓			✓	Reasons for rural settlement locations			
✓									✓				Rural settlement shapes			
✓				✓				✓	✓			✓	Rural settlement hierarchies and spheres of influence			
	✓	✓		✓	✓		✓				✓		Service provision and suburbanisation of villages			

▷ WHAT YOU NEED TO KNOW

 Farming and food supply

Farming is the name given to people's use of their environment to produce food. Farms are the main source of food supply and also provide raw materials (e.g. wool) for manufacturing industry. Food is produced either for farmers and their families (**subsistence** farming) or for sale to other people (**commercial** farming).

In some LEDCs growing crops and rearing livestock for food is a struggle and farming is mainly subsistence. Food shortages occur in the LED countries of Africa, Asia and South America.

World food production has grown faster than world population in recent years, but about half of the food produced is eaten in the MEDCs. These countries have only about a quarter of the world's population.

The changing demand for food matches changes in population and wealth. Farm production has to be increased to meet the ever increasing demand for food. There are two basic ways in which production can be increased:

▶ use more land for farming (**agriculture**);
▶ use farm land more productively so that **yields** (output from a certain area of land) rise.

The box below lists some recent United Nations recommendations for increasing world food supply. Giving everyone a healthy diet is at present partly a problem of distribution. There is a surplus of food in North America and Western Europe. In these MEDCs farming can be called 'agri-business'; farmers work as business people trying to increase their income by adapting their farming to the conditions and by trying to improve some of these conditions (e.g. the soil).

United Nations recommendations for increasing world food supply:

1. Increase the present low level of human inputs into farming in LEDCs (e.g. modern management methods, fertilisers, pesticides, technical equipment).
2. Grow crops more suited to local soils and climates in LEDCs.
3. Grow crops in LEDCs with higher calorie contents.
4. Use all the possible farmland for farming.
5. Encourage freer movement of food from areas of surplus to areas of shortage.

Fig. 10.1 World food production 1995

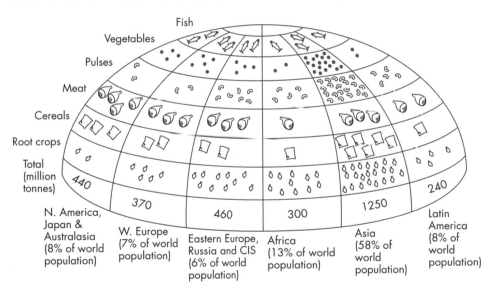

'Feeding the world' is a regional rather than global problem. Africa contains 13% of the world's people but produces only 9% of its food whereas Western Europe produces 10% of the world's food for 7% of its people, as Fig. 10.1 shows.

Sahel

The term **Sahel** is derived from an Arabic word meaning edge or shore. It is now used with reference to countries such as Mali, Mauritania, Burkina Faso, Niger, Chad, Sudan, Ethiopia and Somalia which are on the southern edge of the Sahara Desert, where the rainfall and vegetation conditions are transitional between those of the true desert and those of the savannah (e.g. the Kenyan Game Parks). (See the map in Fig. 10.2.)

These Sahelian countries have been a disaster area in recent years and are often referred to as the 'famine belt' of Africa, where hunger and absolute poverty have affected millions of people. A mixture of factors are to blame for this sub-Saharan crisis:

▶ **rainfall** has fallen in a rather on-and-off way since 1968, the year of the so-called 'Great Drought of Africa', and as a result harvests in the area have fallen by 15 per cent since then. The desert sands have expanded southwards and replaced the scattered shrubs and trees of some of the Sahel.

▶ annual **population growth rates** are among the highest in the world. The population of the Sahelian countries has doubled since 1968. Poor harvests and more mouths to feed have been causes of hunger and famine.

▶ **civil wars** (e.g. in Chad, Sudan and Ethiopia) have aggravated the problem. They have disrupted farming and caused depopulation of the countryside. People have felt safe in the towns, where they cannot farm! The urban population has been growing twice as fast as the rural population during the 1980s.

▶ **corruption** and **poor food storage, marketing** and **distribution** exist. Government administration of good prices and supply has often favoured the powerful groups in the cities and been designed to keep the peace there. Small farmers have often received low farm prices, which are a disincentive to farm. There has generally been inefficiency in farming and food supply in these countries, partly because of under-investment in training people. For example, rats eat about a quarter of harvests and **deforestation**, which allows the soil to be eroded and the desert to grow further, has been permitted.

Fig. 10.2 The Sahel and the drought in Africa

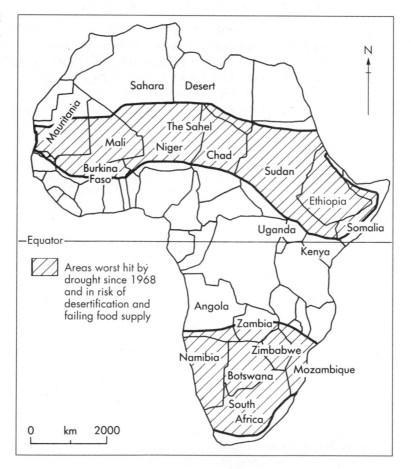

Farming as a system

It is necessary that you understand that farms can be studied as **systems** with inputs, processes and outputs. The terms used in this systems approach include throughputs, stores, processes, outputs, feedback, market, relief. The type of **systems diagram** which you will need to be able to construct or complete is given in Fig. 10.3, which shows the contrasting farming systems.

The nature of the systems diagram varies with the type of farming. The world map (Fig. 10.4) shows the main types of farming. A system diagram drawn for a subsistence farm in Central Africa will be totally different to one for a commercial livestock farm in Britain. You should be able to *recognise* and *distinguish* systems diagrams which are typical of subsistence farming from those typical of commercial farming (i.e. the growing of crops and/or rearing of livestock for sale rather than personal need).

Fig. 10.3

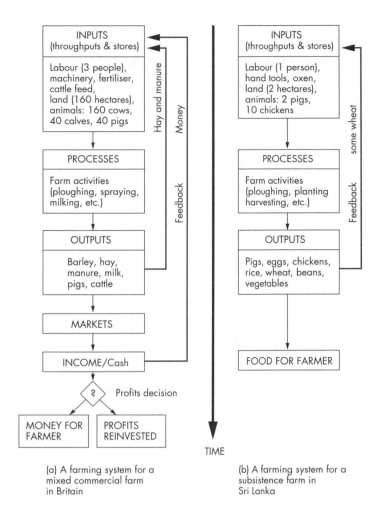

(a) A farming system for a mixed commercial farm in Britain

(b) A farming system for a subsistence farm in Sri Lanka

Fig. 10.4

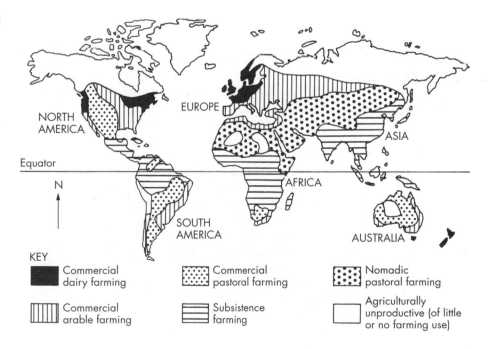

KEY

▪ Commercial dairy farming

▦ Commercial pastoral farming

▦ Nomadic pastoral farming

|||| Commercial arable farming

☰ Subsistence farming

☐ Agriculturally unproductive (of little or no farming use)

Farms can be classified as follows, according to the type of output they produce:

▸ arable – where farmers plough the land so that crops like grain and vegetables can be grown;

▸ pastoral – where farmers keep animals for either meat (e.g. beef cattle), milk (e.g. dairy cattle) or other products (e.g. wool);

▸ mixed – where farmers keep animals and grow crops in equal proportions.

▷ Types of farming

'Make sure you can give examples of the different types of farming'

One very important difference between the types of farming is whether they are **extensive** or **intensive**. These two key terms are defined in the list of major terms given in this chapter (also see Fig. 10.6). Check their meanings.

Extensive farms such as ranches or nomadic pastoral areas are large. They may occupy new and sometimes marginal farming land, that is, land only just suitable for farming, for example the nomadic pastoral farmers of the dry areas of North Africa, with their herds of sheep and goats. They can also only be highly mechanised with a small labour force, as the arable farms on the prairies of North America.

Intensive farms, on the other hand, tend to be smaller and achieve high yields. **Yield** is the amount of output that a farm achieves from a certain amount of land, for example from a hectare. Market gardening is a good example of intensive farming.

Achieving high yields may be the result of using a relatively large labour force on the farm. Many rice farms in South East Asia use **labour-intensive** farming methods. In such densely populated regions, large amounts of labour are available but large amounts of land and capital are not. Other intensive farms use amounts of capital and mechanisation, such as market gardens in the Lea Valley, north of London. They thus use **capital-intensive** farming methods. (See Fig. 10.5.)

Fig. 10.5 Inputs of land, labour and capital needed for three types of farming

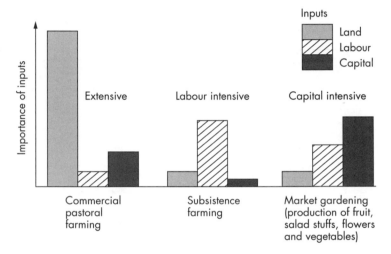

▷ Factors affecting farming

All farms have a land-use decision to make; what shall I produce? (Fig. 10.7). Many factors, both **physical** (environmental or natural) and **human** (economic) affect the farmer's decision. **Relief** (the shape and height of the land) is important, in particular the steepness of slope. Other physical factors affecting land use include **rainfall**, **temperatures** and **sunshine** and the **nature of the soil**. Human factors playing a role here include **transport** and **markets**, **government policy** and **assistance**, etc.

The maps of England and Wales (Fig. 10.8) show that certain **climatic conditions** either favour or discourage certain crops and livestock. Lowland England has a more favourable climate for arable farming than does upland England and Wales. **Soils** have different properties and different soils favour different crops, such as alluvial soil in, say, the Fenland areas of East Anglia is well suited to cereals and vegetables.

Farmers' decisions regarding land use are strongly affected by human factors too, such as transport networks and closeness to the market. Perishable produce that cannot be easily transported to market, because of inadequate road or rail networks, will be less attractive to the farmer. Distance from a farm to its market also has a strong influence on what the farmer decides to produce. It leads to the kind of land-use pattern around many urban areas in Western Europe, shown by Fig. 10.9.

▶ **Market gardening** and **dairy farming** use land with a high value in and around urban areas; they are bulky, perishable goods and rapid, low-cost transport is required. They are only profitable if close to the market, as Fig. 10.9 shows.

▶ **Arable** and **livestock farming** become more profitable than market gardening and dairy farming away from urban areas. Wheat and beef are less perishable products, so speed of transport to market is less important. Also the higher costs to market which these farmers face can be covered by the higher prices that their products fetch.

Profit is of course revenue minus cost, so we need to take account of both the price of the produce (revenue) and the costs of transport, etc. in finding profit levels. The nature of the product is clearly important however in determining the type of transport that is necessary, and therefore where the item can profitably be produced in relation to the market.

This idea that transport and markets affect farmers' land-use decisions is clearly seen at the **national scale** of geography in the case of Uruguay. Fig. 10.11 shows the pattern of agricultural land-use of that country. It shows market gardening around Montevideo, where approximately 39% of Uruguay's population live. Dairying, followed by cereals or stock raising, appear at greater distances from the city.

Fig. 10.6

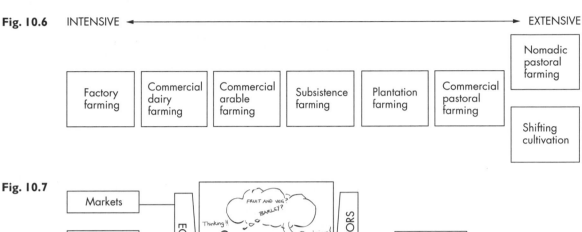

Fig. 10.7

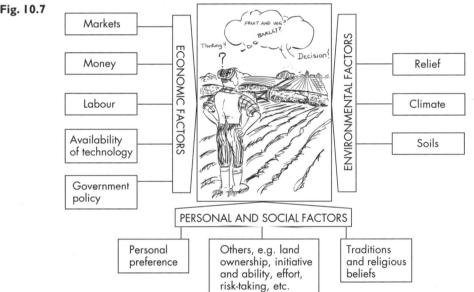

Fig. 10.8 Influences on British farming

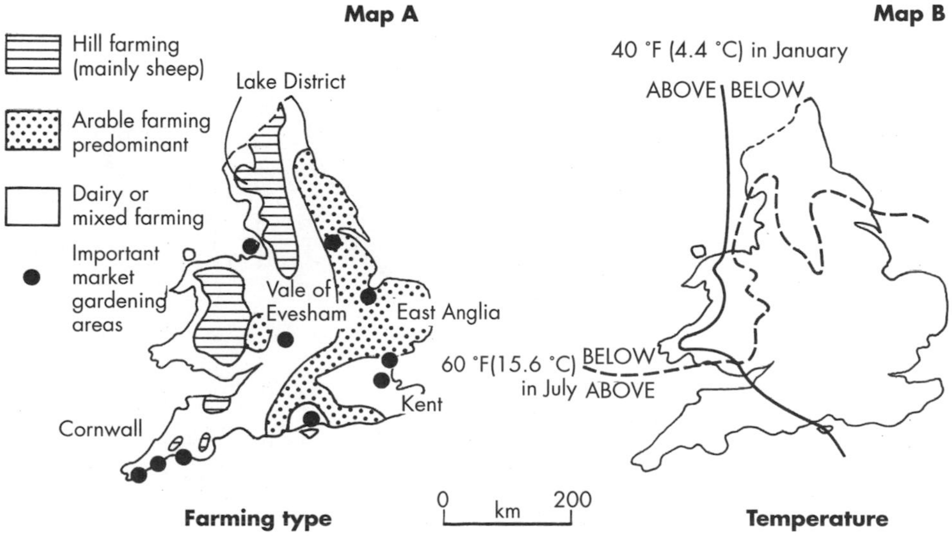

Fig. 10.8 (*cont*)

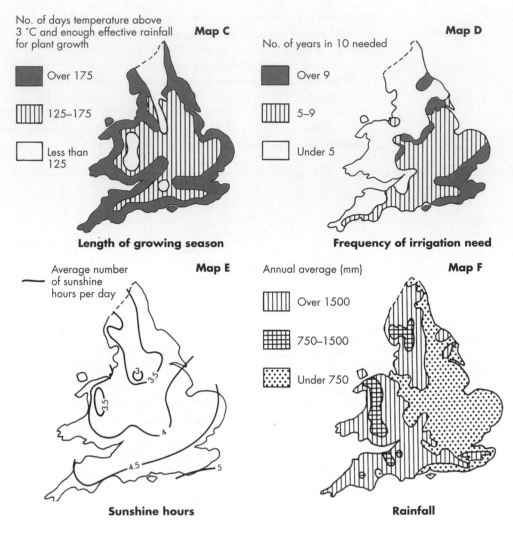

Map C

No. of days temperature above 3 °C and enough effective rainfall for plant growth

▪ Over 175

▥ 125–175

▫ Less than 125

Length of growing season

Map D

No. of years in 10 needed

▪ Over 9

▥ 5–9

▫ Under 5

Frequency of irrigation need

Map E

Average number of sunshine hours per day

Sunshine hours

Map F

Annual average (mm)

▥ Over 1500

▦ 750–1500

▒ Under 750

Rainfall

Fig. 10.9 Rural land use around a town/city

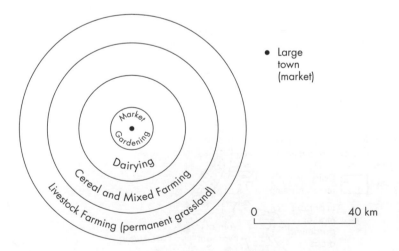

Market Gardening
Dairying
Cereal and Mixed Farming
Livestock Farming (permanent grassland)

• Large town (market)

0 ————— 40 km

Fig. 10.10 The effect of distance from market on profitability of different types of rural land use

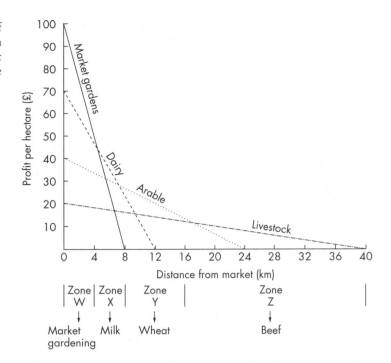

Fig. 10.11 Rural land use around Montevideo

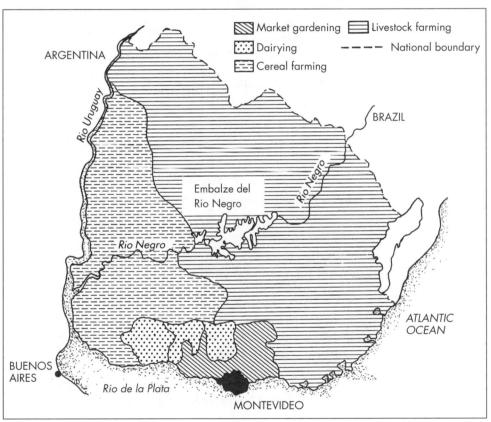

▷ **Rural settlement**   Villages, hamlets and smaller market towns are the dominant **settlement type** in rural areas. These smaller settlements provide a useful context for studying **settlement locations**.

The **site** of a settlement, a factory or any geographical feature is the actual piece of ground on which it stands. This is its **absolute location** rather than its **relative location** (its position in relation to other features), which is known as **situation**. Site and situation are the two kinds of location recognised by geographers.

Many large cities began as a market and meeting place by a ford (a shallow point of a river which could be crossed on foot) where bridges were later built. All settlements, however large now, obviously must have had an original building site. They can be classified according to this original site. Would-be settlers could be expected to choose sites which offered a water supply, a fuel supply, a supply of building materials, farmland for grazing and growing crops, good trading possibilities (e.g. where routes naturally met) and were easy to defend against intruders.

Five different types of settlement sites are shown in Fig. 10.12. It is not difficult to see that water supply, meeting points of routeways and defensibility were important considerations.

Fig. 10.12

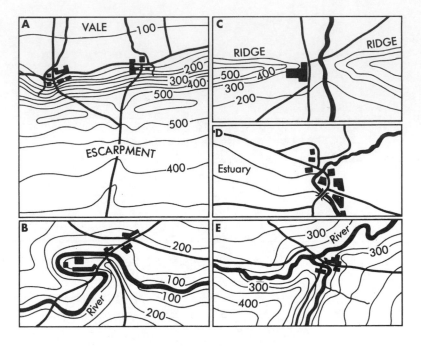

A   Spring-line settlement – at the point where springs are found

B   Defensive site – an easily defended place, usually a hill

C   Gap site – a place where it easy to pass between two ridges

D   Lowest bridging point – the place nearest the sea where a river can be bridged

E   Confluence site – where 2 or more rivers join

As well as more clearly showing the reasons why particular sites were chosen in the past by people for settlement, rural settlements may exhibit distinct **settlement shapes** or lay-outs. Three types of settlement shape are recognised: **nucleated**, **linear** (or **ribbon**) and **dispersed**. Nucleated settlements have a distinct nucleus or centre: for example, they may have developed around a crossroads or market square. Linear settlements (Fig. 10.13) show ribbon development, usually along a road, and are long, narrow settlements. Parts of a nucleated settlement may also show ribbon development as the place has grown out alongside a major road. The plan of the nucleated English village in Fig. 10.14 also shows elements of dispersion around the edges of the village. Truly dispersed settlements are scattered and widespread, with much open space and undeveloped land within the settlement boundary.

Fig. 10.13 A linear settlement

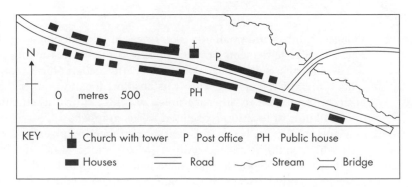

Fig. 10.14 A nucleated settlement

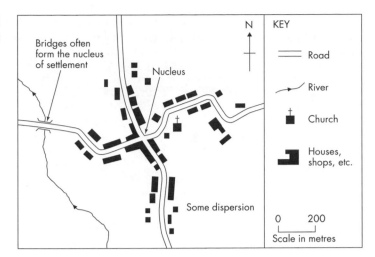

Functions of settlements

Settlements vary in population and size, and so vary in the number and level of **functions** or services they offer. The graph below shows a very important relationship between types of settlement and their functions. It is clear that the number and nature of the functions found in a settlement depend on its size and importance. Large settlements have many services including specialist ones which are not found anywhere else. The graph in Fig. 10.15 shows what is called a **hierarchy** of settlement, ranging from hamlets up to cities, the number of functions rising with the size of settlement.

Fig. 10.15 A settlement hierarchy

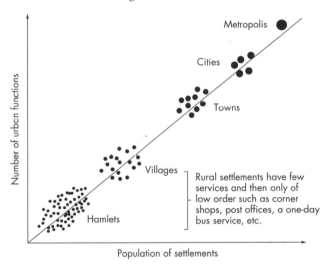

Fig. 10.16 The service area for seven functions provided within Exeter

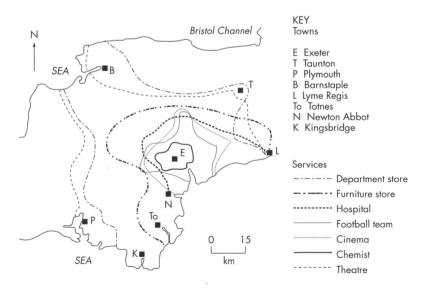

A certain number of people must live in a settlement, or within easy reach of it, before a particular function can profitably survive. This is known as the **threshold population** – as shown in Table 10.1.

Table 10.1 Threshold populations

Function	Threshold population	
General store	200	Low order
Primary school	250	Shops and services found in all towns and cities
Butcher	350	and most large villages. These services are required
Newsagent	750	by most people every week. Everyday goods and
Greengrocer	2500	services with a low threshold population.
Post office	2500	
Public house	3500	
Doctor's surgery	3500	
Branch library	12000	Middle order
Bank	15000	Shops and services found only in towns and cities.
Secondary school	17000	Goods and services used and bought say, two or
Swimming pool	50000	three times a month.
Cinema	50000	
Chain store (e.g. Boots)	50000	
Museum	70000	
Art gallery	200000	High order
General hospital	200000	Shops and services found only in major towns and
Concert hall	300000	cities. Services used infrequently and having a high
Polytechnic/University	300000	threshold population.
Department store	350000	

We can see that a general store is viable with a population as low as 200, with people purchasing items frequently. Other services are used much less frequently and need a higher threshold population, e.g. a department store may need 350000 persons.

Nevertheless some large stores, such as Boots, are found in settlements with less than 50 000 people, because they may serve people living in villages around the town. Settlements, especially larger ones, have a **market area** which includes places outside the town. This is known as the **sphere of influence**, i.e. the area outside the town which it serves and influences. The larger the settlement, the larger this sphere of influence. The distance from a settlement that is reached by a particular function provided within the settlement, is known as the **range** of that function. People travel to buy or use the function provided there.

The work on service areas around Exeter (Fig. 10.16) shows the range for various functions of different 'order'. High-order functions, like a department store, are used much less frequently by an individual. Department stores are relatively few in number, are normally found only in large settlements like Exeter, and have a large range. People travel long distances to use them. Low-order functions, such as a chemist, have a small range. Exeter's sphere of influence for various functions begins to emerge from this map.

People living in rural, farming communities often have considerable distances to travel to reach middle- and high-order services. This poor rural provision is not helped by the arrival in many villages in MEDCs close to urban areas of newcomers from the town or city. Many **commute** (travel to work in the town or city) and purchase goods and services elsewhere. Those without transport find themselves poorly served.

▷ **Issue**   *Overproduction and rural environment damage from European Union farms*

Modern farming has led to overproduction (see Fig. 10.17).

Fig. 10.17

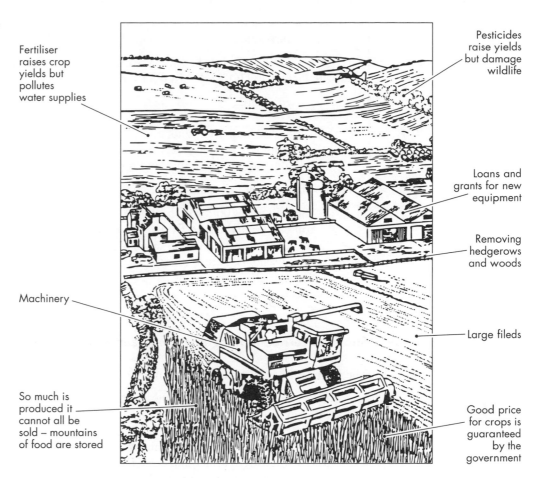

Fertiliser raises crop yields but pollutes water supplies

Pesticides raise yields but damage wildlife

Loans and grants for new equipment

Removing hedgerows and woods

Machinery

Large fileds

So much is produced it cannot all be sold – mountains of food are stored

Good price for crops is guaranteed by the government

Common Agricultural Policy

This policy has also led to overproduction. The 12 European Union (EU) countries work to a **Common Agricultural Policy**, developed to help their farming industries. This policy fixes the price of all farm produce regardless of whether there is too much or too little. The aim was to guarantee farmers a good price and a stable amount of money each year, and to keep prices for shoppers stable. Problems have appeared because the efficient farms of Europe, using modern technology, have been able to increase production too much. All the over-production that was not needed in the shops was bought up by the European Union, so that farmers could still get their money, and knowing this, farmers were encouraged to carry on producing extra. Before long huge stores of crops, meat and milk (the butter mountains, grain mountains, beef mountains and wine lakes) began to build up. The EU could not sell them and they were costing a fortune to store.

In the case of milk, storage was costing so much that dairy farmers were given a top limit which they could produce (known as a **quota**). Anyone going over the quota was fined. Milk production did fall but not by as much as was hoped. The problem was that sticking to the limits led to many marginal farms going bankrupt. This political decision in 1984 caused some farms in Britain to close down and others to change what they produced.

The Common Agricultural Policy also involves loans and grants of money being given to some farmers to enable them to buy new equipment, to encourage them to improve their land or to grow certain crops. The many fields of yellow oil-seed rape we see about us in Britain today were largely the result of the financial subsidies which that crop used to attract.

'One way in which the issue has been managed'

Attention all Farmers

HELP US TO PROTECT THE ENVIRONMENT AND REDUCE OVER-PRODUCTION OF CROPS IN EUROPE.

How can you help?

▶   Choose 20% of your land
▶   This land will be called Set-Aside land
▶   Do not grow crops on this land for 5 years

How will this plan help you?

▶   You will get £200 for each hectare of Set-Aside land
▶   You can leave the land fallow
▶   You can use it for any non-farming purpose, e.g. campsites, games pitches, riding schools, nature reserves
▶   You can plant woodlands

▷ **Case study**   *Subsistence rice farming and the Green Revolution in India*

The features of subsistence farming are:

▶   Farmer lives on 'hand to mouth' basis. No chance of long-term planning.
▶   No form of grant or subsidy. Loans (100% interest charges) have to come from money lender.
▶   Low capital investment. Little money to buy seeds or make farm improvements.
▶   Labour intensive. Farmer and large family 'work' the farm all year.
▶   No outside market except to trade surplus.
▶   Small farm unit, often scattered plots.
▶   Low technology – maybe an ox plough but no other mechanisation.
▶   Grows a variety of food crops to feed family: millet, maize, vegetables, yams, etc.

A farming and climate calendar for subsistence rice farmers on the Ganges Delta, India is shown in Fig. 10.18.

Fig. 10.18

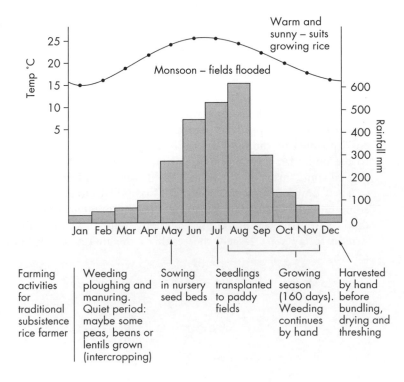

Green Revolution

The term has been used since the 1960s to describe the attempts to improve farming, and the food problems of LEDCs. New fast-growing and high-yielding varieties such as IR8 rice have been developed.

India, especially the state of Punjab, is a good example of the success of the 'Green Revolution'. Over the past 20 years, crop yields per hectare and grain production have grown faster than population, and the use of fertilisers and irrigation has grown significantly. There have been problems though:

▶ educating farmers in new methods;
▶ high-yielding varieties require the correct dose of expensive chemical fertiliser and weedkiller;
▶ the maintenance and high running-costs of technical equipment (e.g. irrigation pumps, cultivators).

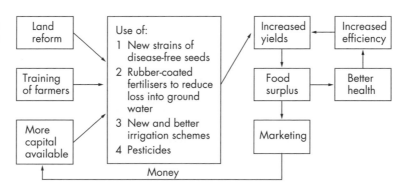

Fig. 10.19 Green Revolution developments

Green Revolution developments offer a way of breaking out of subsistence farming.

Many areas have the possibility of much greater output, particularly when there is invest-ment in fertilisers, pesticides, technical equipment and modern management methods (Fig. 10.19). Crops such as coffee and strawberries are grown productively with the aid of these inputs, for export to developed countries. More financial **aid** for farming, and food mar-kets which give better prices to farmers may help to increase the supply of food for the local population.

▷ Key terms

Make sure you understand and can apply these geographical terms.

Arable farming	Concerned with the production of crops.
Commercial farming	When farmers are principally concerned with producing in order to sell to the market for monetary profit.
Commune	A system for sharing out farm produce from a group of farms in China.
Cooperative farming	A system in which a number of farmers in an area cooperate in the purchase of seeds and fertilisers, etc. and in the sale of their produce.
Dairy farming	Concerned with the rearing of cattle for their milk.
Extensive	The farming of large areas of land often involving considerable mechanisation.
Fodder crop	One grown for the indoor feeding of animals in the winter.
Hill farm	A farm with, in Britain, land over 2000 metres where sheep graze on rough pastures.
Intensive	The production of a large volume of food from a small area of ground.
Irrigation	The addition of water to the land by people in order to improve an area's farming prospects.
Market gardening (or truck farming)	The cultivation of fruit, vegetables and flowers on a small-holding.
Mixed farm	A farm where both crops are grown and animals kept.
Nomadic pastoralism	The farmer follows his herds from pasture to pasture.
Pastoral	Concerned with the rearing of livestock.

Plantation	The usual method of producing rubber, tea, coffee and pineapples in the world's developing countries on a large specialist farming estate.
Ranching	The keeping of very large herds of cattle on vast areas of land.
Shifting cultivation	A system of farming in which people farm an area very intensively for a short period until exhaustion and then move on to another area to do the same again.
Subsistence farming	One on which only sufficient is able to be produced to meet the farmer's own consumption.
Terracing	The cutting of large steps of terraces in a slope in order to produce level areas of ground suitable for farming.
Transhumance	A dairy cattle rearing practice in the Alps, where the cattle are moved between mountain pastures in the summer and valley pastures in the winter.

Make sure you can also define more general geographical terms such as '**physical factor**' '**human factor**', '**relief**', '**input**', ' **process**', '**output**', etc., which commonly 'crop up' in questions on agriculture.

You may find it useful to refer to the list of terms in the urban settlement chapter (Chapter 14) where some of the terms apply to rural settlements too.

Suggestions for further work

▷ Using the enquiry sequence discussed in Chapter 2, you could attempt a useful investigation/enquiry based on any of the following titles:

1 How does land use on Farm X vary with distance from the farm buildings?
2 To what extent do physical factors affect land use on Farm X (or on a number of local farms)?
3 A study of contrasting local farms to show the systems approach to farm study.
4 A study of farming in a National Park to show the conflicts between the needs of farming and the interest of conservation.

These titles would involve fieldwork and could be either teacher-planned or student-planned enquiries. They would require a visit to a rural area.

▷ Classroom-based coursework, using secondary data, could be done on farming in LEDCs. For instance, on the effects and implications of the so-called 'Green Revolution' in India. Alternatively you could investigate contrasting farm organisations and methods, e.g. the collective and cooperative farming in China and Israel, compared to that in the UK, etc. These would need to be teacher-planned.

▷ **STUDENT ANSWER WITH EXAMINER'S COMMENTS**

(a) Study the information on the numbers of farm workers in the United Kingdom, shown in the box below.

Farm workers in	1950	1955	1960	1965	1970	1975	1980
the United Kingdom	760 000	650 000	575 000	490 000	360 000	300 000	250 000

    (i) Plot the number of farm workers employed in 1970, 1975 and 1980 on to the graph (Fig. 10.20). *(3 marks)*

Fig. 10.20

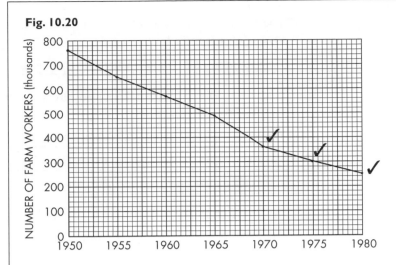

(ii) Between which years was the fall in the numbers of farm workers most rapid?

1965–1970

(1 mark)

(iii) Why has the number of farm workers fallen?

As improvements have been made in agriculture, more machines are being

used such as tractors, combine harvesters, etc. and these are replacing the

farm workers. Machines such as combine harvesters only need 1 operator but

can do the work of hundreds of men. Also people are working more in offices

these days rather than farming. People are mostly family farmers now.

(3 marks)

(b)   Study the systems diagram of an arable farm in the United Kingdom shown in Fig. 10.21.

Fig 10.21

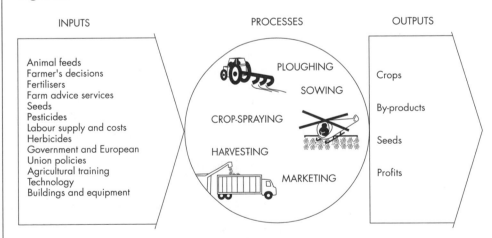

(i)   What is 'arable' farming?

Farming of cereal and grain crops such as wheat and barley.

(1 mark)

(ii)   The physical inputs are not shown on Fig. 10.21. Name TWO physical inputs for an arable farm.

Farmer and workers' labour and farmers learning agriculture methods.

(2 marks)

'Physical inputs are part of the natural environment. Climate, soils, relief, etc.'

(iii)   Describe the links between the inputs, processes and outputs of the farm system shown in Fig. 10.21.

These links are, for example, herbicides which are the input and then crop-spraying which is the process and the output is crops. If one of the three parts was missing there could be no output. They are all dependent on one another. Another link is the farmer's decision: he decides the process and then which one he picks leads to crops, which make profits.

(4 marks)

(iv)   Name an area within a country which is important for arable farming. Explain why arable farming is important within the area you have named.

COUNTRY   *England*   AREA   *East Anglia*

'This section needed expanding'

The relief of East Anglia has large, low-lying land. This is important for wheat farming. The climate is warm, sunny summers with cool winters with moderate rainfall. The soils are light, dry and sandy which are needed for wheat farming. The main town is Norwich where the wheat is sent to the flour mills. It is transported by main roads and motorways such as the M6.

The capital is spent on pesticides and fertilisers and seed to produce higher crop yields. The farmers are usually family farmers but employ people to help with combine harvesting, etc. The farmer is protected by the Common Agricultural Policy (EU) and his prices are guaranteed. All the above factors make East Anglia important for arable farming.

'Not really relevant to the question'

(5 marks)

(c)   As world population increases there is a need to find ways of producing food. Three possible methods of doing this are:
☐   the development of new irrigation schemes;
☑   the increasing use of farm chemicals;
☐   the breeding of new strains of animals and plants.
Choose ONE of the above methods and put a tick in the box next to your choice.
Explain both the advantages and the disadvantages of the method you have chosen.

ADVANTAGES: *The chemicals such as pesticides will control the amount of damage done by pests and insects. Fertilisers added to the soil will make the soils better, with more minerals for the plants. Chemicals such as these lead to a better crop yield and better quality products. Also in dairy farming chemicals are added to the cattle feed to give them more vitamins, make them bigger and fatter and produce more meat.*

'Good points made on both
sides of the argument'

DISADVANTAGES: *When the crops are sprayed with fertilisers such as nitrates, these go through the soil and into the water, then back into seas, where fish swallow them and become poisoned. Also when crops such as apples are sprayed, the chemicals are left in the skins and end up inside our bodies and do damage to us. Also as more organically grown vegetables are coming on the market, people will choose to buy these and much food may be wasted.*

(*6 marks*)
(*Total 25 marks*)
(*SEG*)

'A Level 3 answer (above
grade C in standard)'

A TUTOR ANSWER

(a) Study the two sketches below which show a farming area in a more economically developed country (MEDC) in 1955 and 1995.

Fig. 10.22

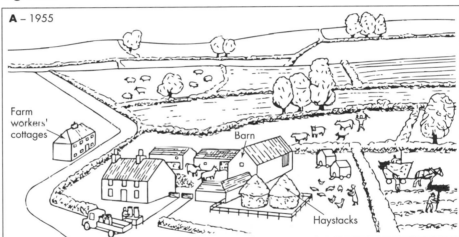

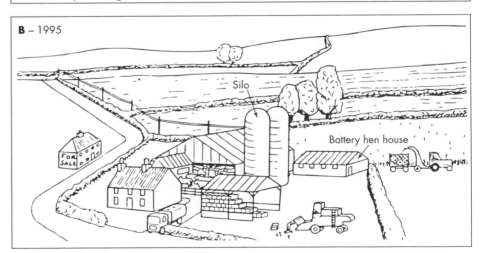

(i) What type of farming is shown taking place in the area in both 1955 and 1995?
Tick the box next to the correct answer
Arable ☐   Pastoral ☐   Mixed ☑   (*1 mark*)

(ii) From the sketches, give a reason for your answer to (a) (i).

There is evidence of both crop growing and animal rearing on both sketches,

i.e. mixed farming.

(1 mark)

(iii) Using evidence from the sketches, suggest how each of the following changed between 1955 and 1995.

1 the use of labour: *As mechanisation has developed less labour is used.*

2 the size of fields: *Hedges have been removed and fields generally grown in size.*

3 the type or use of the buildings: *A silo for hay storage has replaced the*

haystacks

(3 marks)

(b) Give **two** reasons for the change to more scientific and technological farming in MEDCs.

1 *High-technology equipment is now a way of life in MEDCs. It is also available*

for farmers.

2 *It has enabled an increase in farm output and yields per hectare.*

(2 marks)

(c) Suggest why some people believe that some modern farming techniques damage the environment of rural areas.

Some people believe that when farmers remove hedgerows in order to make larger

fields on which they can more easily use large machinery this damages the rural

environment. They may also believe that using large quantities of fertiliser on

fields can lead to water pollution.

(3 marks)
(Total 10 marks)
(NEAB)

► EXAMINATION QUESTION

Tier F only

(a) Study Fig. 10.23 showing two farming systems.

Fig. 10.23   Farm A – Location: Jurunku, a village in Gambia (West Africa)

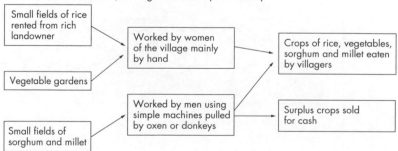

Fig. 10.23 *(cont)*   Farm B – Location: near Ashburton, a market town in New Zealand

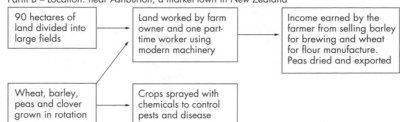

(i) Farm A is a subsistence farm. What is meant by a subsistence farm?
    (2 lines provided here)   *(1 mark)*

(ii) Compare Farm A and Farm B under the following headings:

	Farm A	Farm B
Size of fields	Small fields	
Land ownership		Land owned by farmer
Farming methods	Traditional methods	

(3 marks)

(b) Study Fig. 10.24, which is a cross-section showing farmland around Jurunku, a village in Gambia (West Africa).

Fig. 10.24

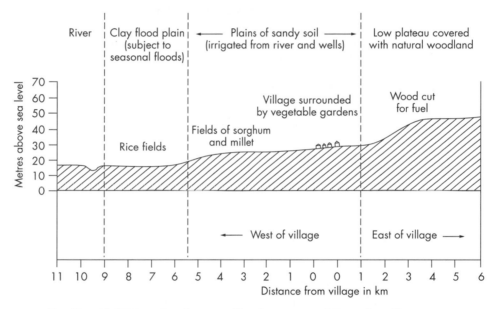

(i) Fig. 10.25 is a sketch map of land use around Jurunku village.
    On Fig. 10.25 shade, using two different colours or types of shading:
    The rice fields.   The fields of sorghum and millet.
    Complete the key below the map to show how you have shaded these areas of land.   *(2 marks)*

Fig. 10.25

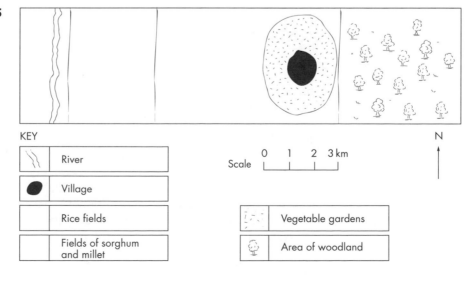

(ii) Suggest **two** reasons why the area to the east of the village is not cultivated.
(4 lines provided here) (*2 marks*)

(c) In many countries farmers have made changes to farming systems to produce more food. For a named country or area which you have studied describe these changes.
Name of country or area (1 line provided here)
Changes (15 lines provided here) (*5 marks*)
(*Total 13 marks*)
(*MEG*)

Tier H only

(a) What is the difference between subsistence and commercial farming? (*1 mark*)

(b) For a commercial farm in a named area which you have studied:
(i) describe the main land uses (*2 marks*)
(ii) explain how both physical and economic factors have influenced the farmer's choice of land use. (10 lines provided here) (*6 marks*)

(c) Study Fig. 10.24 on page 165, which is a cross-section showing farmland around Jurunku, a village in Gambia, West Africa.
(i) At what height is the village above sea level? (1 line provided here) (*1 mark*)
(ii) What crop is grown 7 kilometres west of the village? (1 line provided here)
(*1 mark*)

(d) Study Fig. 10.26 which is a memo listing three possible methods of producing more food from farms in Gambia.

Fig. 10.26

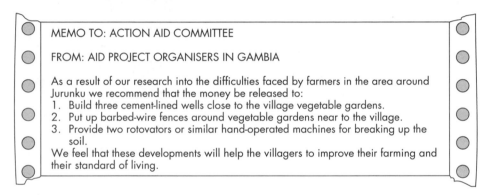

MEMO TO: ACTION AID COMMITTEE

FROM: AID PROJECT ORGANISERS IN GAMBIA

As a result of our research into the difficulties faced by farmers in the area around Jurunku we recommend that the money be released to:
1. Build three cement-lined wells close to the village vegetable gardens.
2. Put up barbed-wire fences around vegetable gardens near to the village.
3. Provide two rotovators or similar hand-operated machines for breaking up the soil.
We feel that these developments will help the villagers to improve their farming and their standard of living.

(i) Explain how any **two** of these measures will result in improvements in food supplies for the people who live in the area shown in Fig. 10.24
(8 lines provided here) (*4 marks*)
(ii) With reference to an LEDC you have studied, describe other changes which have taken place in the farming system in order to improve food supplies.
(15 lines provided here) (*5 marks*)
(*Total 20 marks*) (*MEG*)

▶ EXAMINATION ANSWER

Tier F only

(a) (i) Produce output for self/group/village (*1*)
(ii) Size: large fields
Land ownership: land rented from landowner/owned by rich landowner
Farming methods: modern/advanced methods (*3*)

(b) (i) On map/key (*2*)
(ii) Steep slopes, soil may be infertile, plateau could be too exposed, natural woodland retained as valuable resource for fuel, building, etc. (*2*)

(c) Could be LEDC or MEDC example, therefore changes may vary from agri-business or land reclamation to Green Revolution or irrigation or terracing.
1 mark reserved for named area or country (*5*)
(*Total 13*) (*MEG*)

Tier H only

(a)   Subsistence – output for self
      Commercial – output for sale   *(1)*

(b)   Example may be any commercial farming system
      (i)   e.g. East Anglia – cereals, oil-seed rape   *(2)*
      (ii) Must link to chosen land use
            Physical factors:
            Ideas such as temperate climate is suitable for named crops; land must be rela-
            tively flat to suit modern machinery; soil must be naturally fertile or improved
            to support these crops; climate data/heights/soil types, etc. maybe development
            Economic factors:
            Ideas such as available market for crops grown; named market (dev.); profitabil-
            ity may be affected by price fluctuations; competition from other producing
            areas; costs of inputs; government support; EU influences – subsidies, etc.
            1 mark reserved for named farming area.
            1 mark reserved for physical and economic factors   *(6)*

(c)   (i)   30 m approx.   *(1)*
      (ii) Rice   *(1)*

(d)   (i)   Wells provide more water supply; therefore ensuring better yields (dev.).
            Fences prevent encroachment by animals/thieves; therefore reducing unnecessary
            loss (dev.); machines facilitate faster cultivation; increased depth of soil therefore
            enabling better crop growth (dev.); more rapid planting could facilitate growth of
            another crop (dev.).   *(4)*
      (ii) Ideas could relate to Green Revolution (for example new crop strains, use of fer-
            tilisers, insecticides, herbicides); irrigation; terracing; land reforms; investment;
            introduction of small-scale technology; intercropping; development of storage
            facilities; etc.
            1 mark reserved for named country.
            Single point marking, credit development.
            E.g. investment in agriculture in Cameroons.
            Investment has gone to help small farmers; money comes from government and
            loans from World Bank (dev.); small-scale technologies have been introduced;
            such as ox-drawn ploughs (dev.); half-price fertilisers have been provided; new
            varieties of maize have been introduced; which are higher yielding (dev.); inter-
            cropping maize with vegetables has been encouraged; also with coffee; a main
            export crop (dev.); storage facilities have been built; so that the extra food pro-
            duced does not rot (dev.); most of these developments have been concentrated on
            the women farmers; who produce most of the food to feed the nation's popula-
            tion (dev.).   *(5)*

(Total 20) (MEG)

SUMMARY

▷ A farm or a type of farming can be seen as a system with inputs, processes and outputs of food.

▷ Farming varies from place to place, and can be classified into types which form patterns when mapped.

▷ The natural environment has a strong effect, especially in LEDCs, on the type of farming chosen for a place. Markets, capital, labour, politics and personal preference are also important.

▷ Farming is constantly changing; these changes can be of benefit or harmful. Environmental damage can be done by modern farming if mismanaged.

▷ Rural settlement locations – site and situation – are related to physical and human factors.

▷ Rural settlements vary in shape, size and function. Most have spheres of influence and are part of a regional settlement hierarchy.

▷ The provision of goods and services is an issue in many rural areas.

▷ Many villages in the commuter belts of cities in MEDCs have become suburbanised by urban-to-rural migration.

Employment structures and the swing to tertiary activities

▷ GETTING STARTED

In this chapter we look at the changing size of the sectors of industry and employment between LEDCs and MEDCs and within countries. An important trend is the growth of tertiary and quaternary work in MEDCs as manufacturing industry has declined; unemployment has been a consequence. Retailing (shopping) and tourism are the key tertiary activities focused upon in the chapter. We need to be familiar with the costs and benefits of changes in these two activities, the conflicts of interest that arise and the environmental effects of, for instance, the rapid growth of tourism. Improvements in transport are central to the changes in retailing and tourism, and Chapter 15 might help with a full understanding of this topic area.

Again, case studies to illustrate key ideas are vital but there are few geographical terms specific to this topic area. A short list is included in the chapter but also ensure that you can use general geographical terms such as 'pattern', 'socio-economic' and 'management'.

LONDON A	LONDON B	MEG A	MEG B	MEG C	NEAB A	NEAB B	NEAB C	NICCEA	SEG A	SEG B	WJEC	IGCSE	TOPIC	STUDY	REVISION 1	REVISION 2
✓	✓	✓	✓	✓	✓		✓	✓	✓	✓	✓	✓	Employment structures/industrial classification/sectors of economy			
		✓	✓				✓						Tertiarisation (swing to services)			
		✓	✓	✓	✓	✓	✓				✓		Distribution of retailing/shopping centres			
	✓		✓				✓			✓		✓	Leisure activities and countryside as a recreational resource			
		✓			✓	✓	✓	✓		✓	✓	✓	✓	Tourist development			
	✓	✓	✓		✓	✓	✓			✓	✓	✓	✓	Environmental impact of recreation and tourism			

▷ WHAT YOU NEED TO KNOW

▷ **Classification into sectors of industry**

The jobs or occupations in which people work are so numerous and varied that it is useful to group them. One system of classification in international use has nine groups:

▶ agriculture, forestry, hunting and fishing;
▶ mining and quarrying;
▶ manufacturing;
▶ building and construction;
▶ power and water services;
▶ commerce, insurance and banking;
▶ transportation, warehousing and communications;
▶ other services;
▶ other occupations not classified above.

Fig. 11.1 uses this classification to show how the labour forces of France and Tanzania differ with regard to the type of work done. Classification can be further simplified by grouping jobs and industries into four large and broad categories of economic activity, known as **sectors**:

▶ The **Primary Activities Sector** – this covers the first and second groups listed above. Agriculture is the main single activity in primary industry. The term **extractive industry** is often used to describe activities in this sector because they are concerned with the extraction of material from land or sea.

▶ The **Secondary Activities Sector** – manufacturing which uses the products of primary industry and processes them into finished goods is secondary industry. The third and fourth groups listed above, which include building and construction work, fall into this sector.

▶ The **Tertiary Activities Sector** – the fifth, seventh and eighth groups listed above are concerned with the provision of services rather than goods. The production is of intangible and invisible items that cannot be touched, felt or readily seen, like the outputs of a banker, train driver and teacher.

▶ The **Quaternary Activities Sector** – this last category is a relatively new addition to the occupational classification by sector. Research work, higher education (university lecturers), the so-called professions (doctors, lawyers, etc.) and other services concerned with providing information and expertise are covered. Such occupations may barely exist in some LEDCs and are often grouped with the Tertiary Sector who they also often serve.

Fig. 11.1 A comparison between the type of work done by the labour forces of France and Tanzania

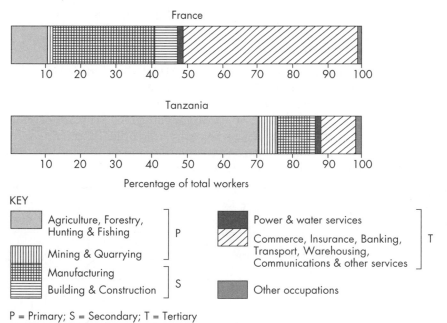

The proportion of workers employed in each of the three main sectors; primary, secondary, tertiary/quaternary can be presented in a diagram, using either a pie chart, a triangular graph or a bar chart (Fig. 11.2). Make sure that you can both read and plot triangular graphs of the type shown.

Fig. 11.2

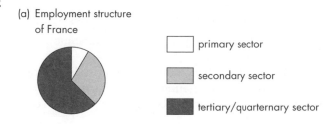

Fig. 11.2 *(cont)*

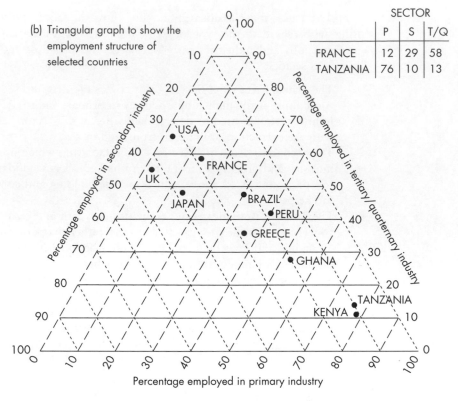

(b) Triangular graph to show the employment structure of selected countries

	SECTOR		
	P	S	T/Q
FRANCE	12	29	58
TANZANIA	76	10	13

Stages of growth

You can see from Fig. 11.2 that MEDCs, with their high GNPs per head, such as France, the USA and the UK, have a large proportion of their workforce in tertiary and quaternary employment. In contrast, LEDCs with their lower GNPs per head, such as Tanzania and Kenya, rely heavily on *primary* industry. As a country develops economically, the proportion of its labour force employed in the primary sector *declines* while the secondary sector grows in importance; and continued economic development sees the eventual decline of secondary industry and the rise of the tertiary and quaternary sectors. (See Fig. 11.3.)

Fig. 11.3 Stages in the economic development of a country and changes in its employment structure

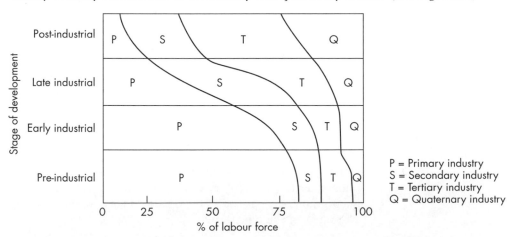

P = Primary industry
S = Secondary industry
T = Tertiary industry
Q = Quaternary industry

▷ **The structure and growth of the service sector**

Tertiary and quaternary employment has grown to become the major sector in MEDCs as:

▶ the needs and demands of people have become more complex. The supply and range of services has increased.

▶ working hours have fallen and the amount of **leisure** time has increased. The 'leisure age' and a more leisure-orientated life has emerged.

▶ economic growth has raised income levels per head so that people can afford to be more pleasure-seeking.

▶ manufacturing, particularly heavy manufacturing (e.g. textiles, mining, etc.) has declined. This is known as de-industrialisation.

The growing number of service jobs in MEDCs has meant a way of classifying them is useful. Table 11.1 shows a method of classification.

Table 11.1 The structure of the service sector

Group	Type	Examples of establishments
Trade	Retail	Superstore, launderette, used-car dealer
	Wholesale	Warehouse
Financial	Banking	Building society, local bank
	Insurance	Insurance broker's office
	Real estate	Estate agency
Other services	Recreation	Theatre, sports stadium, restaurant
	Vacation	Hotel, camp site
	Transport and communications	Petrol station, airport, bus depot
	Medical	Hospital, surgery
	Research and teaching	School, college, university, research laboratory
	Public administration	Government offices, Town Hall
	Business and repair	Advertising agencies, accountants, TV repair premises, computer consultancy

Location of tertiary activities

Tertiary and quaternary industrial activities tend to congregate in the centres of towns and cities. Offices, shops, entertainment, hotels and public/social services are **customer-orientated** and so are strongly attracted by the substantial demand within large urban area locations.

More than half of London's jobs are in the service sector, such as wholesale and retail distribution, government administration, etc. London has a major role in office location and employment in Britain; about 40% of all office jobs in the country are located in central London, especially the head offices of large companies and the offices of financial institutions in the 'square mile' around the Bank of England, known as 'the City'. Approximately 30% of all Britain's jobs are office work; some of these have in recent years been relocated away from central London and south east England. Some of the reasons for this 'decentralisation' of offices are:

- High cost of labour
- Busy roads/ traffic jams
- Old buildings not always suitable
- Increased demand for space
- Not enough parking space
- Very high rates and rents (London £300 per sq. m, Newcastle £75 per sq. m)
- Local house prices very high
- 70% of area is conservation area
- Not enough workers nearby
- Difficult to get planning permission

Office clustering at city centre locations, whether in London or Sheffield, is common, especially among commercial offices (e.g. insurance companies, solicitors, etc.) because:

- they need strong links with other offices and associated businesses (e.g. estate agents, solicitors, banks and building societies, all concerned with buying and selling houses, find it convenient to be close together so that face-to-face contact is possible). Modern telecommunications (e.g. telephone calls, telex machines, computer terminals, etc.) have reduced the necessity for offices to cluster around other offices.
- They are the most accessible sites for both staff and customers.
- It is the traditional office area which carries prestige, is very visible to the public, has access to business contacts and other services for the staff, and has office premises available.

Fig. 11.4 shows some examples of government offices which have relocated from South East England.

Fig. 11.4

The skylines of cities show the high-rise office tower-blocks at the centre, built upwards because of the competition for land.

▷ Distribution of retailing/shopping centres

Not all service industries choose CBD (Central Business District) locations. Clustering at city centre locations is common among commercial offices, but some retailers, especially superstores like Sainsbury's, Tesco, etc., favour **out-of-town** sites where people can shop 'one-stop', using their cars. Large cities too have OBDs (Ordinary Business Districts) or suburban high street shopping areas. Offices are often attracted to these locations. Fig. 11.5 shows the location within a city of the different types of shopping centre.

Fig. 11.5

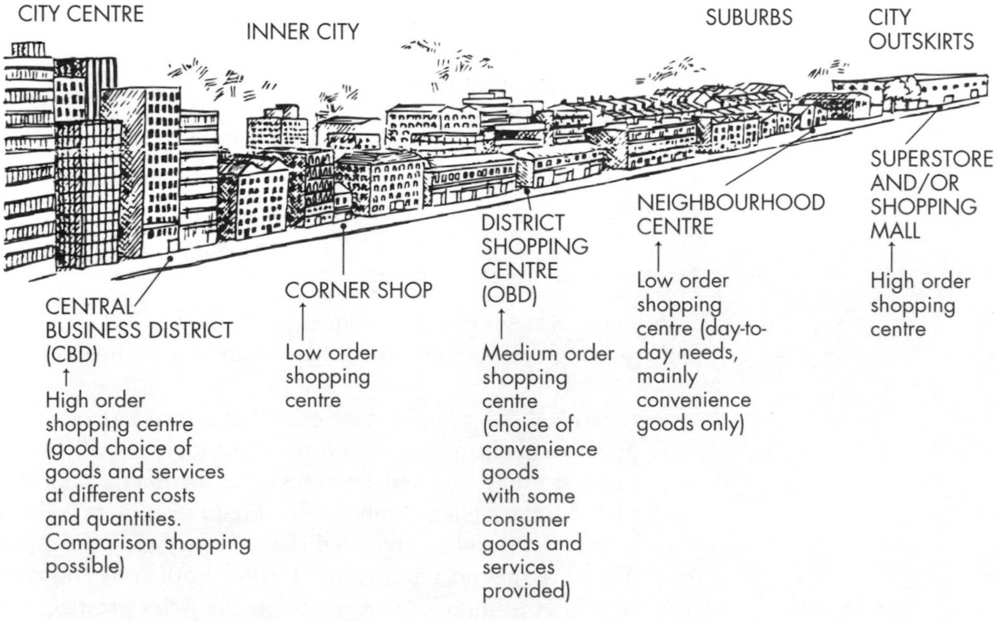

CITY CENTRE   INNER CITY   SUBURBS   CITY OUTSKIRTS

CENTRAL BUSINESS DISTRICT (CBD)
↑
High order shopping centre (good choice of goods and services at different costs and quantities. Comparison shopping possible)

CORNER SHOP
↑
Low order shopping centre

DISTRICT SHOPPING CENTRE (OBD)
↑
Medium order shopping centre (choice of convenience goods with some consumer goods and services provided)

NEIGHBOURHOOD CENTRE
↑
Low order shopping centre (day-to-day needs, mainly convenience goods only)

SUPERSTORE AND/OR SHOPPING MALL
↑
High order shopping centre

In many MEDCs, e.g. USA, Britain, Sweden, France, etc., huge shopping schemes known as **shopping malls**, which include superstores or hypermarkets have been built on the outskirts of many towns and cities, surrounded by facilities such a cinemas, restaurants, swimming pools and playgrounds. Brent Cross in north London and the Metro Centre in Newcastle are examples of the change towards the American locational pattern of out-of-town shopping. (See Table 11.2.) Out-of-town superstores owned by a few leading retailers (e.g. Asda, Tesco, Sainsbury's) have been replacing small independent shops. It is said that one new supermarket replaces between ten and fifteen small shops. Has bigger been better in retailing?

Some of the effects of the superstore revolution in Britain are:

▶ some people have further to travel to shop – a problem for the old and infirm, and for those without their own transport or living where public transport is inconvenient or unreliable;

▶ congestion and pollution in the suburbs due to the increased use of cars for shopping;

▶ loss of large areas of countryside for purpose-built superstores and their car parks;

▶ loss of shops in villages and suburbs;

▶ 'one-stop' shopping (with a wide range of goods under one roof); using the car and free on-site parking makes shopping convenient and easy;

▶ people have to shop less often but have to buy their own storage facilities (e.g. freezers).

▶ less expensive prices are charged because buying and selling can be in bulk;

▶ restricted choice of brands for shoppers.

Table 11.2 Out of town shopping malls in Britain 500 000 sq. feet and over

Shopping Centre	Size (sq. ft)
Blue Water, Dartford	1.5 m
Lakeside, Thurrock	1.2 m
Merry Hill, Dudley	1.2 m
Metro Centre, Gateshead	1.2 m
Meadowhall, Sheffield	1.1 m
Cribbs Causeway, Bristol	1.0 m
Trafford, Manchester	1.0 m
Brent Cross, London	0.6 m
White Rose, Leeds	0.6 m
Grafton Centre, Cambridge	0.5 m

The development of out-of-town shopping centres is threatening to kill town-centre trade in many British towns/cities. There is a growing conflict between established town centre shopping and new out-of-town shopping centres. Local authority Planning Departments, faced with this conflict, consider the following points when deciding whether to grant planning permission for new superstores:

▶ will it harm the future of shops in established shopping centres?
▶ will it be readily served by public transport?
▶ will it cause traffic congestion?
▶ will it harm the amenities of the surrounding area?

Informal sector

So far we have referred only to the formal and official work in an economy; jobs known to and recorded by the authorities. There is also an informal sector of work, often services, especially in LEDCs. It has been estimated that 40% of South America's population of working age work in this informal section of irregular hours in small-scale service enterprises, such as street trading, shoe cleaning, etc.

▶ **Tourism**   Tourism is the most rapidly growing industry in the world. In Britain it employs 22% more people that it did ten years ago, and in some countries it is their most important industry. Spain is a good example, where tourism is the country's biggest earner of foreign currency. The Spanish population is now 38 million; in 1973 it received 21 million foreign tourists, but as many as 30 million in 1995.

We live in an age of recreation and leisure compared with the times of our predecessors. Mass international tourism is only one example of this. Any tourist flow map of north west Europe reveals a complicated picture. Britons holidaying in Spain, France and Italy;

Germans holidaying in these countries and Austria, Switzerland and Yugoslavia; French holidaying in Spain; Americans holidaying in Spain, Britain and Germany, etc. The pattern becomes even more complicated as still more countries become destinations for tourists, and tourist movement becomes an all year round activity.

A 'sun rush' is largely responsible for the development of mass international tourism. This has in turn been made possible by cheaper air travel and by cheaper 'package holiday' arrangements. Most of the international tourist centres which attract foreign visitors are close to an airport. This is becoming an essential requirement for a successful tourist resort.

The role of sunshine in the growth of international tourism can be illustrated by looking at the climatograph for Malaga in Southern Spain (Fig. 11.6). The hot, dry summers of Malaga, with winter temperatures similar to those of a British summer, are typical of much of the area around the Mediterranean Sea. The demand for 'winter sun' from some people living in the MEDCs of north west Europe, and North America has resulted in international tourism becoming *less of a seasonal activity* and *more of year round* activity.

Fig. 11.6 Climatograph for Malaga, Spain

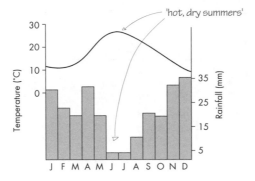

Fig. 11.7 (right)

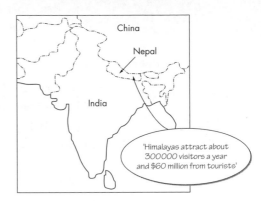

The dependency of tourism on the natural environment, especially the weather, has resulted in tourism within Britain being a highly seasonal activity. The sandy beaches and picturesque scenery of Britain are not enough in themselves, in the absence of good weather. The importance of an attractive natural environment to tourism can also be seen in the growth of winter sports holidays in mountain resorts, e.g. the Alps, the Cairngorms of Scotland, etc.

Tourism *can* help an LEDC like Nepal (see Fig. 11.7). It can increase a country's earnings and lead to balanced development. Tourism can pay for improved health, hygiene and food production, and can even pay for conservation measures to protect precious forests and rivers. It can create pride in local culture. Sadly these things are *not* happening in Nepal.

Tourism has not helped many local people. Some tourists treat the Himalayan people badly by invading their privacy. Children are encouraged to beg and hustle rather than to learn traditional village ways of life. Few locals can afford the prices and facilities that cater for tourists.

▷ Leisure pursuits

Leisure and recreation can be different from tourism. **Recreational pursuits** can be experienced without travelling from your home area. There has been an explosion of recreational and leisure facilities available in many areas of Britain, Europe and North America to cater for local people. Country parks, theme parks, dry ski slopes, sports centres, leisure centres, golf courses, sailing areas, etc. are developing all around us. Think of your own local area and list all the *new* leisure and recreational facilities you can. Their value to people is, of course a matter of personal judgement.

This leisure age has two basic causes:

1   Working hours have fallen. The amount of leisure time has therefore increased; both for those people in work and those out of work.
2   Economic growth over the last 30 years or so has raised general income levels per head. People can now afford a more pleasure-seeking, leisure-orientated life.

EuroDisney, a new theme park

The biggest theme park ever seen in Europe was opened in April 1992 in quiet countryside on former farmland (see Fig. 11.8).

Fig. 11.8

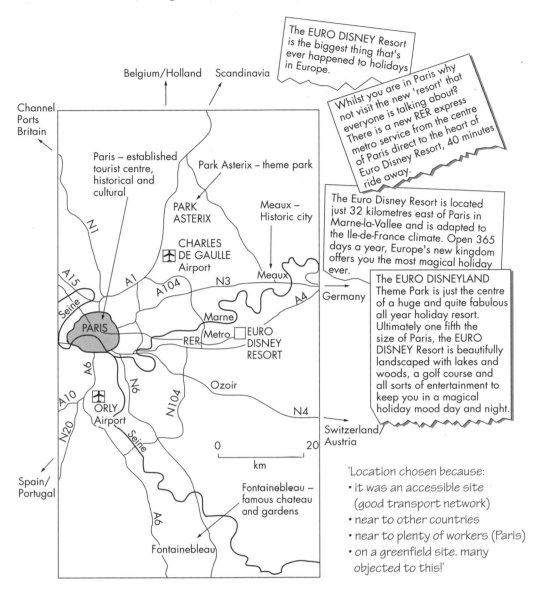

▷ Issue   Tourism and the Lake District National Park

Fig. 11.9 Number of resident visitors to Windermere in 1995

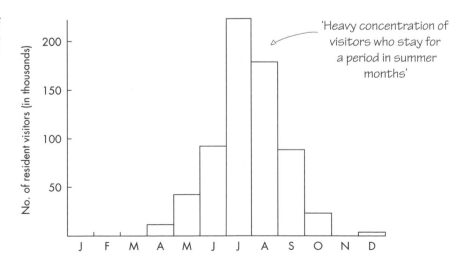

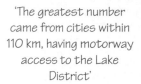

'The greatest number came from cities within 110 km, having motorway access to the Lake District'

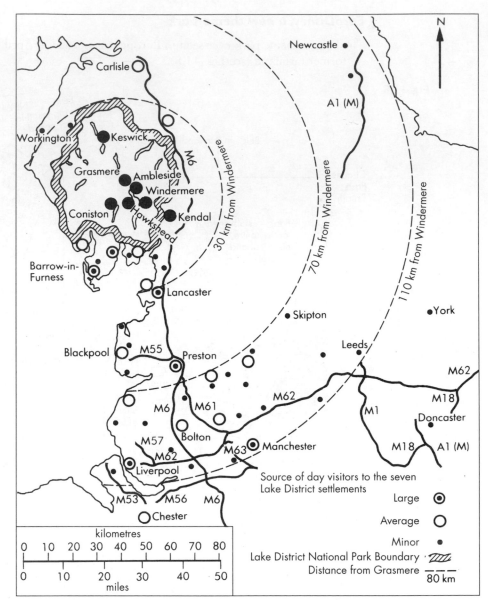

The Lake District is Britain's most visited National Park. It is an upland area containing fells and glacial valleys of outstanding natural beauty.

The seasonal nature of the visiting (Fig. 11.9) poses problems for jobs, with many local people facing winter unemployment. The summer visiting poses other problems in areas and places attracting lots of visitors such as Windermere and Grasmere, which are called 'honeypots'.

The problems include congestion on narrow roads, inadequate official car parking, unauthorised parking, increased noise and 'pollution' related to vehicles (exhausts) and persons (litter), etc. The wish of many people, including the National Park authorities, to conserve and protect the countryside creates a **conflict** with those who wish to use the land in other ways (Fig. 11.11).

The livelihoods of those who benefit from the greater spending of tourism must be offset against the costs of litter, footpath erosion and large numbers of cars. What schemes might overcome these problems and prevent the environmental changes depicted by Fig. 11.12?

Fig. 11.11 Conflicts of interest over land use in National Parks

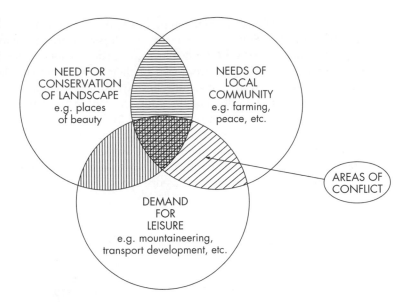

NEED FOR CONSERVATION OF LANDSCAPE e.g. places of beauty

NEEDS OF LOCAL COMMUNITY e.g. farming, peace, etc.

AREAS OF CONFLICT

DEMAND FOR LEISURE e.g. mountaineering, transport development, etc.

Fig. 11.12 Environmental changes and the growth of leisure, recreation and tourism in rural areas

Past

Present

Future?

▷ **Case study**   *Tourism in an LEDC: Jamaica*

Jamaica is the home of just over two million people. Today many of them are found in the rapidly growing towns such as Kingston and Montego Bay, but the majority remain in the villages, farms and plantations helping to produce the crops for which Jamaica is famous – sugar, bananas, coffee and citrus fruit. Jamaica is a major world producer of bauxite and is increasingly processing this ore into alumina. The island occasionally suffers from hurricanes during the summer.

Tourism is now Jamaica's second biggest earner of foreign currency, after the export of bauxite and aluminium. Jamaica is well-placed for the development of a tourist industry; a tropical climate within easy access of the affluent (rich) continent of North America. Around 60% of visitors arrive from the USA and Canada. They are part of a 'sun rush', attracted by an annual average temperature of 26 °C and an annual average daily sunshine rate of 7.4 hours. Some people in the 'developed' world are willing and able to pay large sums of money to travel long distances, in order to spend their greater leisure time in an environment very different from that of their home country. The growth of tourism (Fig. 11.13) has benefited the Jamaican economy. Tourist spending has created jobs and brought general economic benefits, but these have not been fully available to all the local people. The 'honeypot' tourist area of Montego Bay has seen some tension between tourists and local people. Some of the resentment may be of a racial nature. Growth of hotels at Runaway Bay, Port Antonio and Negril, as well as at Montego Bay, has 'commercialised' areas of natural beauty. The influx of tourists has also influenced established local patterns of life, in ways which some view as disruptive.

Fig. 11.13

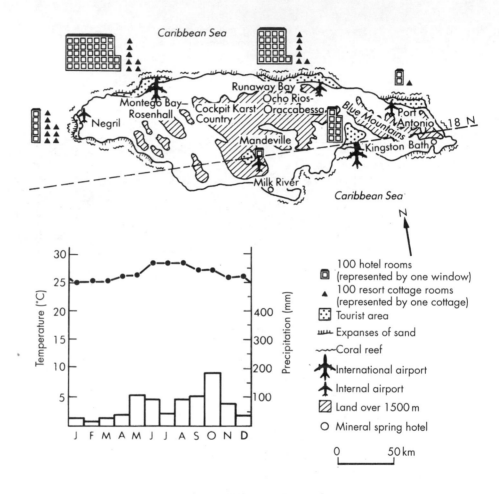

Some of the plans for the future for Jamaican tourism and tourist income are to:

▶ build chalet-style accommodation instead of hotel blocks
▶ develop local craft workshops
▶ create national parks in the interior
▶ build more tourist accommodation on new sites
▶ grow more food on local farms
▶ redevelop slum areas.

▷ **Key terms**   *Make sure you understand and can apply these geographical terms.*

CBD	Defined and explained on page 172.
De-industrialisation	The contraction of the secondary sector (manufacturing industry).
Honeypot	A place attracting lots of visitors for leisure, recreation and tourist purposes, usually in the countryside.
National Park	An area whose scenic beauty or attractiveness because of its uniqueness (e.g. mountains, moorland or coast) is preserved and improved so that people, especially those from urban areas can see it, get to it and enjoy it.
OBD	Defined and explained on page 172.
Primary	Defined and explained on page 169.
Quaternary	Defined and explained on page 169.
Secondary	Defined and explained on page 169.
Shopping mall	Defined and explained on page 172.
Superstore	A very large supermarket.
Tertiarisation	The growth of the tertiary/quaternary sectors of employment.
Tertiary	Defined and explained on page 169.

Suggestions for further work

▷   This topic provides a number of possible areas for fieldwork enquiry, e.g.

  1.   What effects has Meadowhall had on the CBD of Sheffield and other surrounding towns?
  2.   Are the leisure facilities of your area/town adequate for the needs of the people?
  3.   What impact has tourism had on your area/town and has this impact been 'good' or 'bad'?
  4.   The smaller the population the fewer the services in a settlement.
       Is this true and how does it affect people in village X?

▷   There will be many opportunities for studying the provision and location of both indoor and outdoor amenities for recreation and leisure and shopping within a small locality, such as your own area. You can look at their sphere and range of influence, the conflicts that arise and the costs and benefits to different residents. Teacher-planned, classroom-based coursework can be set on the National Parks, major tourist/holiday areas, a holiday resort or the effects of tourism upon an LEDC.

STUDENT ANSWER WITH EXAMINER'S COMMENTS

▷ **Longer structured question**

(a) Study Fig. 11.14 showing the main tourist attractions in Cyprus.

Fig. 11.14

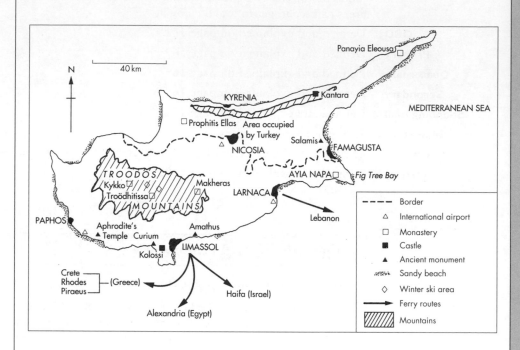

Cyprus attracts many visitors with a variety of interests.

Using Fig. 11.14, complete Table 11.3 below.

Table 11.3

People interested in:	Recreation Activity	Location
A summer beach holiday	*swimming*	*Panayia Eleousa*
A winter sports holiday	*skiing*	*Troodos*
The history of Cyprus	*site seeing*	*Amathus*

(6 marks)

(b) Study Fig. 11.15, showing the origin, distance and number of visitors to Cyprus
   (i) On Fig. 11.15, draw and label the flow line for Germany. Use the information given below.

	DISTANCE	VISITORS
Germany	2800 kilometres	90 000

(2 marks)

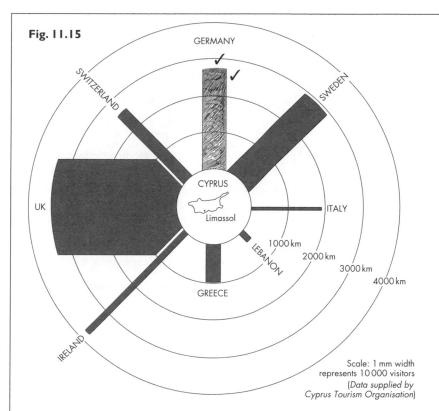

Fig. 11.15

Scale: 1 mm width
represents 10 000 visitors
(*Data supplied by
Cyprus Tourism Organisation*)

'Good, sufficiently accurate'

(ii) Describe and suggest reasons for the pattern shown by Fig. 11.15.

The UK will have a lot of visitors for the hot weather and perhaps as a skiing
holiday. Switzerland is well known for having winter sports and there would
be no need for the travel of about 2500 km. Not very warm Sweden, Cyprus
quite cheap warm holiday. Germany not very warm again. Cyprus hot and
cheap. Italy have good sun and are near to winter sports although distance
not far perhaps prefer something a bit different. Lebanon visitor might go for
winter sports, very close. Easy to get away. Greece quite near.

(*6 marks*)

'Do you mean UK visitors to Cyprus?'

'Very poor grammar, little geography and question not really answered'

'Good Level 1 only'

(c) The Government of Cyprus is concerned about the rapid increase of tourism.
Study the news report below.

THE CYPRUS WEEKLY

June 2–8, 1989 25c UK 60p No. 500

Government moves to limit development

ENOUGH!

The Government announced measures to control tourism. There is concern that the development of the coastline for tourism is out of control.

The measures include stopping permits for building new hotels for 10 months; making stricter financial controls; withdrawing incentives for the tourist industry.

The Government are concerned with the damage to the environment. Planning is required to solve problems such as overcrowded beaches, insufficient water supplies, traffic on the narrow coastal and hill roads and unsightly buildings along the coastline.

However, there is another immediate problem. There is a shortage of labour. This will become worse as the tourist industry grows for there are 12 000 tourist beds under construction, e.g. new hotels, apartments, villas, etc.

(The Cyprus Weekly, *June 1989*)

(i) Using information in the news report, describe the problems resulting from increased tourism in Cyprus.

Overcrowded beaches, insufficient water supplies, roads not fit for so much

traffic. Coastlines filled with tourist development, hotels, unnatural concrete

jungle. Damage to environment. Demand for work but not enough workers.

(4 marks)

(ii) The news report shows that people may cause damage to the environment. However, people's actions can lead to environmental disasters. Describe an example of an environmental disaster you have studied.

Name of example *Mediterranean Sea*

The Med. has been used as a waste dumping ground. Raw sewage has been

dumped into it by the surrounding countries (and others). Rubbish from

tourists and pollution from boats (water sports etc.) have polluted the waters.

Because of the position of the Med. and the surrounding land it is unable to

flush out its pollution as it is more or less closed in.

(6 marks)

'Level 2 because main points are there but very badly written'

'Good'

'I understand what you mean. Med. is landlocked'

'A good Level 2 response. I like the way you've linked it to rest of question on Cypriot/Med. Tourism'

(d) Study Fig. 11.16 showing the number of visitors to tourist areas in Cyprus for 1973, 1983 and 1993.

(i) Complete the pie chart for 1993 using the following information:

Limassol 27%	Larnaca 16%	Paphos 18%
Troödos Hill Resorts 2%		

(4 marks)

(ii) Fig. 11.14 shows the area of Cyprus occupied by Turkey in 1974. Many Greek Cypriots moved from this area after it came under Turkish rule. Using Fig. 11.14 and 11.16 describe the changes in the number of visitors to the tourist areas in Cyprus between 1973 and 1993.

In 1973 the number of tourists visiting Famagusta was about 53% but in 1983

and 1993, although the total number of tourists has risen from 1.33 million to

3.87m no one visited Famagusta. Ayia Napa has gradually become the most

popular place attracting about 32% in 1993 whereas in 1973 no one visited

it. Larnaca increased in 1983 and became non-existent by 1993. Areas out of

the Turkish border have become more popular.

(6 marks)

'A bit of a rambling answer. A more logical development would have been to say how numbers have grown overall, and then which resorts have grown or shrunk, and why'

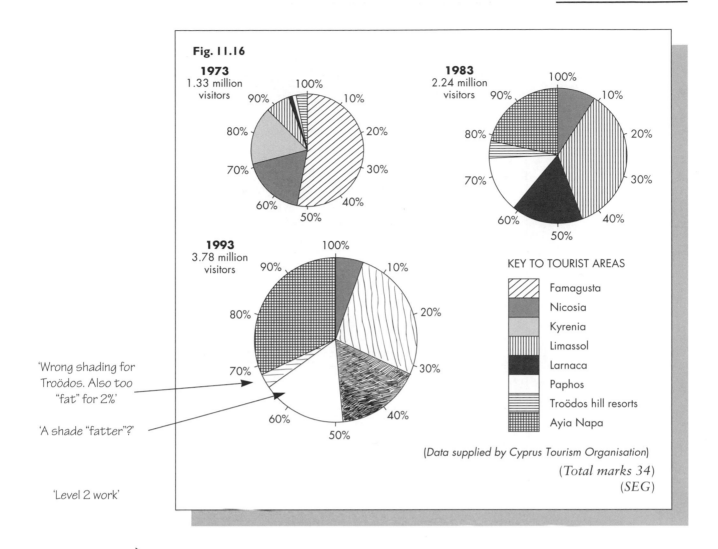

Fig. 11.16

1973
1.33 million visitors

1983
2.24 million visitors

1993
3.78 million visitors

'Wrong shading for Troödos. Also too "fat" for 2%'

'A shade "fatter"?'

'Level 2 work'

KEY TO TOURIST AREAS

Famagusta
Nicosia
Kyrenia
Limassol
Larnaca
Paphos
Troödos hill resorts
Ayia Napa

(*Data supplied by Cyprus Tourism Organisation*)

(*Total marks 34*)
(*SEG*)

A TUTOR ANSWER

▷ **Short structured question**

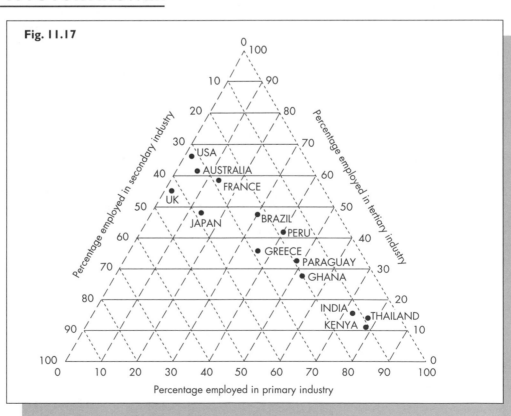

Fig. 11.17

Percentage employed in secondary industry

Percentage employed in tertiary industry

USA
AUSTRALIA
FRANCE
UK
JAPAN
BRAZIL
PERU
GREECE
PARAGUAY
GHANA
INDIA
THAILAND
KENYA

Percentage employed in primary industry

1   What is the difference between 'primary industry' and 'secondary industry'?

Primary industry includes the extraction of materials from the land or the sea whereas secondary industry is the processing of these materials into finished or semi-finished goods.

(1 mark)

2   (a)   Use the information on the graph in Fig. 11.18 to complete Fig. 11.19 below by placing each of the following countries in the correct box **A**, **B**, or **C**:

Australia, Ghana, Japan, Kenya, Paraguay, USA

Fig 11.18

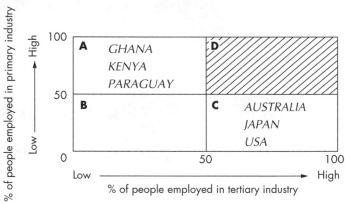

(2 marks)

(b)   Countries in box **A** are often referred to as less economically developed countries (LEDCs). Give THREE characteristics of LEDCs other than those concerned with industry.

(i)   *Lower incomes per head than in more economically developed countries.*

(ii)   *A large proportion of the population living in rural areas, say, around 50%.*

(iii)   *A higher infant mortality rate than in more developed countries.*

(3 marks)

(c)   Gross National Product her head of population is often used as a measure of development. Give TWO full reasons why this may be a misleading measure of development.

(i)   *As an average figure it hides how incomes are distributed among the population. A 'good' average might result from many millionaires even though there may be many paupers too.*

(ii)   *It does not tell you how income is spent. A country could have a high GNP per head, spend a lot of it on the military so that people's daily living standards are not high.*

(4 marks)
(Total 10 marks)
(NEAB)

> ### EXAMINATION QUESTION

(a)   Study Fig. 11.19, a sketch map of a tourist area in mountains.

Fig. 11.19

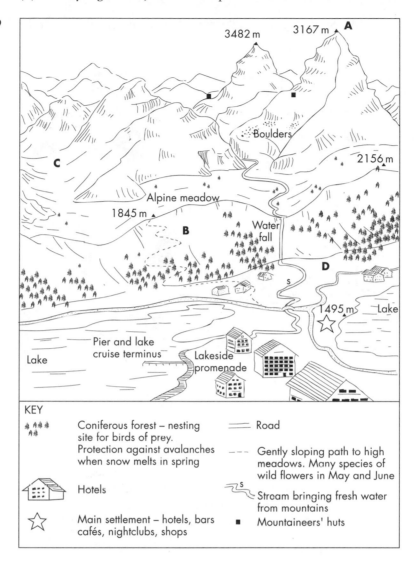

(i)   What is the height of the highest mountain?
............Metres   *(1 mark – Tier F only)*

(ii)   Why is the stream important for the village? (2 lines provided here)
                                                                                 (1 mark – Tier F only)

(iii)   Why might the coniferous forest be interesting for tourists?
(5 lines provided here)   *(3 marks – Tier F only)*

(iv)   The letters **A** to **D** on the sketch map show different areas of the mountains.
Match each letter to **one** of the descriptions in the Table 11.4 below.

Table 11.4

Description of area	Letter
An area of fairly flat land lower than its surroundings	D
A steep mountain	
A steep slope on one side of a large valley with lakes in it	
A broad valley higher up than the main valley it leads into	

(3 marks – Tiers F and H)

EITHER (TIER F)

(v)   Describe the attractions of this area for **summer** visitors with **outdoor** interests.
(7 lines provided here)   *(4 marks – Tier F only)*

OR (TIER H)

(vi) Physical (natural) features provide opportunities for leisure. Explain how the area shown could be used for leisure activities. (16 lines provided here)

(7 marks – Tier H only)

(b) Study Fig. 11.20, the map showing National Parks in England and Wales.

Fig. 11.20

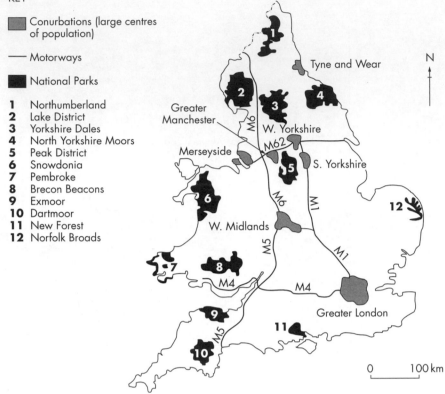

KEY

▨ Conurbations (large centres of population)

— Motorways

■ National Parks

1 Northumberland
2 Lake District
3 Yorkshire Dales
4 North Yorkshire Moors
5 Peak District
6 Snowdonia
7 Pembroke
8 Brecon Beacons
9 Exmoor
10 Dartmoor
11 New Forest
12 Norfolk Broads

0 ____ 100 km

(i)   State which National Park is surrounded by motorways and conurbations. (1 line provided here)   *(1 mark – Tiers F and H)*

(ii) Name the most northerly National Park (1 line provided here)

(1 mark – Tier F only)

EITHER (TIER F)

(iii) National Parks attract many tourists, leading to the growth of 'honeypots'. Using an example from your own studies, describe a place which has become a tourist honeypot. (11 lines provided here)   *(5 marks – Tier F only)*

(iv) Problems occur when an area attracts a large number of tourists. Describe these problems and give examples. (12 lines provided here)   *(6 marks – Tier F only)*

(Total 25 marks – Tier F)

(SEG)

OR (TIER H)

(iii) National Parks attract many tourists. This may lead to land-use conflicts with others such as farmers and landowners.
     Using examples from your own studies, describe conflicts which may occur.
     (17 lines provided here)   *(7 marks – Tier H only)*

(c) (i) Explain the meaning of 'tourist honeypot'. (5 lines provided here)

(3 marks – Tier H only)

    (ii) Name an example of a tourist honeypot which you have studied.
        (1 line provided here)
        Name of tourist honeypot
        Explain why it has become a tourist honeypot. (19 lines provided here)

(9 marks – Tier H only)

(Total 30 marks – Tier H)

(SEG)

▷ **EXAMINATION ANSWER**

(a) (i)   3482 (m)   *(1) (Tier F)*

(ii) Idea of fresh water or water supply.   *(1) (Tier F)*

(iii) (Any 3 x 1) Nesting sites; birds of prey; woodland idea.
(Might be interesting for walking or picnics).   *(3) (Tier F)*

(iv) D (given) A B C   *(3) (Tiers F and H)*

(v)   Marks for picking out and realising the opportunities for **summer** tourists with
outdoor interests (e.g. walking activities, scenery, wild flowers, birdwatching).
Level One: Brief points; partial use of the data.   *(1–2)*
Level Two: Full use made of data to give relevant points.   *(3–4) (Tier F)*

(vi) Marks for recognising the opportunities for leisure provided by the physical
environment (e.g. Walking, skiing, birdwatching, scenery, wild flowers, water
sports, cruises on lake).
e.g. There are steep mountain peaks, which climbers could scale. The lake in the
valley provides opportunities for cruises, etc.
Level One: Brief points; partial use of data.   *(1–2 marks)*
Level Two: Incomplete use of data, but some development of points and linkages
established.   *(3–5)*
Level Three: Full use of data, with clear linkages between physical features and
leisure opportunities to make developed points.   *(6–7) (Tier H)*

(b) (i)   Peak District   *(1) (Tiers F and H)*

(ii) Northumberland   *(1) (Tier F)*

(iii) Accept any tourist location which fits in with the idea of the question (e.g. a seaside resort, an inland area such as Cotswolds, a theme park, a National Park, a
location within a National Park, etc.). Description of the natural/physical sur-
roundings which attract visitors or the built environment (e.g. York, Chester,
Durham, Canterbury, etc.) or the range of facilities provided to attract visitors
(e.g. AltonTowers, etc.).
e.g. Blackpool has a long, sandy beach and faces the Irish Sea. It has developed a
huge range of built attractions. There is a large funfair area at the southern end
of the resort. In the centre is the Golden Mile with traditional seaside amuse-
ments. Of special interest is the Tower, a listed building. Special attractions such
as the Autumn illuminations extend the tourist season until the beginning of
November. An electric tramway along the coast provides a good internal transport link and is an attraction in itself. The resort can be reached by the M55
which links to the M6 or by rail, etc.
Level One: Brief points, perhaps not clearly linked to an identified place.   *(1–3)*
Level Two: Points are developed or are linked to a stated place.   *(4–5) (Tier F)*

(iv) The emphasis is on problems (e.g. overcrowding, traffic flow, footpath erosion,
conflicts with other land users, etc.).
e.g. Castleton in Derbyshire suffers from its own popularity. In the summer
months, good weather attracts large numbers from nearby Sheffield and Greater
Manchester so that car parking cannot cope and the A625, the main access road,
is congested. This leads to difficulties for the many pedestrians as the village
streets are narrow and sometimes without pavements, creating an accident risk.
A popular centre for hikers and ramblers with its focus of footpaths, the surrounding area experiences footpath erosion (e.g. the path up the western side of
Mam Tor). Land use conflicts arise between visitors and local residents who experience large crowds passing by their homes at close quarters. The local quarrying
of limestone gives rise to visual pollution (the cement work is clearly visible from
certain viewpoints) and there is the disturbance of blasting.
Level One: A few very brief points with some link to the idea of a problem *(1–2)*
Level Two: Problems are stated, perhaps not with great clarity. Focus on one
problem.   *(3–4)*
Level Three: A coherent account of different problems with examples. Focus on
one problem in considerable depth.   *(5–6) (Tier F)*
(Total 25)
(Tier F) (SEG)

(iii) Credit each conflict given as follows:

1 mark for correctly stated conflict (e.g. farmers with walkers)

2 marks for development

Conflicts must be with others users (not between different types of tourist)

e.g. In the Peak District, walkers and hikers enjoy the walks around Castleton through varied scenery, e.g. limestone to the south and grits or shales to the north. The Hope Valley cement works, to the east of the village, can be seen clearly from the surrounding hills; an eyesore. Regular blasting at quarries disturbs the peace and quiet. In many National Parks visitors may cross farmland leaving gates open and allowing farm animals to stray on to busy roads.

Level One: Brief points loosely bearing upon the land use issue.   (1–2)

Level Two: Conflicts are identified, perhaps with limited development.   (3–5)

Level Three: Conflicts clearly stated with good development based on examples studied.   (6–7) (Tier H)

(c) (i) For full marks the explanation should include any three of the following types of idea:

popularity; many tourists; overcrowding, especially on Bank Holidays and other days; built or natural attractions. (3 x 1 mark)   (3) (Tier H)

(ii) Accept any appropriate example from the wide range of possibilities, e.g. areas of countryside, particular villages, heritage sites or towns (York, Chester, etc.), theme parks, etc.

Emphasis should be on **explanations**:

▶ good accessibility to centres of population and transport (e.g. Lake District, Peak District)

▶ quality of built environment (e.g. York, Chester, Salisbury)

▶ quality of natural environment (e.g. a National Park, coastal area, etc.)

▶ appeal of built attractions (e.g. Blackpool)

▶ car factors

▶ advertising

▶ variety of attractions, etc. (not all necessarily applying to one example)

Level One: Brief points, which scratch the surface of the issue.   (1–3)

Level Two: Some depth achieved, combined with a range of reasons. Perhaps one aspect explained but not as thoroughly as required in Level Three   (4–6)

Level Three: A range of points explained in detail or with good development clearly linked to the chosen area. One point thoroughly explained if appropriate (e.g. unusual/interesting scenery or high quality of built environment).   (7–9) (Tier H)

(Total 30)

(Tier H) (SEG)

SUMMARY

▷ Industrial activity can be classified into four sectors – primary, secondary, tertiary and quaternary. These employment structures vary over time and space, and are an indicator of economic development.

▷ Changes are taking place in most MEDCs in the structure and location of employment, with a swing to service industries and land on the urban–rural fringe being popular. Accessibility, transport and the size of markets is important to the location of tertiary activities.

▷ Changing shopping habits have affected the distribution and nature of retailing, with many traditional urban shopping centres in decline and new centres emerging.

▷ Recreational activities and leisure facilities have grown in many MEDCs in recent years. The countryside is increasingly used as a recreational resource though leisure activities occur in both physical and human (urban) environments.

▷ A wide range of factors besides the physical environment and climate explain the pattern and nature of tourism.

▷ Tourism is a way of creating economic growth, though care has been taken to avoid conflicts between people, ensure maximum benefit for local people and sustain the industry long-term.

▷ Recreation and tourism put pressure on some environments and some very accessible rural environments are in danger of being over-used by visitors.

Manufacturing systems, locations and changes

▷ **GETTING STARTED**

In this chapter we look at the major ideas relating to manufacturing industry, give some examples of places where these ideas apply, and raise a number of current issues associated with the changes and effects of manufacturing industry in both MEDCs and LEDCs. Its general decline in MEDCs, its migration to greenfield sites in these countries, and its growing emergence in some countries, especially those in the Pacific Rim of South East Asia, need to be studied.

You may need to support your work in this chapter by referring to Chapters 9, 11 and 15. The latter deals with trade and interdependence; international trade and interdependence is an essential feature of most industries. Multinational companies draw raw materials and chase markets around the world.

LONDON A	LONDON B	MEG A	MEG B	MEG C	NEAB A	NEAB B	NEAB C	NICCEA	SEG A	SEG B	WJEC	IGCSE	TOPIC	STUDY	REVISION 1	REVISION 2
✓				✓		✓			✓			✓	Industry as a system			
✓					✓				✓		✓	✓	Classifying industries			
✓	✓	✓		✓	✓	✓		✓	✓	✓	✓	✓	Location of manufacturing industry			
✓	✓	✓	✓	✓	✓	✓	✓	✓	✓	✓	✓		Areas of industrial growth, newly industrialising countries (NICs) and High tech industry			
✓	✓	✓	✓	✓	✓	✓	✓	✓		✓	✓		Areas of industrial decline			
✓			✓	✓	✓		✓		✓	✓	✓		Industry and the environment			

▷ **WHAT YOU NEED TO KNOW**

'Make sure you can explain how different parts of manufacturing depend on other parts'

Manufacturing industry works as a **system** and each firm or plant/factory may be seen as a set of objects, some being **inputs** (things which are put into production), some being **processes** (the actual art of producing) and others being **outputs** (things which are produced, including by-products and waste). The idea of a system is that all these objects involved in the production of goods are linked together. It is these interrelationships or links which make it a system, so that a change in one part of the system will have effects on other parts. For example, if the demand for a product rises it will be necessary to increase inputs if the output is to rise to meet this increased demand. Equally, if the inputs fall, perhaps through a strike or problems with raw material, the output is also likely to fall in terms of finished products (goods) or financial gain to the factory owner. You only get out what you put in! As some plants may be linked with other plants through the transfer of materials and product, a change in one part of the system may influence other parts of the system. For instance, if the component producer fails to deliver the required items, the manufacturer of the finished product will be left with partly finished items. Fig. 12.1 shows the manufacturing system for iron and steel as a flow diagram with the inputs, processes and outputs arranged in sequence, that is, in the order in which they occur.

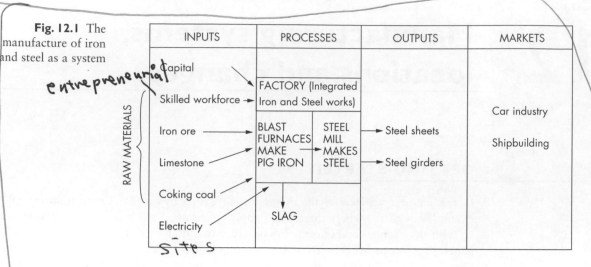

Fig. 12.1 The manufacture of iron and steel as a system

Fig. 12.1 The manufacture of iron and steel as a system

Factor inputs

All production requires the input of resources called **factors of production** of which there are four groups:

1   **Land** This includes all the free gifts of nature, the land and soil itself, the minerals in the earth's crust, and all the other natural resources around.
2   **Labour** All the physical and mental characteristics of working people ranging from enterprise and initiative to sheer manual work are referred to as labour.
3   **Capital** Tools, machinery and all other humans aids used to produce goods and services for consumers are called capital.
4   **Knowledge** This fourth type of resource is a special type of capital, human capital; and includes all the information and understanding that people have accumulated over the years which is stored in books, people's heads, etc. and is available to producers.

Manufacturing industry uses varying combinations of these factors to produce goods. Many modern industries have increased output by increasing the input of capital and knowledge.

▷ Manufacturing location

One of the three major decisions that manufacturers have to take is: where do we **locate** the factory? These decisions and how they are interrelated are shown by the flow diagram in Fig. 12.2. Location concerns finding an accessible position at which inputs can be gathered and output distributed to markets. An accessible location will allow the manufacturer to operate profitably, not necessarily maximising their profits but providing sufficient profits to keep shareholders happy with the location chosen. A range of factors may influence the location decision taken by manufacturing (Fig. 12.3).

Fig. 12.2

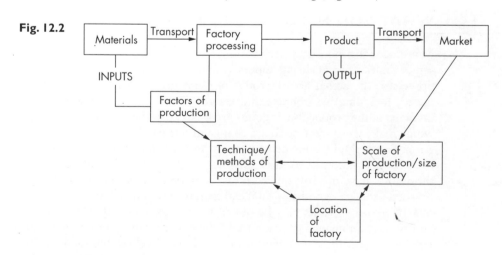

Fig. 12.3 The factors which influence the location of a factory

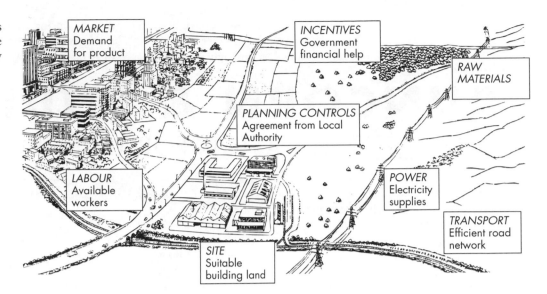

The importance of each of these factors can vary from industry to industry, and even within the same industry may vary from place to place and time to time.

The **pulp and paper industry** is clearly attracted by **raw materials**, and is generally located close to forested areas, often those which also enable the generation of hydroelectricity. **Bakeries** are, on the other hand, generally **market-orientated** with quick and cheap transport to customers being of prime importance in the location decision. Pulp and paper mills in Britain can be found around Fort William in Scotland; large bakers are found in major town and cities.

Cost and price factors for a computer game factory looking for a new location are show in Fig. 12.4.

'It helps to give examples of industries affected by particular locational factors'

Table 12.1 Industries classified according to location

Group	Characteristic
Raw material-orientated	Located near the source of the raw materials they process
Market-orientated	Located near their consumers
Footloose	Free from the restriction of materials and markets and not tied to any location

Many modern industries are **footloose**, that is to say they are not tied to any particular type of location. Government policy, personal factors and transport availability are the sort of factors influencing the locational decisions that footloose industries make.

Fig. 12.4 Production costs and market prices for a computer game factory looking for a new location

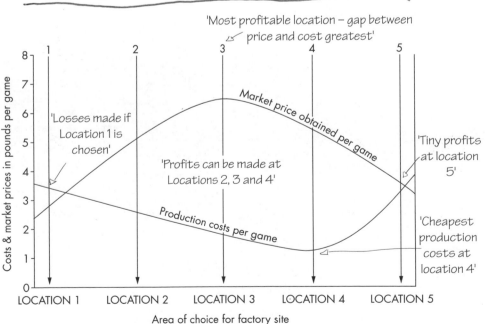

Advertising is thought to have a strong influence on industrial location decisions. Fig. 12.5 is a recent advertisement placed in *The Times* on 13 November 1996 by Halton Borough Council to highlight the advantages of Runcorn and Widnes for industry.

Fig. 12.5

RUNCORN & WIDNES
THE <u>RIGHT</u> LOCATION FOR YOUR BUSINESS

- *The <u>right</u> location.*
  Halton is bounded to the North and West by the Merseyside conurbations. It straddles the River Mersey and consists of the two towns of Widnes and Runcorn. It is a UK Intermediate Area, with European Objective 2 status. A massive market of five million people live within a 25 mile radius.

- *The <u>right</u> labour, education and training.*
  Halton can offer you an unbeatable customised workforce which is skilled, productive, adaptable, committed and fully supported by educational and training facilities.

- *The <u>right</u> environment.*
  Halton is home to large World Class companies and rapidly growing small businesses, with everything in between. It is well supported by a comprehensive service sector plus excellent conference facilities and top quality accommodation for business visitors.

- *The <u>right</u> land and premises.*
  Widnes and Runcorn represent one of the North West's major employment areas and have an impressive choice of sites and premises in prime locations within the M62 and M56 corridors - available now!

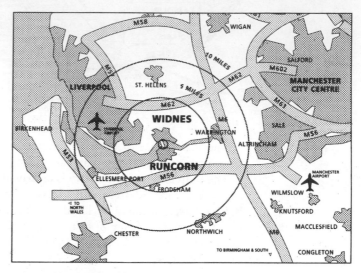

- *The <u>right</u> package.*
  We can help you find the perfect premises, secure maximum finance and assist with recruitment and training, so ...

Ring or fax the Economic Development Unit *Right now* for an information pack

Tel: 0151 424 2061
Fax: 0151 471 7301

HALTON
BOROUGH COUNCIL
RUNCORN · WIDNES
WORKING FOR BETTER LIVES

Right Here · Right Now

Agglomeration

Manufacturers concerned with similar types of work may come to similar decisions about where to locate their plant. Equally, manufacturers may consider closeness to factories producing component materials or similar products an important locational factor. Manufacturing firms and similar types of manufacturing work often group together in certain areas: e.g. at ports, at the site of raw materials and increasingly today in the main market regions close to customers. Regions and smaller areas specialise (as do countries and people) in producing those goods and services in which they have either a **comparative advantage** (they can produce better or cheaper than any other producer) or an **absolute advantage** (they can produce better or cheaper than any other area). This concentration of firms and specialisation of areas is known as **industrial agglomeration** or **localisation**; it occurs at both regional and local levels.

There are often clear economic benefits to a firm when it locates in a manufacturing area close to a number of other firms. External economies of scale (or economies that result from larger-scale production made possible by the local concentration of firms and shared by these firms) encourage the clustering together of manufacturers. External economies are of two main types:

- ▶ linked processes – e.g. the production process might be divided up, with individual plants specialising in a limited number of stages; there might be marketing links between firms, such as the sharing of a lorry's load;
- ▶ the local infrastructure of services – e.g. the availability of services such as water supply, banking, transport, etc. and of a pool of skilled labour.

A localised industry is one which concentrates its firms in one area. The extent to which an industry is localised and a region specialised in their production can be measured using the following simple formula:

$$\frac{\% \text{ of workers in the region employed in the industry}}{\% \text{ of the country's workers employed in the industry}}$$

The number produced is known as the **labour quotient** (LQ); it is useful for studying the distribution of industry. Light industry tends to be less localised than heavy industry and more widely dispersed. For instance, food, drink and tobacco manufacturing in Britain have regional LQs which range from 0.6 in Wales to 2.2 in East Anglia; metal manufacturing LQs range from 0.1 in East Anglia to 3.8 in Wales.

The agglomeration of Japanese industry is shown in Fig. 12.6.

Fig. 12.6

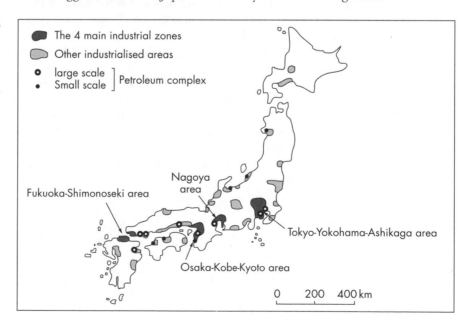

▷ High-tech industry, science (technology) parks and greenfield sites

The idea of industry and business being in a park-like setting has grown during recent years in MEDCs. They are known by various names – business parks, research parks, technology parks, science parks, office parks – and are most common in the USA. In Britain they are either on university sites (e.g. the Cambridge Science Park), in New Towns (e.g. Llantarnam Park, Cwmbran), in **Enterprise Zones** (e.g. Dundee Technology Park) or in a few forward-thinking towns and cities with access to airports and motorways (e.g. Bristol, Swindon, Birmingham, etc.). **High-tech** industry or '**sunrise**' industry, producing computers, micro-electronics and telecommunication equipment and using techniques involving micro-electronics, rather than old-style heavy manufacturing or low-tech industries, seems to be attracted to these parks. In these industries no special inputs or facilities are needed and neither the raw materials nor the finished products are bulky or heavy; they are 'footloose' and the availability of good modern transport facilities is important. Road and air are used to transport the small raw materials and products, and factories are usually single-storey, modern and may be automated. Studies in the USA show that high-tech industries are attracted to these industrial parks because:

▷   the immediate environment is of a high quality, e.g. a pleasant environment of fully grown trees and lakes, attractively designed buildings with open spaces between them, plenty of facilities like restaurants, tennis courts, etc. They normally occupy a '**greenfield**' site, which will have a high amenity value (top-quality environment) as it will not have been built on before.

▷   they are close to universities and colleges, where there is expertise in science, computer research, etc. Industry and business working closely with university departments is a major feature of many industrial parks.

▷   they have been developed on sites with good communications (e.g. close to motorways and/or airports; helicopter pads, etc.)

▷   they can be close to other established high-tech firms. Links with other firms are seen as important.

One of the earliest, and now most famous, of British industrial parks is the Cambridge Science Park, opened in 1973 on 130 acres on the northern edge of the city, close to major roads. Sixty-eight science-based firms and research institutes have located in this attractive, well-landscaped park. It is developed to a very low density, with only about a sixth of the total area being building floor space. One condition of locating in the Park is that firms must be involved in the research and development of products rather than their large-scale manufacture, and must take advantage of links with the University. University-linked industry marrying scientific brains and business is the basis of the Science Park. Most firms are small and are mainly involved in laser, telecommunication, precision electronics and pharmaceutical production.

Today's 'sunrise industries', using and producing high-tech equipment such as computers, lasers, micro-electronics, favour greenfield sites. A high-quality environment with green open space around has become a locational factor for manufacturing industry. Modern manufacturing tends to be light (makes small, easily transported items) and footloose but transport-dependent; the locations chosen are often on green land in pleasant environments close to motorway junctions.

This trend in MEDCs for industry to relocate away from traditional urban areas to edge-of-town or out-of-town greenfield sites contrasts with that to be found in many LEDCs, as Fig. 12.7 shows.

Fig. 12.7 Changing industrial locations in MEDCs and LEDCs

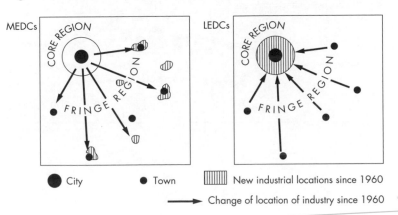

Fig. 12.8 Reveals manufacturing industry in Ghana, an LEDC, becoming agglomerated or concentrated in a few areas of the country.

Fig. 12.8

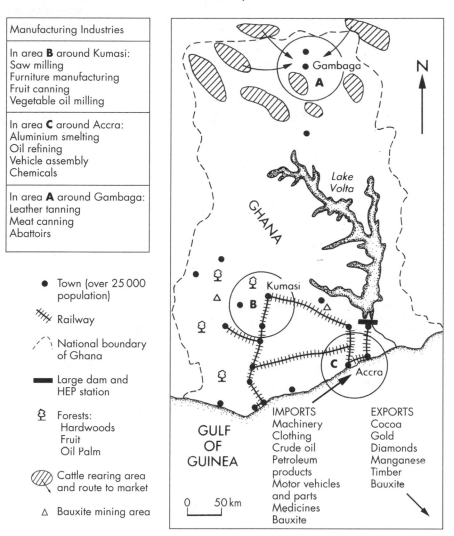

Manufacturing Industries
In area **B** around Kumasi: Saw milling / Furniture manufacturing / Fruit canning / Vegetable oil milling
In area **C** around Accra: Aluminium smelting / Oil refining / Vehicle assembly / Chemicals
In area **A** around Gambaga: Leather tanning / Meat canning / Abattoirs

● Town (over 25 000 population)

✕✕✕ Railway

⌒⌒ National boundary of Ghana

▬ Large dam and HEP station

♉ Forests: Hardwoods Fruit Oil Palm

Cattle rearing area and route to market

△ Bauxite mining area

Ghana, like most LEDCs, believes it has insufficient manufacturing industry, and much of what little there is is dominated by foreign companies and capital. Only 20% of the Ghanaian labour-force is employed in manufacturing. Cheap labour has attracted multinational companies, run by foreign managers, to the coastal cities, especially to Accra. The Ghanaians are keen to develop manufacturing and 'Ghanaianise' it. The Volta scheme was an attempt to produce a large supply of cheap hydroelectricity in order to provide energy, vital in transforming the country from a non-industrial to an industrial one (Fig. 12.8).

▷ **Issue** *Environmental impact of manufacturing industry*

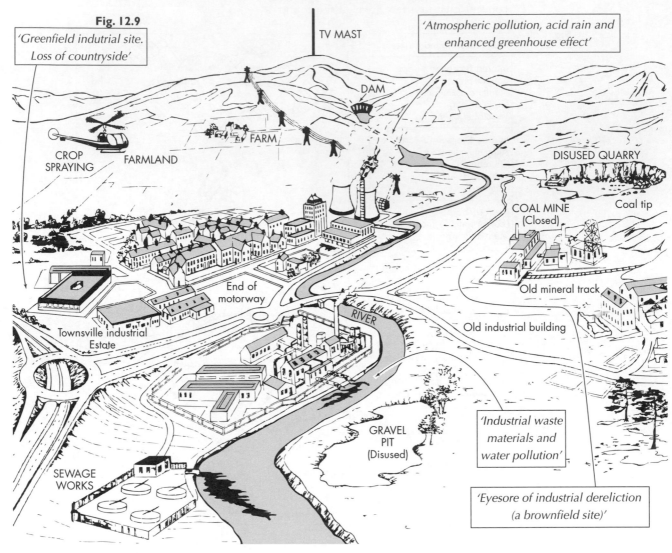

Fig. 12.9

'Greenfield indutrial site. Loss of countryside'

'Atmospheric pollution, acid rain and enhanced greenhouse effect'

TV MAST

DAM

FARM

CROP SPRAYING   FARMLAND

DISUSED QUARRY

COAL MINE (Closed)   Coal tip

End of motorway

Old mineral track

Townsville industrial Estate

RIVER

Old industrial building

GRAVEL PIT (Disused)

'Industrial waste materials and water pollution'

SEWAGE WORKS

'Eyesore of industrial dereliction (a brownfield site)'

▷ **Case study** *Sheffield's industrial estates*

Fig. 12.10 Sheffield's major industrial estate

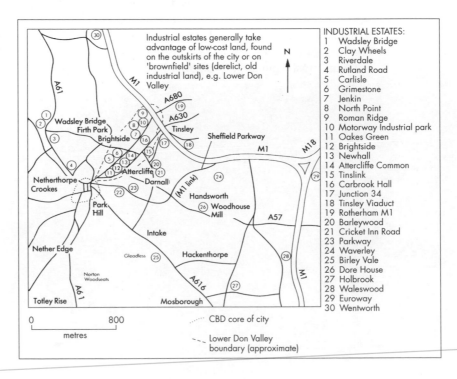

Industrial estates generally take advantage of low-cost land, found on the outskirts of the city or on 'brownfield' sites (derelict, old industrial land), e.g. Lower Don Valley

N

A61
M1
A680
A630
Wadsley Bridge
Firth Park
Brightside
Tinsley
Sheffield Parkway
M18
M1
Netherthorpe
Crookes
Attercliffe
Darnall
(M1 link)
Park Hill
Handsworth
Woodhouse Mill
Intake
Nether Edge
Gleadless
Hackenthorpe
A57
Norton Woodseats
A616
Totley Rise
Mosborough
A61

INDUSTRIAL ESTATES:
1 Wadsley Bridge
2 Clay Wheels
3 Riverdale
4 Rutland Road
5 Carlisle
6 Grimestone
7 Jenkin
8 North Point
9 Roman Ridge
10 Motorway Industrial park
11 Oakes Green
12 Brightside
13 Newhall
14 Attercliffe Common
15 Tinslink
16 Carbrook Hall
17 Junction 34
18 Tinsley Viaduct
19 Rotherham M1
20 Barleywood
21 Cricket Inn Road
22 Parkway
23 Parkway
24 Waverley
25 Birley Vale
26 Dore House
27 Holbrook
28 Waleswood
29 Euroway
30 Wentworth

0   800
metres

········· CBD core of city

~~~ Lower Don Valley boundary (approximate)

Fig. 12.10 shows the location, within the city, of Sheffield's 30 major industrial estates. The importance of road transport, the clustering of estates in the old industrial areas of the Lower Don Valley, and the edge-of-city location of many estates can be seen. A study of the Roman Ridge Industrial Estate (Fig. 12.11) shows its good road transport facilities, especially its accessibility to the M1 motorway. The estate was designed almost entirely for light industry and service industry. There are small factory units producing glass, laboratory equipment, industrial diamonds and frozen food, small warehouses and cold stores.

Fig. 12.11 Roman Ridge Industrial Estate, Sheffield

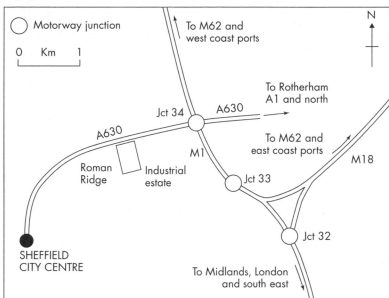

A study of the industries locating on most industrial estates shows that they are often:

▶ 'footloose' light industries, with no particular orientation to materials or to specific markets, transport improvements having reduced the importance of the old factors of nearness to materials or markets;

▶ directly consumer-based industries dependent on road transport, especially for the distribution of products;

▶ small- or medium-sized firms employing relatively few people.

▶ **Key terms**   *Make sure you understand and can apply these geographical terms*

Agglomeration	The clustering of similar types of industry at one location.
Capital intensive	A high proportion of capital equipment (e.g. machinery) relative to labour in the production process.
Cottage industry	Small-scale industrial enterprise, often based in the worker's home.
Decentralisation	Industries relocating and being spread around a region/country.
Development area	Region of Britain which has been selected for government financial aid, perhaps because of the decline of its manufacturing industries.
Greenfield site	New land for building and development that was not used for that purpose before, perhaps because it was countryside.
Heavy industry	Industries making very bulky products, often from steel, that need very large sites.
Industrial inertia	When industry remains where it was originally sited even though the original reasons for its location there are no longer of any importance.
Labour intensive	High proportion of labour relative to capital equipment.
Light industry	Industries making small, easily-transported items.
Manufacturing	Processing industries which produce goods in a finished or partly finished form.
Multinational or transnational company	Large international firm operating across national boundaries.

Raw materials   Products of **primary sector** industries, e.g. iron ore and coal.

Science park   Science-based industries located in a park setting.

Terms like 'footloose', 'raw material-orientation', 'market-orientation', and 'capital', are also important, and are defined in the text of this chapter. Note their definitions when you come across them.

Suggestions for further work

There is ample scope for fieldwork investigations of manufacturing industry. Suitable titles might be:

▶ What factors have influenced the location of particular industries in your area?

▶ To what extent do the industrial estates of your area fit the textbook model of the location and features of an industrial estate?

▶ What changes have occurred in the pattern of industry and employment in your area in the past 25 years? Can you suggest reasons for these changes?

▶ Consider the environmental impact of the growth (if there has been growth!) of industry in your area. What conflicts have arisen, and why?

▷ ## STUDENT ANSWER WITH EXAMINER'S COMMENTS

▷ **Short structured question**

Study the two sketches below which show a valley in a more economically developed country (MEDC) in 1750 (Fig. 12.12) and in 1950 (Fig. 12.13).

Fig. 12.12

RURAL PHASE – 1750

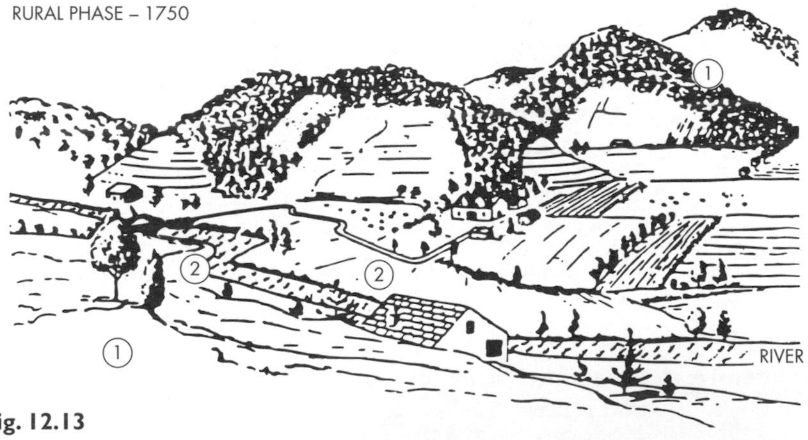

Fig. 12.13

INDUSTRIAL PHASE – 1950

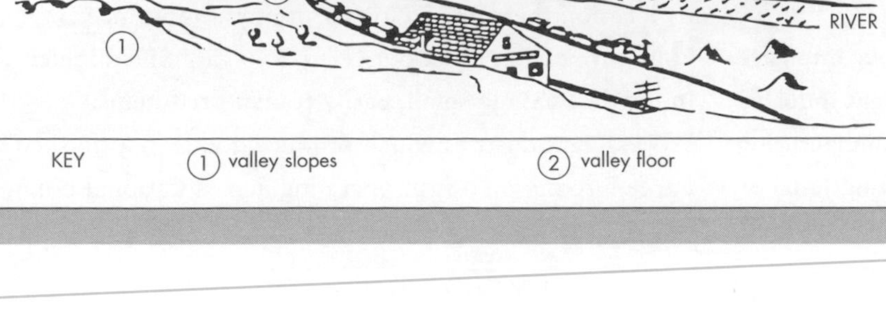

KEY   ① valley slopes   ② valley floor

(a) (i) State **two** changes which took place between 1750 and 1950.

1 A mine shaft has been sunk and a village has been built

2 All the forests have been knocked down in the industrial place

(*2 marks*)

(ii) Name a resource which the sketches suggest was important in the industrialisation of the valley.

Wood (from trees)

(*1 mark*)

(b) After 1950, the industries shown on Fig. 12.13 closed, unemployment rose and the valley needed redevelopment. By 1992 redevelopment had taken place.

Fig. 12.14

'Suitable title'

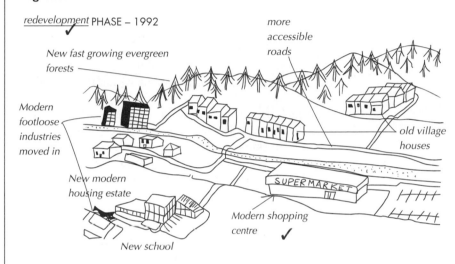

redevelopment PHASE – 1992   ✓

New fast growing evergreen forests

more accessible roads

Modern footloose industries moved in

'Excellent geography as well as artwork'

New modern housing estate

old village houses

SUPER MARKET

Modern shopping centre   ✓

New school

(i) On the outline sketch in Fig. 12.14, draw and label the features you would expect to find in the valley in 1992. Complete the title for the sketch in the space provided.   (*5 marks*)

(ii) Suggest how the members of a family with two teenage children might feel about the changes in the valley between 1950 and 1992.

They are happier with the prospects for work and jobs in 1992 than after

1950. The redevelopment has also improved the valley, it has been cleaned

up. Access out of the village to big towns is easier for shopping and work so

their children will probably get jobs, whereas after the pit closed,

unemployment was high.

'You rightly referred to why all members of family might be in favour of redevelopment'

(*2 marks*)
(*Total 10 marks*)
(*NEAB*)

'Level 2 quality (grade C and above)'

A TUTOR ANSWER

▷ **Multiple-choice questions**

Fig. 12.15

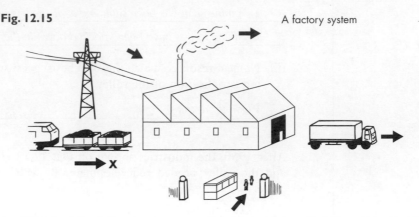

A factory system

'The correct answer. Raw materials are the name for the "things" brought into a factory by, say, train, to be processed into commodities'

1   Which of the following is correct for the arrow marked X on Fig. 12.15 above?
  A   Power   D   Commodity
  B   Water   E   Labour
  Ⓒ   Raw materials

Most new steel-making plants built within the past 30 years have been located on coasts.

'The correct answer. Iron ore is bulky and expensive to transport, so the nearer the plants can get to the source of iron ore overseas, the cheaper it will be for them'

2   Which one of the following has encouraged this change to take place?
  A   An increase in demand for steel.
  Ⓑ   Imports of cheap iron ore.
  C   The development of the motorway network.
  D   A decrease in the price of coal.
  E   An increase in the length of the railway network.

'The correct answer. Modern integrated steel-works are automated; this is expensive to install but less labour is then required'

3   The building of these new plants has been accompanied by
  Ⓐ   increased investment and a decrease in the work force.
  B   decreased investment and an increase in the work force.
  C   no changes in either investment or the work force.
  D   decreased investment and a decrease in the work force.
  E   increased investment and an increase in the work force.

Many LEDCs have little or no manufacturing industry.

'The correct answer. Lack of capital to invest is one of the causes of insufficient manufacturing in "developing" countries. It's the best answer here!'

4   Why is this so?
  A   Shortage of suitable sites.
  Ⓑ   Low capital investment.
  C   Shortage of raw materials.
  D   Low population growth.
  E   Shortage of unskilled labour.

5   The map in Fig. 12.16 shows part of the 'high-tech' corridor west of London. With the help of the map evidence, state which one of the following group of factors (**A** to **E**) is responsible for attracting high-tech industries to the area.

'Not true'
'Not important to high-tech!'

A cheap land, large market, cooling water from the river

'False and unimportant'

B open countryside, nearby docks, coal supply from South Wales

'Next best'

C large workforce available, near major towns and cities, clean water

'Not a locating factor'
'Best answer, all true'

Ⓓ easy access to airport, many research laboratories, motorway links

'A factor!'

E fast rail links, local raw materials, near to European market

'Doesn't apply to high-tech!'

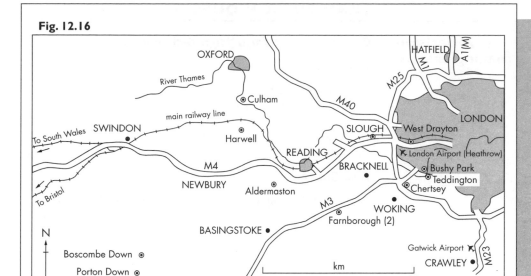

Fig. 12.16

6   The map in Fig. 12.17 shows the location of industrial estates in a city in an MEDC.

Fig. 12.17

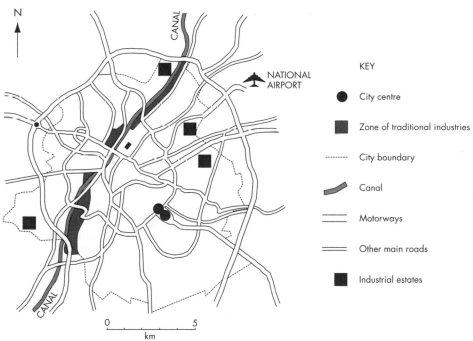

What does the map suggest is the most important locating factor for the industrial estates?

    A   the city centre
    B   the national airport
    ⓒ   motorways and main roads
    D   the canal
    E   the zone of traditional industries

'This is clearly the main factor. Both your own knowledge and the map point to this'

EXAMINATION QUESTION

▷ **A decision-making exercise**

Choosing a site for a 'High-tech' industry

Instructions

1. Analyse again all the information provided on the task sheet and information sheets.
2. Read carefully through the three tasks.
3. You may give the answers in ANY order, but make sure they are numbered correctly.
4. Try to answer all parts of the exercise.

Task Sheet

Read the following instructions and guidelines thoroughly.

Introduction

In this exercise you are to imagine that you are a Chief Executive of a successful European 'high-tech' electronics company.

The company wants to expand in the UK but has yet to decide **where**. The company wants you to find out about a possible location site in the UK because

(a) it will be in a better position to serve its existing UK customers;
(b) to try to attract more UK orders.

Your task is three fold

1. In this task use **Information Sheets One and Two** (*Either* Tier F *or* Tier H version).
   You have to go back to your company headquarters and describe to the shareholders, the present distribution of 'high-tech' electronic firms in the UK, and suggest reasons for this distribution.

2. In this task use **Information Sheets Two** (*either* Tier F *or* Tier H) **and Three**.
   You have narrowed down your choice of a site to FIVE possible locations.

   (a) Bradford
   (b) Cumbria
   (c) Livingston
   (d) Mid Glamorgan
   (e) North Kent

   You have now to explain to the shareholders **briefly** what you consider to be the main advantages and disadvantages of each location.

3. Using all the information you have been given (including **Information Sheet Four**), which of the 5 possible locations do you consider to be the best site for your future UK factory?

   (*MEG*)

Information Sheet One – Tier F

Background information
Terms used:

(a) **'High-tech'** or **'high-technology'** is used to describe industries where micro-electronics processes are important.
(b) **'Information technology'** industries usually produce computers and telecommunication equipment.
(c) Computer **hardware** is the machinery.
(d) Computer **software** is the term for the programs produced.

Where high-tech industries are located
Unlike older industries they *do not* need:

(a) Special power supplies, e.g. coal or oil.
(b) Large quantities of water.
(c) Bulk transport such as trains or lorries.

In the computer industry they *do not* need large amounts of raw materials – they only need small quantities of plastics, rubbers, glass, etc.

The finished product is small, (e.g. compare a computer with a car or farm product), so it can be moved by road or small aircraft.

They *do* need highly trained people as they are hoping to improve their computers or software all the time. So they *do* like to be close to universities or colleges where they can employ experts. They also like to be in areas that are regarded as pleasant, e.g. nice countryside, good weather.

In the USA, studies have shown that high-tech industries seem to be attracted to areas where:

(a)   They are close to universities or colleges with expertise in computer research.
(b)   Land prices are low.
(c)   There is an attractive climate.
(d)   There is attractive countryside.

Information Sheet One – Tier H

Background information

(a)   The term '**high-technology**' or '**high-tech**' for short, is now used to describe industries whose manufacturing processes use techniques usually involving micro-electronics.
(b)   '**Information technology**' industries involve the production of computers, micro-electronics and telecommunication equipment.
(c)   **Hardware** is machinery.
(d)   **Software** is the term for the programs produced.

Location factors

Traditional location factors for the manufacturing industry do not really apply to the computer industry. For example the industry does *not* need special power supplies, large quantities of water, or access to bulk transport facilities.

In the computer industry, neither the raw materials nor the finished products are bulky; transport, therefore, tends to be by road or by air freight, and the small volume means that even minor airports are suitable.

Research and Development are an integral part of the industry because of the rapidity of innovation, so the labour needs are specialised and will become more so as the basic factories go on to automation.

Most 'hardware' is produced in small, single-storey factories. The production of 'software' can be described as a **footloose** industry.

Amenity factors i.e. the quality of the immediate environment, are extremely important in location, e.g. a recent study of the town of Boulder, Colorado in the USA, which is a growing centre of high-tech industry, suggests that four main factors attracted firms there:

(a)   The presence of well-established electronics industries and technical government bodies.
(b)   Low property prices.
(c)   The University of Colorado.
(d)   An attractive climate and countryside.

Information Sheet Two

Tier F

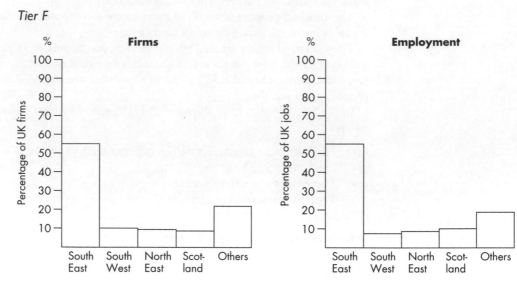

Tier H

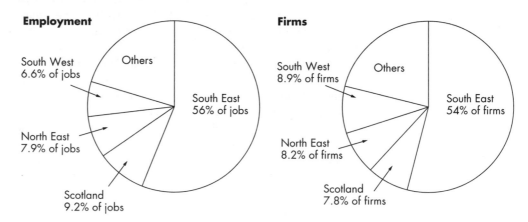

Information Sheet Three

A map showing five possible locations for the new 'high-tech' electronics factory.

Information Sheet Four

Government incentives for 'new' industries

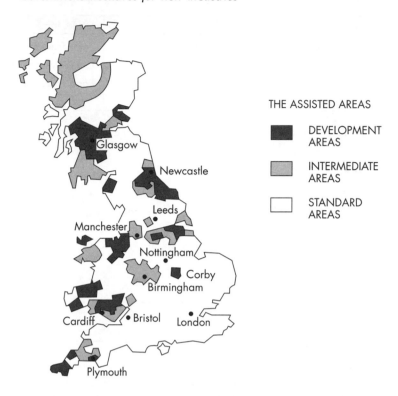

THE ASSISTED AREAS

▪ DEVELOPMENT AREAS

▦ INTERMEDIATE AREAS

☐ STANDARD AREAS

	Standard Areas	Intermediate Areas	Development Areas
Government built factories	Not available	Available at low rents and rates possibly up to 2 yrs, and free	Available at low rents and rates possibly up to 2 yrs, and free
Factory buildings	None	25%–35%	Up to 45%
Government loans available	No	No	Yes
Grant to clear derelict land	50%	75%	85%
Training grants	No	£10.00 a week with smaller grants for women	£10.00 a week with smaller grants for women
Grants for moving and housing key workers	No	Yes	Yes
Other grants for training centres	No	Yes	Yes

(MEG)

 EXAMINATION ANSWER

▷ **Decision-making exercise**

Task 1

Tackle this in two stages:

1. Describe the distribution of the firms in the UK. For example, 56% of UK's high-tech jobs and 54% of UK's high-tech firms are in South East England; South East dominates, etc. Information Sheet Two gives you the answer.

2. Use Information Sheet Two to explain this South East domination. You will need to write about being near to expertise, universities and other high-tech firms, and attractive environments, and apply these ideas to the geography of the UK while, at the same time, linking it up to the pattern you previously described.

Task 2

A table might be a good way of answering this e.g.

Site	Advantages	Disadvantages
Bradford etc.	University of Bradford Cheap land prices Nice countryside	Away from main high-tech area of UK Cooler, wetter climate Poor image/unattractive old urban area

Be brief but do all five sites!

Task 3

Make a choice from the five locations. All can get you good marks provided the decision is justified well. There is no right answer; the marks are awarded for the quality of the reasons, not the name of the site. Remember to add government support if you choose a site in a 'Development' or 'Intermediate' area, i.e. Cumbria, Bradford and Mid Glamorgan.

SUMMARY

▷ An industry can be seen as a system with inputs, processes and outputs.

▷ Industrial activity can be classified according to the type of work, the type of goods, its location and the relative quantity of the various inputs.

▷ A number of factors affect the location and changing characteristics of manufacturing industry. Industry changes over time as locational factors change.

▷ Many urban/industrial areas have seen a decline in their traditional secondary industries, often heavy industry.

▷ Some areas and countries are currently developing a broader manufacturing base.

▷ Industrial activity and change have an impact on the environment and on local industries.

Population distribution, changes and policies

▷ **GETTING STARTED**

Population changes provide some of the burning issues for geographers today to study. Overpopulation, ageing populations and refugee migrations are newsworthy! These issues are dealt with in this chapter where the different situations in the MEDCs and LEDCs with regard to population matters are pointed out. Case studies to illustrate these issues and ideas are given, and a list of the key geographical terms used in the topic area is included for you to work through.

You might find it helpful to use Chapter 9 – Economic development and human welfare – in conjunction with this chapter.

LONDON A	LONDON B	MEG A	MEG B	MEG C	NEAB A	NEAB B	NEAB C	NICCEA	SEG A	SEG B	WJEC	IGCSE	TOPIC	STUDY	REVISION 1	REVISION 2
✓		✓		✓		✓		✓	✓	✓	✓	✓	Population densities and distribution; patterns and reasons			
✓	✓	✓	✓	✓			✓	✓	✓	✓	✓	✓	Population structure, and change in size and structure due to births, deaths and migration			
✓		✓		✓		✓		✓	✓	✓		✓	Causes and consequences of population growth/overpopulation			
✓	✓	✓	✓	✓	✓			✓	✓		✓	✓	Population migration; causes and effects			
		✓		✓				✓	✓				Population control policies/strategies			
✓	✓	✓	✓	✓				✓		✓			Urban and rural population differences			

▷ **WHAT YOU NEED TO KNOW**

▷ **Population distribution**

Population is distributed unevenly. There are high densities in some places and low densities in other places on the earth's surface. These variations from one part of the world to another result from a variety of physical, political and socio-economic factors. People tend to live between 15 and 200 metres above sea level, close to exploitable sources of energy. They tend to avoid certain climates, such as extremes of heat and cold.

Some parts of the world are overpopulated, whilst others are underpopulated. There are five types of hostile environment in the world which tend to be underpopulated:

'Type of hostile environment'

1 the **polar ice deserts** of Antarctica and the North Polar region;
2 the **boreal/taiga** (coniferous forests) and **tundra** regions of Scandinavia, Northern Canada and the Soviet Union;

金于業木幇权·

3   the **hot deserts** of Africa, Australia and the Middle East;
4   the **hot, wet forests** of Brazil, the East Indies and Central Africa;
5   **desert basins**, such as south west USA, and the **mountains** in the interior of continents, e.g. the Urals.

Fig. 13.1 The most densely and sparsely populated areas and the relationship with hostile environments

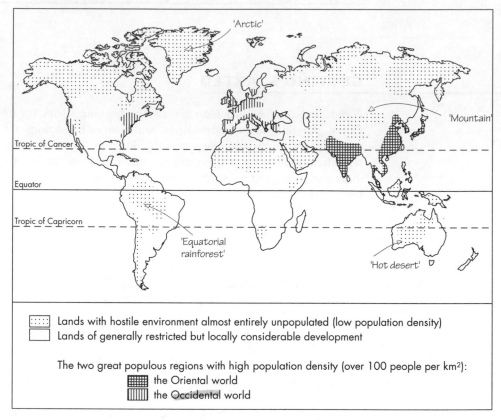

Physical conditions can make some environments unsuitable for comfortable human life. At the same time, you should note that there are two great belts of dense population:

▶ the **Orient** (Japan, east China, south east Asia and India)
▶ the **Occident** (north west Europe, north east USA and California)

where people find natural environments more positive. The distribution of population is uneven within countries and can be partly related to physical factors, as Fig. 13.2 for Japan shows. Building is difficult on sloping ground, so the mountains of central Japan have deterred settlement.

Fig. 13.2 The population distribution of Japan by density

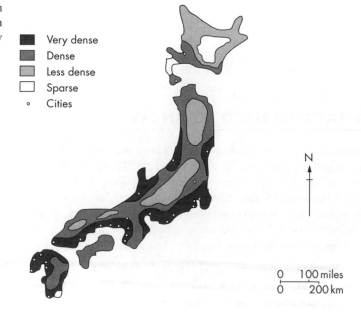

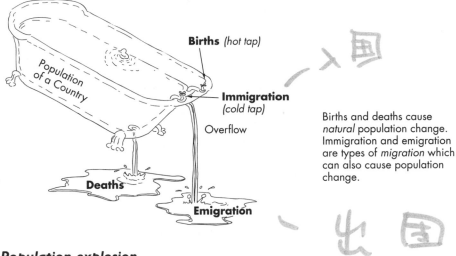

▷ Population change

Changes in population size can be depicted as a bath. **Births** and **immigration** which *add* to a country's population are shown as the two taps which add to the amount of water in the bath (Fig. 13.3). **Deaths** and **emigration** cause population *loss* just as water is lost through the plug and overflow on a bath.

Fig. 13.3

Births and deaths cause *natural* population change. Immigration and emigration are types of *migration* which can also cause population change.

Population explosion

The world's population has exploded in size during the present century (Fig. 13.4).

The length of time it takes to add each 1000 million human beings to the earth's population has fallen from about 100 years for the second 1000 million, to 12 years for the fifth. The 'human snowball' or '**population explosion**' has rolled on faster and faster! On a world scale there has been a **positive** replacement rate, that is, the **birth rate** has exceeded the **death rate**. This has resulted, as Fig. 13.5 suggests, from a falling death rate in LEDCs.

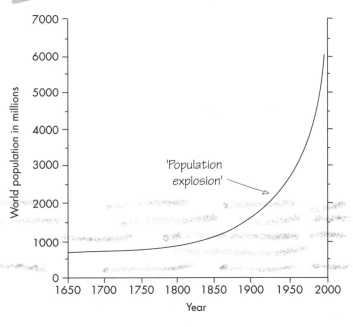

Fig. 13.4 Rapid population growth in the twentieth century

The relationship between birth rates and death rates in different parts of the world is shown by the graph in Fig. 13.5.

▶ Countries falling in Group 4 on Fig. 13.5 (e.g. Tanzania, Syria, India, Thailand, etc.) account for the 'population explosion'. Fig. 13.6 shows the large contribution made by LEDCs in Africa, Asia and Latin America to the growing world total.

▶ Countries falling in Group 1 on Fig. 13.5 (e.g. the USA) have stable populations, with low birth rates largely being cancelled out by low death rates. Fig. 13.6 shows the stability of population size in MEDCs.

Fig. 13.5

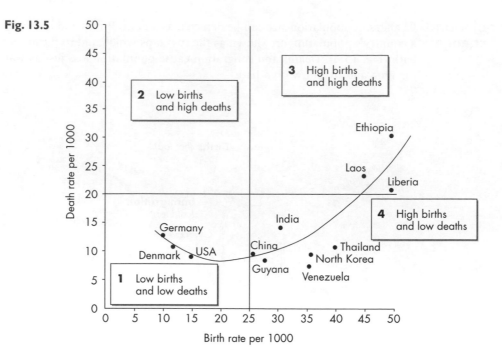

Fig. 13.6 Population by region of world, including predictions to 2100

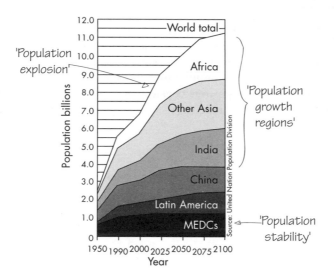

Populations in MEDCs have evolved through four basic stages (see Fig. 13.7).

Stage 1 high birth rate and high death rate, therefore population stability
Stage 2 high birth and falling death rate, therefore population explosion
Stage 3 high but falling birth rate and falling death rate, therefore slowing down in rate of population growth
Stage 4 low birth rate and low death rate, therefore population stability.

Fig. 13.7

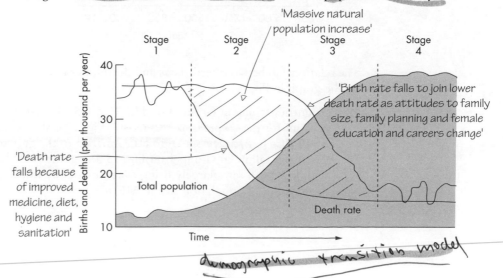

The 'population explosion' is linked with Stage 2 and 3 of this population change model. Falling death rates in the LEDCs are associated with a reduction in infant mortality (deaths before one year) and an improvement in life expectancy. Medical advances, improved hygiene and sanitation, and better diet help explain these changes. Even though the major cause of high population growth may be falling death rates, the fact remains that birth rates in LEDCs are higher than in the MEDCs. The graph shown in Fig. 13.8 shows the falling birth rates in the USA, Japan and the UK since 1960. It corresponds to the later stages of the population change model. Contraception has helped to curb the birth rate, as have changing attitudes in the MEDCs, e.g. greater female employment and more concern to preserve living standards by having smaller families.

Fig. 13.8 The birth rate in some MEDCs

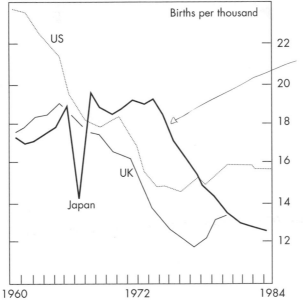

'Low birth rates. Improved contraception has enabled choices with regard to having children. Children can be seen as a financial liability. There is more to life for some women than having children'

▷ Population migration

The urban populations of many LEDCs are at present growing rapidly. There are two reasons for this: first a high rate of general population increase due to high birth rates and falling death rates, secondly large-scale migration from rural areas as a result of the influence of various 'push' and 'pull' factors on the rural population.

The 'push-pull' influences on people living on the Ganges Delta that can lead to them migrating into Calcutta are shown in Fig. 13.9.

Fig. 13.9 Rural-to-urban migration.

The population explosion is largely localised to the LEDCs and it is partly localised even within that area of the world, namely to the **cities**. Cities such as Sao Paulo, Mexico City, Bombay, Bandung, Lagos, Karachi, Bogota, Baghdad, Bangkok, Teheran and Lima have more than doubled their populations since 1980. All the ten fastest growing cities in the world are in LEDCs. The population explosion is associated with an 'exploding' city problem. Up to 1930, the 'millionaire' cities of the world were almost entirely restricted to the MEDCs in North America, Europe and Australasia; now more than half the number are in the LEDCs. One reason for the rapid population growth in the cities is **migration from rural areas**. At present, 30% of the Brazilian population lives in the countryside. However, it is estimated that, as a result of the rural-to-urban migration of people, only 10% will live there by the end of the century. The picture is similar in India, as shown in Table 13.1, with shanty towns an inevitable consequence.

Table 13.1 India – Urban growth, natural increase and migration 1961–91

Years	Growth in urban population (in millions)	Natural increase in urban population (in millions)	(as %)	Migration (number of people moving from rural to urban areas) (in millions)	(as %)
1961–71	22.0	13.3	61	8.7	39
1971–81	29.4	19.0	65	10.4	35
1981–91	49.2	26.1	53	23.1	47

Fig. 13.10 Migration models for MEDCs and LEDCs

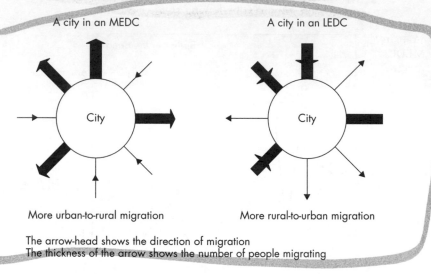

A city in an MEDC — More urban-to-rural migration

A city in an LEDC — More rural-to-urban migration

The arrow-head shows the direction of migration
The thickness of the arrow shows the number of people migrating

Population change and MEDCs

As Fig. 13.10 shows, the migration pattern in the MEDCs is at present in the opposite direction to that in the LEDCs. Urban areas in Britain (Table 13.2) continue to lose population as urban-to-rural migration, or large city-to-smaller-town migration, occurs.

Table 13.2

By Region			By City	
South West England	+10	More rural regions gain population	Inner London	−12
East Anglia	+10		Manchester	−10
East Midlands	+4		Liverpool	−14
Wales	+2		Newcastle	−9
South East England	−1	Population loss from more urbanised regions	Birmingham	−7
Northern England	−3		Sheffield	−3
Scotland	−2		Leeds	−4
North West England	−3			

▷ **Population structure**

The age and sex structure of a population (which is affected by the birth, death and migration rate changes just looked at) can be presented as a diagram known as a **population pyramid**. Though many now drawn in MEDCs are more pillar- or onion-shaped than pyramidal.

Fig. 13.11 Structures for MEDCs and LEDCs

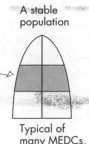

A stable population

'Not pyramidal as size of age-groups not too dissimilar. The old are a major group'

Typical of many MEDCs, an ageing structure

Age (years): 52+, 26–50, 0–25

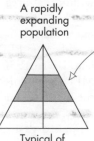

A rapidly expanding population

'A pyramid with a wide base and sharp peak, showing far more young people than older ones'

Typical of many LEDCs, a youthful structure

Population pyramids for four populations are shown in Fig. 13.12.

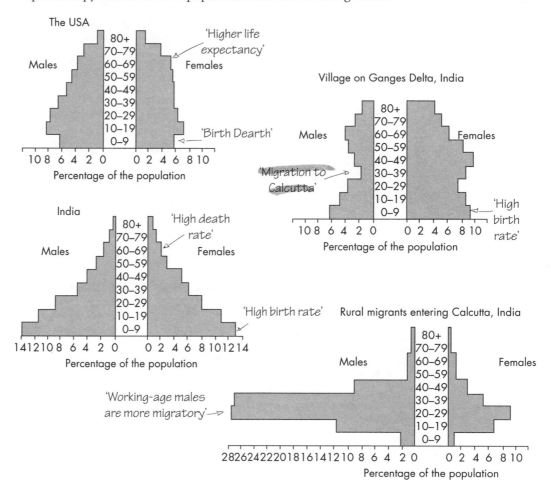

Fig. 13.12

Population structure is important for future planning. When a large proportion of the population is in either the over-60 age-group or the under-19 age-group it is said that the 'burden of dependency' is high. By comparing the size of the working-age population (people aged 19 to 60) with that of non-working age (under 19 and over 60) a **dependency ratio** can be calculated. The dependency ratio in MEDCs worsens as their population structures age. Paying for the growing army of older dependants is a mounting issue in MEDCs.

▷ **Population control**

Many LEDCs recognise that **population control** is necessary if they are to eliminate poverty and generally raise living standards. The 'rush to the towns' has led to the appearance of a new group of urban poor people. They live in appalling shanty towns or on the streets in filth and squalor, without money, and are usually malnourished. This has increased the urgency for tackling population growth. There are, however, those who believe a large population is an asset, rather than a liability, and who would prefer to concentrate on raising the country's productive output.

A number of countries have had some success in lowering their birth rates by, for example, educating people about contraception, or by introducing government incentives or penalties to curb family size. In India there has been a government drive to better educate people about family planning and to encourage sterilisation, with payments to those who accept it. Other countries have done little or nothing to try to stabilise their populations.

▷ **Issue** *China's one-child population policy to better balance population and resources*

Fig. 13.13 The dangers without any control

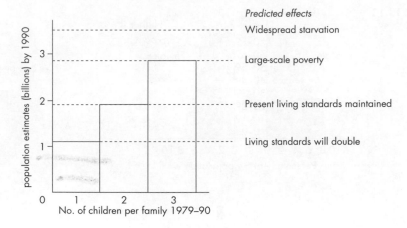

More details of China's policy are given in the following extract (Fig. 13.14).

Fig. 13.14

China's population policy

Its success? – Evidence and Reasons

China's population accounts for 21% of the world total! China's attempts to curb its population growth are therefore significant for the whole planet.

The average number of children per Chinese family has plummeted from 5.8 to 2.4 in the space of 20 years, but this has not been achieved without controversy.

China's communist government has laid down a series of rigid five-year plans for the country's development since coming to power in 1949. The government's policy towards population growth has varied from plan to plan. At first families were encouraged to have many children but recent plans have promoted family planning programmes encouraging birth control, sterilisation and abortion. In 1979 the government took the most drastic measure of all by introducing a 'one-child' policy. Married couples were to be limited to a single child. This would achieve a population ceiling of 1.2 billion by the year 2000, falling to 700 million within 75 years.

Couples breaking the one-child rule could expect to be fined 15% of their earnings, lose pension benefits and child allowances and have to pay for their children's education.

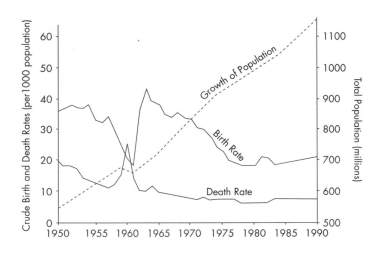

Wan-xi-shao!
Later, longer, fewer,
? ? ?
Family planning slogan
Health care

Education?

Communication of and enforcement policies?

China – some facts

Life expectancy (1991) — 69 years
Infant mortality rate (1991) — 33 per 1000

Average number of births to illiterate mothers (1981) — 4.7 per 1000

Average number of births to mothers with senior secondary education — 2.4 per 1000

Average age of 1st female marriage:
(1949) — 18.5 years
(1979) — 23 years

You cannot convince all the people, all the time
Account of a 46 year old mother in Sichuan province, China

I've borne nine children. The first was a boy but he died. Then I had seven girls and the sixth one died. Only the ninth time did heaven send another son. ...

'Girls are no use. They can't inherit your house or your property. You struggle all your life, but who gets your house in the end? Your daughters all marry out and belong to someone else. ...

'Of course my elder brother will inherit everything in my old home. ... You can't rely on a son-in-law. A son-in-law isn't family – so you can only depend on your son. ...

'Of course, they don't let you have many babies any more. If you have another without permission you get fined. ...

'They fined me the 1,300 yuan (£200). We had to borrow 900 of it. Took us two years to pay it back. Having sons is what women come into the world for. What's the point of it all if you don't have a son? It's what we live for.'

STOP PRESS
The government has relaxed its one-child ruling in many rural areas, particularly if the first born child is a daughter.

Source: 'Chinese Lives' by Zhang Xinxin and Sang Ye, *People* 16, no. 1, 1989

(NEAB)

▷ **Case study** *In-migration to Sao Paulo from rural Brazil*

Fig. 13.15

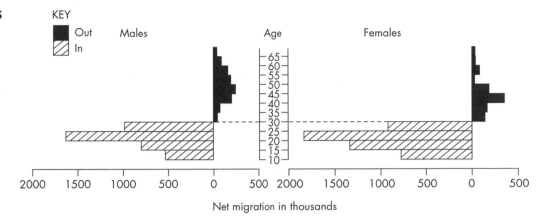

Net migration in thousands

The population of Sao Paulo grew from 7.8 million in 1970 to 18.8 million by 1991 (Fig. 13.15), a growth rate of 140%. 7.8 million of this population growth was thought to be the result of rural-to-urban migration; people from the rural north east, with its drought and crop failure, moving to the more economically successful coastal cities of southern Brazil. The results of a survey of migrants who have moved into Sao Paulo's **favelas** (nine shanty towns on the edge of the city) are shown in Table 13.3. The survey records their reasons for migrating, and any obstacles they encountered. Migrants flock to Sao Paulo as if it were a magnet. The consequence may be another doubling of population by the next century.

favelas

Table 13.3 A survey amongst migrants moving into Sao Paulo

	Reasons		
	Push factors	Pull factors	Migration obstacles
There has been a poor harvest	✓		
There is a greater variety of work in the town		✓	
There are factories in the town		✓	
The wages are higher in the cities		✓	
There is not enough money to improve old farms	✓		
You have very little money for transport			✓
There is little chance of education in the countryside	✓		
There are many entertainments in the town		✓	
Relations may already live in the city		✓	
Relations do not want you to leave the village			✓
Floods damage your land and house	✓		
There are more hospitals in the towns		✓	

Canalisation : straightening river
Irrigation : addition of water to the land by people in order to improve farm prospects

▷ **Key terms** *Make sure you understand and can apply these geographical terms*

Ageing population   Growing proportion of older people in population.

Birth rate   Number of births per 1000 of the population. *PER YEAR.*

Death rate   Number of deaths per 1000 of the population.

Density of population   Number of persons per unit of area, e.g. people per sq. km. = $\dfrac{\text{Population}}{\text{Area}}$

Dependency ratio   Proportion of working-age people to non-working age.

Hostile environment   Inhospitable and unwelcoming natural conditions.

Infant mortality   Number of deaths before the age of one year as a ratio of the number of live births.

Life expectancy   Average length of an individual life.

Migration   Movement of people from one place to another.

Counter urbanisation : urban → rural migration
Land Reclamation : 土地を復旧する. Zuyder Zee scheme, Netherland.

Natural change	A change in population size as a result of the difference between births and deaths.
Population pyramid	A bar graph showing the age and sex structure of a population.
Shanty town	A collection of temporary, makeshift dwellings on the edge of a city, perhaps in a developing country.
Youthful population	A growing population because of a high birth rate.

Refugee: escaping abroad without visas/passport, for political social issues etc.

Suggestions for further work

▶ This is not a particularly suitable topic for fieldwork investigation. Generally speaking, population studies use census data; secondary data not easily collected in the field by GCSE students. It may be possible to carry out a field study, say, of migration patterns affecting an inner city area.

▶ Population study does, however, make a suitable topic area for classroom-based coursework using census data and perhaps planned and directed by your teacher.

▷ STUDENT ANSWER WITH EXAMINER'S COMMENTS

▷ **Longer structured question**

(a) Study the graph, Fig. 13.16, showing world population.

   (i) What is the estimate of the world's population in the year 2000?

   6.1 billion

   (1 mark)

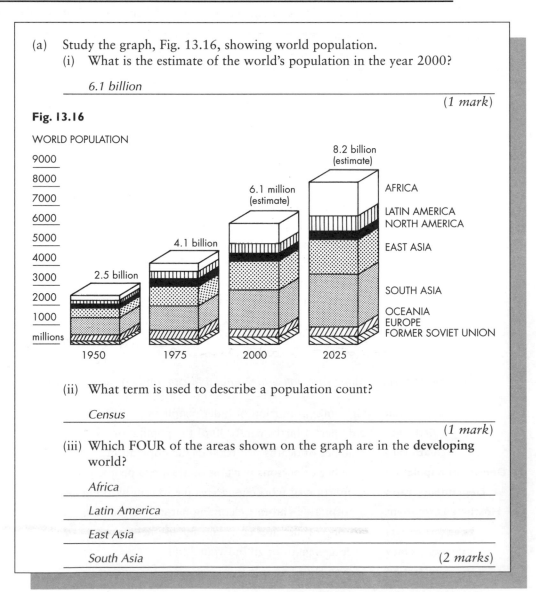

Fig. 13.16

   (ii) What term is used to describe a population count?

   Census

   (1 mark)

   (iii) Which FOUR of the areas shown on the graph are in the **developing** world?

   Africa

   Latin America

   East Asia

   South Asia

   (2 marks)

(iv) Why is the population increasing more rapidly in the developing world?

The developing world tends to experience a lot of infant deaths due to lack of

medical technology, therefore families are required to be bigger to improve

the chances of offspring surviving. Furthermore, a large number of children in

a family can help with the family income, so go to work at an early age.

More children means more income.

Contraception and birth control methods are generally scarce due to lack of

awareness or slow medical technology. Therefore there are no preventative

measures against 'accidental' conception.

Religions and traditions in a lot of countries encourage large numbers of

offspring. Many of these developing countries like India, Bangladesh have

predominant religions practised by many. Therefore children are constantly

tried for.

(6 marks)

'Very good point'

'Lower level 3 response (grade A/B quality)'

(b)   Study Table 13.4, which shows details of five large recent migrations of refugees.

Table 13.4

Origin	Numbers	Destinations	Reasons
Afghanistan	5.9 million	Iran and Pakistan	Civil war
Israel	2.5 million	Occupied Territories (eg Gaza Strip), Jordan and Kuwait	Palestinians resettled after Israeli occupation
Vietnam	1.2 million	Hong Kong, Japan, China and other SE Asian countries	Political and economic factors
Ethiopia	1.1 million	Sudan and Somalia	Drought and civil war
Mozambique	1.0 million	Zimbabwe, South Africa and Malawi	Civil war

(i)   What is a 'refugee'?

A refugee is a person who leaves their country often without passports or

visas in desperation to escape hardship, etc. in their homeland.

(2 marks)

(ii) Use Table 13.4 to state the main cause of people becoming refugees.

War and political unrest.

(1 mark)

(iii) What are the political and economic factors which may have caused people to migrate as refugees?

Political factors *Very often it's government oppression of a group of people*

which causes them to migrate. Civil war often drives those caught in the

crossfire away. Sometimes the government regime can drive people away.

Racial prejudice can be a reason behind political pressure.

Economic factors *Lack of work, lack of jobs, often caused by political unrest*

'Okay, civil war!'

'An example!'

'A good level 2 (grade C) answer; the difference between economic and political migrants is made'

can drive people away. If they have no money to support often large families and no job can be found then those in this situation will leave to try to find work elsewhere.   (*4 marks*)

(c)   Study the world map, Fig. 13.17, showing the major refugee migrations during the 1980s.

Fig. 13.17

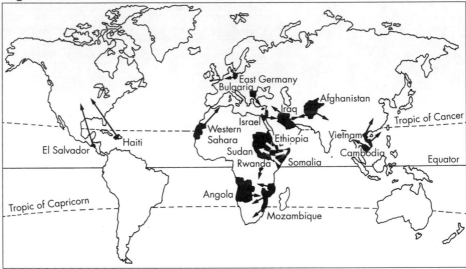

(i)   Comment on the pattern of refugee migrations in the 1980s as shown in Fig. 13.17.

'Good, a number of types of migration recognised'

It seems that, firstly, most countries experiencing emigrating citizens are what we call third world countries; the developing countries perhaps with many unemployed or poor. Secondly, these countries have in the main, suffered political strife resulting in war, e.g. Iraq, Afghanistan, Ethiopia. Some places have harsh governments which people flee from, e.g. E. Germany before German reunification. Some places have desert conditions like W. Sahara, so people leave as the land is unworkable in agriculture and the desert is spreading. The refugees head for developed, 'rich' countries e.g. in the 1980s Mozambique people – S. Africa, E. Germany – Europe, Haiti – USA. (*4 marks*)

'Examples; good!'

'Top Level 2 work'

(ii)   Suggest why the governments of some countries are reluctant to receive refugees and other migrants.

If a government gives permission for an influx of refugees, those possible thousands left behind who decided not to go as no one would have them would suddenly all leave for the new land. That government could have its own problems without having them added to by refugees overcrowding the place. This acceptance could cause religious or cultural friction causing trouble in the country. This acceptance could also worsen relations with a volatile government from which the refugees came, causing international unrest. The accepting government will have to pay for housing, transport, military supervision, etc. which costs a lot and encourages the situation.

'A valid point'

'Some key reasons offered but often not made crisply enough, i.e. high cost; open door for everyone etc.'

(*4 marks*) (*Total 25 marks*) (SEG)

A TUTOR ANSWER

▷ **Short structured question**

(a)   Study the graph in Fig. 13.18 which shows changes that can take place in a country's birth rate, in its death rate, and in its total population over time.

Fig. 13.18

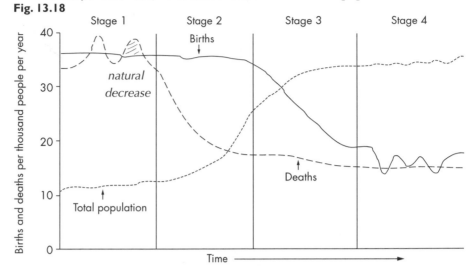

Natural decrease in population: death rate greater than birth rate
Natural increase in population: birth rate greater than death rate

(i)   On the graph, shade and label a period of natural decrease in population.
                                                                    (1 mark)

(ii)   State the natural increase in population per 1000 people per year at the very end of Stage 1.

   3   *(1 mark)*

(iii)   Give two possible reasons for *either* the falling death rate in Stage 2 *or* the falling birth rate in Stage 3.

   Chosen rate: *falling birth rate*

   1 More and better family planning, for example, contraceptives, sterilisation,

   abortion, etc.

   2 Increased desire for material possessions (e.g. cars) and less for large families.
                                                                    (2 marks)

(b)   A country's total population can rise or fall for reasons other than changes in the birth and death rate. With reference to a named country, explain why this can happen.

   Chosen country: *Hong Kong*

   The wealth of Hong Kong in an economically fairly poor part of the world

   has traditionally attracted migrants into the country. Its return in 1997 to

   China is expected to encourage some people to migrate elsewhere, so

   lowering its population.
                                                                    (2 marks)

(c)   Read the following headline which appeared in a British newspaper. (Bangladesh is a less economically developed country – an LEDC.)

> ## Bangladesh problem is 'too many births'

(i) In which stage on the graph does the headline suggest that Bangladesh is?

_2_

(1 mark)

(ii) Suggest why some people in Britain believe that 'too many births' is a problem in Bangladesh and some other LEDCs.

A large birth rate produces quite quickly a large population of young people

of non-working, school age. They are dependent on the older, working-age

population and so put pressure on the country's other resources, especially

finance and food. However, it can be said that a large young population is an

asset; it will lead to a large and cheap labour supply.

(3 marks)
(Total 10 marks)
(NEAB)

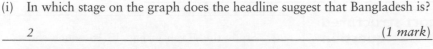

EXAMINATION QUESTION

Tier F only

(a) Study Fig. 13.19, showing birth rates in selected countries.

Fig. 13.19

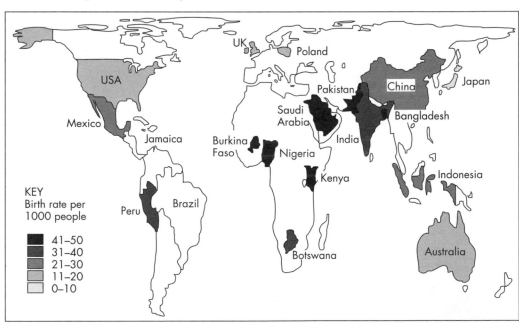

(i) In Brazil the birth rate is 25 per 1000. Show this information by shading the country on Fig. 13.19. (1 mark)

(ii) Use the information in Fig. 13.19 to complete Table 13.5 below by putting the following countries in correct rank order:

Japan   Kenya   Australia   India

Table 13.5

Birth Rate	Country
Highest	1
↑	2
	3 Mexico
↓	4
Lowest	5

(1 mark)

(iii) Give **three** reasons why many people have large families in countries like Nigeria.
(6 lines provided here)   (*3 marks*)

(b) Study Fig. 13.20 showing birth and death rates in China.

Fig. 13.20

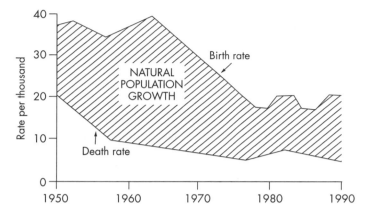

(i) What was the birth rate per thousand in China in 1960? (1 line provided here)
                                                                          (*1 mark*)

(ii) During which one of the following 10-year periods was there most rapid natural population growth in China? **Underline your answer.**
1950–1960   1960–1970   1970–1980   1980–1990   (*1 mark*)

(iii) State **two** problems caused by rapid population growth in LEDCs
(less economically developed countries) (4 lines provided here)   (*2 marks*)

(iv) Give **two** reasons why the death rate in LEDCs has been reduced since 1950.
(4 lines provided here)   (*2 marks*)

(v) For either China, or another named country which you have studied, describe the attempts being made to influence population growth.
Name of country (1 line provided here)
(9 lines provided for rest of answer)   (*4 marks*)
                                                                  (*Total 15 marks*)
                                                                          (*MEG*)

Tier H only

(a) Study Fig. 13.19, showing birth rates in selected countries.
   (i) Use the key to rank any five countries according to the categories given. The country ranked 1 should have the highest birth rate. (5 lines provided here)
                                                                          (*1 mark*)
   (ii) State **one** significant feature of the pattern of birth rates shown in Fig. 13.19.
   (1 line provided here)   (*1 mark*)
   (iii) Name the other **two** factors which must be considered when studying population change in a country. (2 lines provided here)   (*2 marks*)
   (iv) Explain why birth rates vary between countries. (15 lines provided here)
                                                                          (*7 marks*)

(b) Study the news headline on population control in China shown in the box below.

> # Hefty fines for Shanghai couples with second child
>
> They will pay three times their annual income

   (i) With reference to China, or another named country which you have studied, describe the attempts made to influence population growth. (12 lines provided here)   (*6 marks*)
   (ii) Describe how people react to these efforts to influence growth. (6 lines provided here)   (*3 marks*)
                                                                  (*Total 20 marks*)
                                                                          (*MEG*)

EXAMINATION ANSWER

Tier F only

(a) (i) Shading on figure   *(1)*
     (ii) Kenya, India, (Mexico), Australia, Japan   *(1)*
     (iii) Ideas such as high infant mortality rate; lack of birth control; little knowledge/availability of contraception; lack of education; tradition – for example children are wage earners, children look after the old; religious beliefs, etc.*(3)*

(b) (i) 36–38 per 1000   *(1)*
     (ii) 1960–1970   *(1)*
     (iii) Lack of jobs/unemployment; lack of houses; overcrowding; overpopulation; pressure on resources; lack of food/water; crime; lack of health care/medical facilities; more disease; growth of squatter settlements/shanty towns; low standard of living; poverty; lack of education; rapid urban growth; migration of labour; lack of transport; pollution (specified); soil erosion; desertification; deforestation. *(2)*
     (iv) Improvements in health care, sanitation, diet, social conditions, housing conditions, etc.   *(2)*
     (v) For example, attempts to reduce or increase population growth. Ideas such as one child policy, free abortions, later marrying age, government 'spies', family planning clinics, making contraception widely available, immigration restrictions; incentives such as free education, guaranteed work, guaranteed pension, priority in housing, priority in medical care, extra food rations.
     Disincentives such as no state allowances, heavy pay deductions, extra taxes, revoking rewards on birth of second child, etc.
     No mark for name of country.   *(4)*
                                                                         (Total 15)
                                                                            (MEG)

Tier H only

(a) (i) One country from each category   *(1)*
     (ii) High in LEDCs; higher in Africa, S. Asia, S. America, etc.   *(1)*
     (iii) Death rate; migration   *(2)*
     (iv) Ideas such as: availability of contraception/birth control facilities; awareness of contraception; education towards small family size; working women; infant mortality rate; availability of state benefits; effect of government incentives; economic requirement for large family; social requirement for children to look after old; cost of raising children; etc.
     Look for contrasts, development marks may be explaining the contrast.
     Single point marking, credit development.   *(7)*

(b) (i) Example may be of attempts to reduce or increase population growth (e.g. China). Ideas such as: one child policy; free abortions; later marrying age; government 'spies'; family planning clinics; making contraception widely available; immigration restrictions.
     Incentives such as free education; guaranteed work; guaranteed pension; priority in housing; priority in medical care; extra food rations.
     Disincentives such as no state allowances; heavy pay deductions; extra taxes; revoking rewards on birth of second child; etc.
     Also credit pro-natalist ideas such as: to develop the economy in underpopulated countries; build up to war; been through a period of declining population; etc.
     Single point marking, credit development.   *(6)*
     (ii) Ideas such as hostile to policy; infringement of personal freedom; can appreciate need for policy; obey laws; appreciate benefits which accompany policy; limit family size; infanticide; increase in abortions; etc.
     Credit ideas which relate to more than one country.   *(3)*
                                                                         (Total 20)
                                                                            (MEG)

SUMMARY

▷ The distribution of population is not even. Population densities vary from place to place due to physical, social, economic and political factors. More people live in some places than others so that there are densely populated areas and sparsely populated areas within countries and globally.

▷ The size and structure of populations change from place to place and over time. Changes result from birth rates, death rates and migration.

▷ The population size of some places, especially in LEDCs is growing as births exceed deaths. Overpopulation is a major problem in some places.

▷ The population structure of countries, which is important for their future planning for services and employment, varies between countries and is affected by changes in population size. LEDCs with growing populations tend to have a youthful structure; MEDCs a more ageing one. These characteristics are shown by age/sex pyramids.

▷ People migrate in response to their perceptions (view) of opportunities ('pull' factors in the receiving area) and problems ('push' factors in the source area) because population and resources are not balanced. Migration can be international or within countries and has economic and social consequences for both the source and receiving areas. Some migration is voluntary, other involuntary due to political force.

▷ Population change presents opportunities and problems for governments, some of which try to manage these by means of policies and strategies.

Urban structure, change and planning

GETTING STARTED

Most of us live and/or work/study in urban settlements. Whether you are one of this majority or not, try thinking about the present use of land in your home or local town: where are the areas of manufacturing industry, or of more expensive housing? Are there any suburban high street shopping areas, known as OBDs (Ordinary Business Districts)? Do certain types of shop tend to cluster and congregate together in the centre (CBD)?

Urban geography is all around most of us, and this should help your study of this topic area. Important in this topic area is the idea that towns and cities are constantly changing and that this change needs managing and planning if decent environmental quality is to be maintained. You will need to know about changes in both MEDC and LEDC cities so case studies for you to familiarise yourself with are provided in the chapter. This is a key topic area for issues and conflicts of interest between people, and as the topic chart shows, figures in all GCSE syllabuses. Chapter 11 on tertiary activities, and Chapter 15 on transport and traffic clearly support some of the ideas raised in this chapter. Try cross-referencing chapters a little.

LONDON A	LONDON B	MEG A	MEG B	MEG C	NEAB A	NEAB B	NEAB C	NICCEA	SEG A	SEG B	WJEC	IGCSE	TOPIC	STUDY	REVISION 1	REVISION 2
✓	✓	✓	✓	✓	✓	✓		✓	✓	✓	✓	✓	Urbanisation/urban growth/LEDC cities			
✓	✓	✓	✓	✓		✓	✓	✓	✓	✓	✓		Counter-urbanisation/MEDC cities/rural–urban fringe land			
✓	✓			✓	✓	✓	✓		✓	✓	✓	✓	Areas and other processes of urban change/inner cities			
✓	✓	✓	✓	✓	✓	✓		✓	✓	✓	✓	✓	Urban functions and structure/land use zones, and socio-economic and ethnic areas/ urban inequalities			
✓	✓	✓	✓		✓	✓	✓	✓	✓	✓	✓		Urban planning			

WHAT YOU NEED TO KNOW

▷ **Urbanisation**

About 30 per cent of the world's population live in urban areas, that is, settlements with a population greater than 20 000 (towns and cities). The percentage is increasing. In Britain the percentage was roughly 25 in 1800; it is nearer 80 today. This increase in the number of people living in towns and cities is called **urbanisation**.

The rate of urbanisation in LEDCs has been very rapid in recent times, and the trend is predicted to continue as Fig. 14.1 shows.

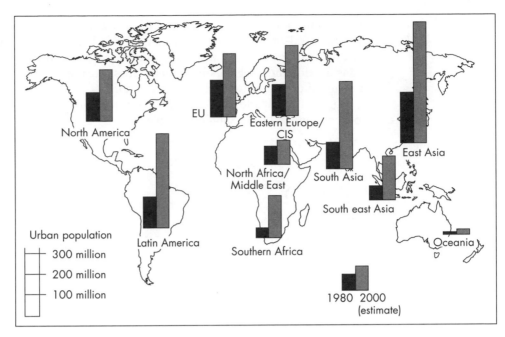

Fig. 14.1 Urban population changes 1980–2000

Urban sprawl

Urban sprawl is the process involved in urbanisation. Towns and cities grow outwards, spreading into the countryside. Sprawl can be a result of ribbon development along major roads. Outlying villages become suburbs of the town/city, as can be seen in Fig. 14.2 for London.

Urban sprawl through suburbanisation can proceed to such an extent that towns and cities merge, producing a **conurbation**. It has been predicted that if urban sprawl continues at its present pace in south-east England, in the next century a massive, continuously built-up area will cover the region. Fig. 14.3 shows the so-called 'Spread City' of south-east England during the next century. The opposite of urbanisation – **counterurbanisation** is also partly to blame as urban dwellers migrate into rural areas and expand villages commutable to and from London.

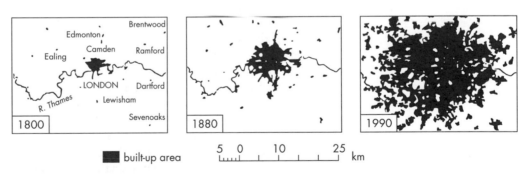

Fig. 14.2 The urban sprawl of London, 1800–1990

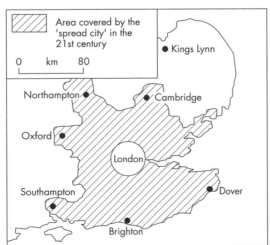

Fig. 14.3 'Spread City' may exist in south-east England by the twenty-first century

Suburbanisation is the process by which a town/city's outer suburbs spread, reaching out into the rural–urban fringe (the **rurban**). Towns become cities, cities become 'million' cities (i.e. populations exceed 1 million), large cities become the core of conurbations, conurbations develop into megalopolises, mega-cities (i.e. populations in teens of millions) form as a result of urban sprawl and suburbanisation.

Fig. 14.4 is a world map showing the distribution of large cities, with populations of 3 to 5 million, and over 5 million people.

Fig. 14.4

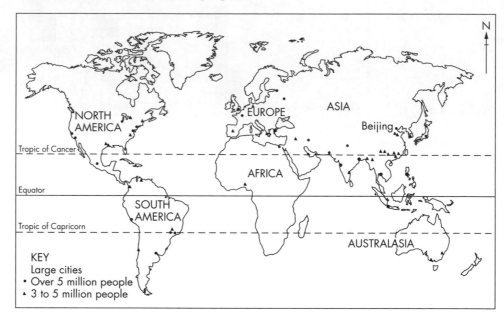

KEY
Large cities
• Over 5 million people
▲ 3 to 5 million people

Conurbation

A **conurbation** is a very large urban area formed by the joining together of several separate expanding towns/cities. Most of the 'green' land which formerly separated them becomes urbanised and a large, continuous, built-up area is produced. Conurbations normally have populations in excess of 1 million. They are the result of urban sprawl. Britain's seven conurbations – Greater London, the West Midlands, south-east Lancashire (Greater Manchester), Merseyside, West Yorkshire, Tyne and Wear, and Clydeside – together contain almost half the population of Britain.

Continued urbanisation in the world has seen not only the development of **'mega-cities'**, with populations of 10 million plus (e.g. Mexico City, Tokyo), but also **super-conurbations** (**megalopolises**). These are continuous, built-up areas covering very large areas and/or very large numbers of people; hundreds of square miles and perhaps 20 million people! Three examples occur in the USA; Boswash (*Bos*ton–New York–Philadelphia–Baltimore–*Wash*ington);Chipitts (*Chi*cago–Detroit–Cleveland–*Pitts*burgh); and Sansan (*San* Francisco–Los Angeles–*San* Diego). Conurbations have themselves coalesced into megalopolises. With continued suburbanisation of people and jobs, and long-distance **commuting** to work developing, will the Boswash megalopolis on the north-east seaboard and the Chipitts megalopolis around the Great Lakes one day coalesce?

Land use zones

Those providing the various functions in a large settlement tend to group together in certain areas, producing a pattern of **zones**. Shops, offices and tall buildings tend to cluster in the centre, which usually coincides with the original site where the settlement began centuries ago. This zone is known as the **CBD** (**Central Business District**). Land is limited and expensive here, so developments are multi-storey. The resident population is low in this part of the town/city. The **population density** (numbers per unit of area) rises rapidly as you travel outwards into the inner-city areas. The inner-city zone may be a zone of transition, i.e. one of mixed and changing land use. Thereafter the density of the resident population tends to fall steadily as you move towards the outer suburbs.

There are various models (simplified generalisations) which have been developed by geographers for American, British, LEDC, etc. cities. Fig. 14.5 shows one developed for British cities which reasonably fits some of them. (The Examination Question at the end of this chapter contains a model for an LEDC city.)

Fig. 14.5 Model for structure of a British city

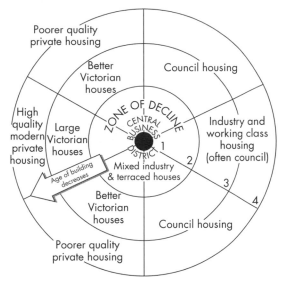

Such land use patterns largely mirror the pattern of land values within the city. The CBD is where land values are highest; housing where it is lowest (Fig. 14.6).

Fig. 14.6 Land values model for an urban area

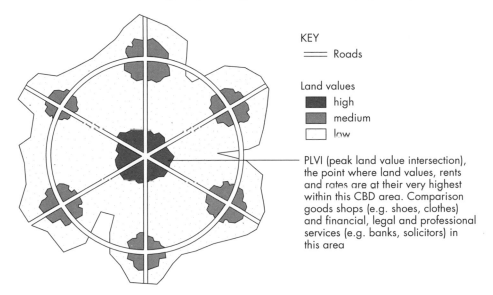

KEY

═══ Roads

Land values
■ high
▨ medium
□ low

PLVI (peak land value intersection), the point where land values, rents and rates are at their very highest within this CBD area. Comparison goods shops (e.g. shoes, clothes) and financial, legal and professional services (e.g. banks, solicitors) in this area

Fig. 14.7 The distribution of ethnic neighbourhoods in Indianapolis, USA

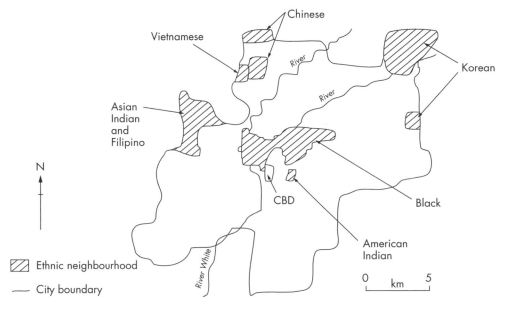

In addition to being able to identify land use zones within urban areas, it is also possible to recognise marked differences between residential areas. These **socio-economic** (i.e. occupational groups) and **ethnic** (i.e. racial and cultural groups) areas often show major inequalities in housing and the provision of services. Many inner-city areas in MEDCs are run-down, decaying, polluted, violent, crime-ridden, lack education and job opportunities, and community amenities, and are in great need of urban renewal/redevelopment. Fig. 14.8 shows the inequalities in income, education and jobs between those living in the black ethnic neighbourhood of Indianapolis and the white population of the city (Fig. 14.7).

Fig. 14.8 Socio-economic information for Indianapolis, USA

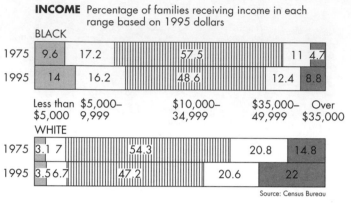

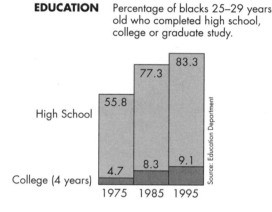

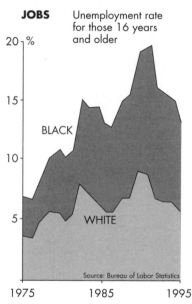

▷ Urban planning

As towns and cities or areas of the town/city grow or decay planners have to develop schemes to improve the quality of the environment.

Planning decisions to tackle problems of CBD congestion, inner-city decay, shanty town development and sprawl around the rural–urban fringe are influenced by property developers, financial institutions, local authorities, governments and, occasionally, local pressure groups such as residents. Conflicts obviously arise between them, and clearly not everyone wins. There are winners and losers, but environmental quality is increasingly recognised as highly important, especially in MEDCs.

Examples of schemes proposed by the planning committees of LEDC and MEDC cities may include decisions to:

▷ develop derelict dockland areas
▷ improve run-down inner-city flats and houses (slum areas)
▷ develop a scheme to reduce traffic congestion
▷ get rid of shanty towns and rehouse residents
▷ clean up the rivers and create a more attractive environment, perhaps a leisure park
▷ improve water supply and sewerage facilities.

Shanty towns

A **shanty town** is an illegal squatter settlement built of tents and shacks made out of scrap material on unoccupied land on the edge of or within the city. They develop spontaneously and grow very quickly; the number of migrants from the countryside is so large that the city authorities cannot house them. They arrive penniless but hope 'to make it' in the city. Shanty towns are features of many large cities, especially in LEDCs. While they are usually to be found on unused land on the edge of the city, there are examples on unused land within the city.

Fig. 14.9 Issues which shanty towns pose for urban planners

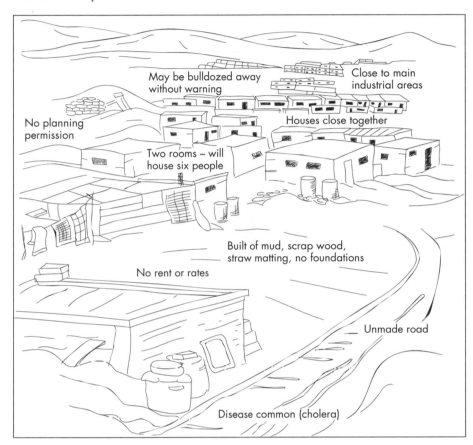

Issue Pressures on the outerland and rural–urban fringe land of Rio de Janeiro, Brazil

Fig. 14.10 The structure and urban sprawl of Rio

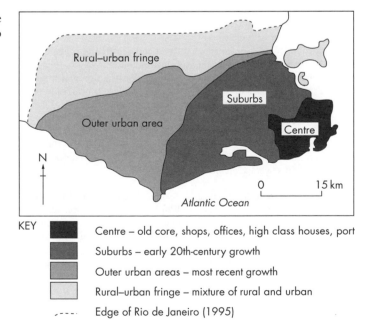

Fig. 14.11 Rio's changing population 1955–95

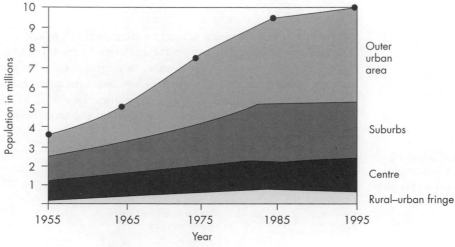

Fig. 14.12 The growth of Rio's Favela (shanty town) households, 1985–95

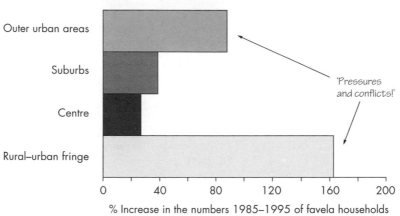

% Increase in the numbers 1985–1995 of favela households

▷ **Case study**   *Urban planning to improve Madras, India: The work of the Madras Metropolitan Development Authority (MMDA)*

MMDA presents to the people of Madras, the plan for a better city.

Madras will undergo a major transformation following on from the work of the Madras Urban Development Project. This World Bank assisted Project is designed to promote low cost solutions to the problems of the metropolis and ensure its orderly growth in future.

Sites and Services:
The Project provides for development of three sites at Arumbakkam, Villivakkam and Kodungalyur to provide housing primarily for the economically weaker section and will benefit 74 000 people. Serviced land for commercial and small scale industrial uses and community facilities at the three sites to provide employment and develop self-sufficient communities.

Slum Improvement:
In 85 slum areas 1 26 500 persons will be provided with community facilities such as common lavatories, baths, drinking water fountains, lighting, paved pathways and sewerage facilities.

Small Scale Business:
This component would created 4000 jobs in small scale activities and 5000 jobs in cottage industries in the three sites and service areas and the 85 slums selected for improvement.

Maternal and Child Health:
This component would provide pre-school education for 17 000 children under the age of 6 years.

All these children and 7000 expectant and nursing mothers will be provided with supplementary nutrition and immunisation against disease.

Water Supply and Sewerage:
Interim measures are being undertaken to improve the existing distribution system. Extensions and additions will also be effected.

Road and Traffic Improvement:
Construction of a 12 km long inner ring road to relieve traffic congestion. Construction and improvements of 200 km of footpaths, 50 km of bicycle tracks, nine pedestrian subways and one overbridge are in progress.

Bus Transport:
285 buses to be added to the existing fleet; construction of 3 depots, 8 terminals and 400 passenger shelters will also be undertaken.

Technical assistance to MMDA:
While the major components of the Project will be implemented by nine other government agencies, MMDA will play the crucial role of long-term planning and overseeing the entire Project so that benefits accrue to the city quickly.
And in time, MMDA will have initiated a change which will make Madras a better place to live in.

 – building a better Madras. For you.

Fig. 14.13 Plans for development at Kodungalyur, Madras

Residential	152 090
Community facilities	65 709
Roads/paths	87 701
TOTAL AREA	305 500
POPULATION on completion	12 065
COST OF PLOTS	R2300 - R7000

The Madras Urban Development Project

This earlier project had a so-called 'master plan' for Madras (Fig. 14.14). The main features were a series of urban nodes and satellite towns designed to relieve congestion and pressure in the city proper.

There were to be six **urban nodes** (an urban node is simply a new, planned concentration of urban growth), all close to the city and connected to it by public transport, and each planned to contain a population of between 200 000 and 300 000. Beyond the urban nodes, about 20 kilometres from the edge of the city, four new satellite towns were to be built, each one of which would be self-sufficient in terms of employment and facilities, commerce and housing.

Fig. 14.14 The 'master plan' for Madras

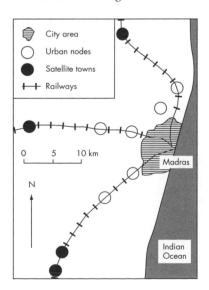

▷ **Key terms**   *Make sure you understand and can apply these geographical terms*

Bridge point	A convenient place to build a bridge over a river.
Central business district	A central zone characterised by shops and offices; often coincides with the historical centre of settlement.
Conurbation	A very large urban area formed when two or more towns grow and take over most of the land separating them.
Counterurbanisation	The loss of urban population as urban livers relocate in rural areas.
Land-use zone (or functional zone)	An area of an urban settlement within which the majority of the land is used for similar purposes.
Range	The maximum distance people are prepared to travel to obtain a good or service.
Site	The exact location; actual plot of land of a settlement, building or feature.
Sphere of influence	The area served or influenced in some way by a settlement.
Suburb	An area of mainly residential land use in the outer part of an urban area.
Threshold population	The number of people needed to provide sufficient trade for a function to break even.
Urban redevelopment	Existing buildings redeveloped.
Urban renewal	Urban areas cleared and new buildings/land uses put in place.
Urban sprawl	The outward growth of an urban settlement.
Urbanisation	The growth of towns and cities with perhaps an increasing proportion of the total population living in these settlements.
Zone of transition	An area in a town surrounding the CBD in the which the CBD is growing – an area of mixed and changing land use. It is also known as the **inner city, inner suburbs** or **twilight zone**.

Suggestions for further work

▷   There are endless possibilities for fieldwork with this topic area. We give just a few examples:

1   To what extend does land use vary in the CBD of the town and why?
2   What factors influence the size and shape of the town's sphere of influence?
3   To what extent does the range of services offered by a settlement relate to its population size and vary within the city?
4   How does quality of life and environment vary between the residential areas of the town/city?

▷   Many students undertake urban enquiries, especially on functions, zoning and urban inequalities.

STUDENT ANSWER WITH EXAMINER'S COMMENTS

(a)   Study Fig. 14.15, showing the population size and growth rates of some South American cities (1990).

Fig. 14.15

'Good, height and shading correct'

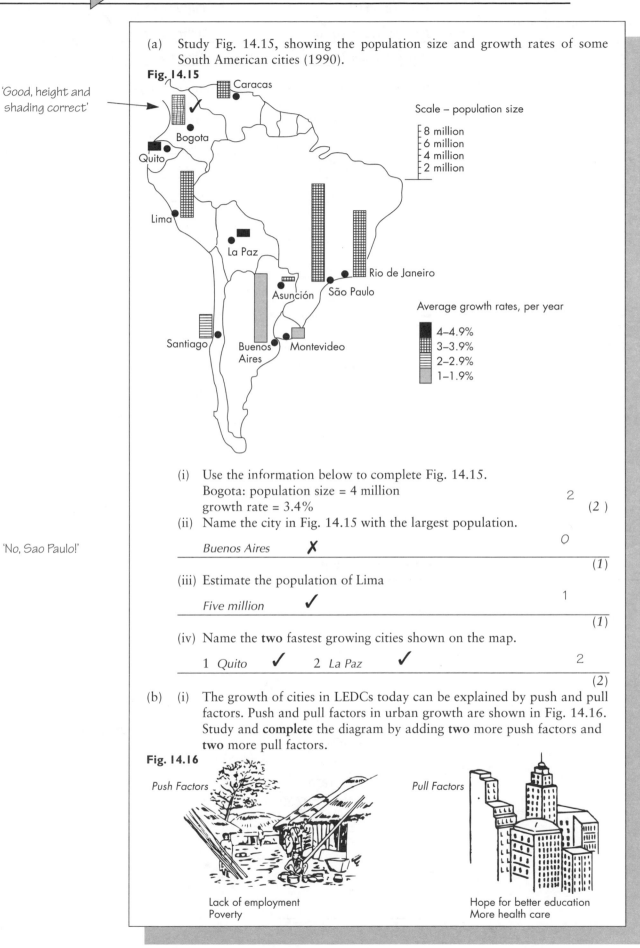

Scale – population size

8 million
6 million
4 million
2 million

Caracas
Bogota
Quito
Lima
La Paz
Rio de Janeiro
Asunción
São Paulo
Santiago
Buenos Aires
Montevideo

Average growth rates, per year

4–4.9%
3–3.9%
2–2.9%
1–1.9%

(i)   Use the information below to complete Fig. 14.15.
Bogota: population size = 4 million
growth rate = 3.4%

2

(2)

(ii)   Name the city in Fig. 14.15 with the largest population.

'No, Sao Paulo!'

Buenos Aires   ✗

0

(1)

(iii)   Estimate the population of Lima

Five million   ✓

1

(1)

(iv)   Name the **two** fastest growing cities shown on the map.

1 *Quito*   ✓   2 *La Paz*   ✓

2

(2)

(b)   (i)   The growth of cities in LEDCs today can be explained by push and pull factors. Push and pull factors in urban growth are shown in Fig. 14.16. Study and **complete** the diagram by adding **two** more push factors and **two** more pull factors.

Fig. 14.16

Push Factors

Pull Factors

Lack of employment
Poverty

Hope for better education
More health care

Push Factors	Pull Factors	
Poor housing conditions ✓	Better job prospects ✓	
Bad water, sanitation supplies i.e. disease ✓	Better housing with basic needs ✓	4
		(4)

'Watch your SPG mark!'

'Clear factors – good!'

(ii) When people come to the city from the countryside they often have to live in areas of poor housing called shanty towns (squatter settlements). Describe **three** features of a shanty town.

1   Lack of basic sanitation, e.g. water supply ✓

2   Vast areas of slum houses ✓

3   Poor housing conditions, leads to disease and illness ✓   3
(3)

(iii) How do city authorities attempt to improve the quality of life for people living in shanty towns?

City authorities attempt to improve the quality of life for people living in shanty towns by trying to improve the area, by trying to upgrade the area, e.g. building water supplies, ✓ try to help with health care of the people. ✓   1
(3)

'Used nearly all the space and said nothing!'

'Ha! Ha! A point made but do try to be specific. Name places and schemes if you can'

(iv) City authorities are not always successful in improving the quality of life for such people. Explain why.

Some people do not like interference from city authorities and see this as an ✓ invasion of their space and privacy. ✓ Also people are set in their ways and do not want to be helped.   2 ✓
(4)
(Total 20)
(NEAB)

'Again, too broad and vague. Haven't you studied a shanty town development in a specific city that wasn't successful?'

A TUTOR ANSWER

▶ **Short-answer questions**

1   The map in Fig. 14.17 shows the changing boundary of a city in an MEDC.

Fig. 14.17

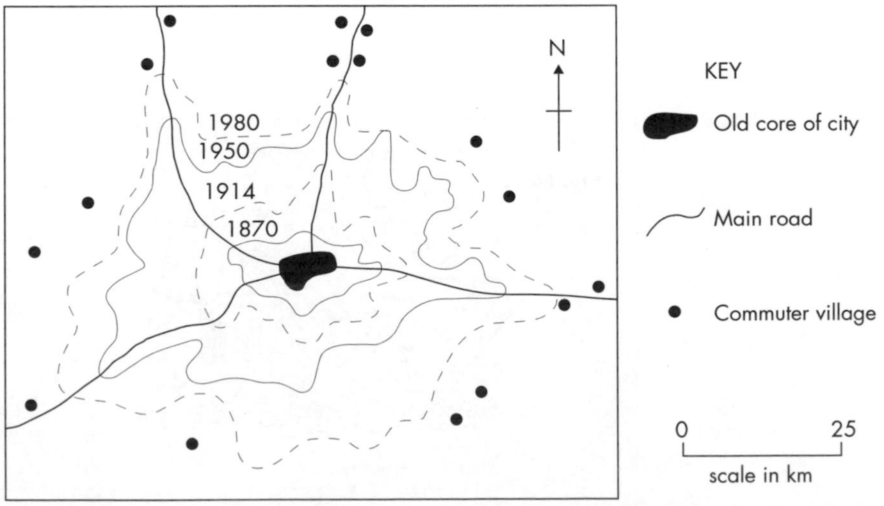

KEY

Old core of city

Main road

Commuter village

scale in km

(a) The map shows urban sprawl. What is urban sprawl?

When a town or city grows outwards so that its boundary spreads.

(1 mark)

(b) Describe **two** features of the urban sprawl of the city shown on the map

(i) *has been greatest along the main roads. This is known as ribbon*

development.

(ii) *The greatest recent (1950–1980) sprawl has been to the north of the city.*

(2 marks)

2   The graph in Fig. 14.18 shows how population density changes with distance from the centre of a city.

Fig. 14.18

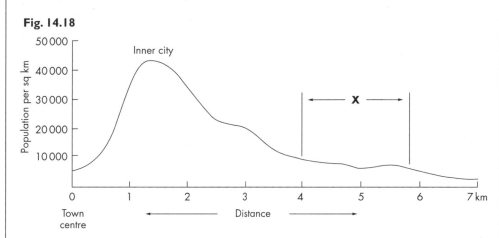

(a) The area marked **X** on the graph corresponds to the part of the town known as
A   the Green Belt
B   the twilight zone
C   the Central Business District
D   the rural fringe
E   the suburbs   (1 mark)

'The correct answer. The area marked is in the town but close to its edge'

(b) State the relationship between population density and distance from the town centre to the inner city.

Increases approximately fivefold.

(1 mark)

(c) Give **one** reason for this relationship.

Densities are low in the town centre where few people live. Inner cities

are major residential areas.

(1 mark)

(d) State the relationship between population density and distance from the inner city to the outer city.

Decreases, falling roughly to the density of the town centre

(1 mark)

(e) Give **one** reason for this relationship.

Towards the outer city, houses become larger, gardens more sizeable and

open spaces generally increase as environmental quality of the town improves.

(1 mark) (Total 8 marks)
(ULEAC London)

EXAMINATION QUESTION

(a) Study Fig. 14.19, showing estimates of the world urban population from 1955 to 2015.

Fig. 14.19

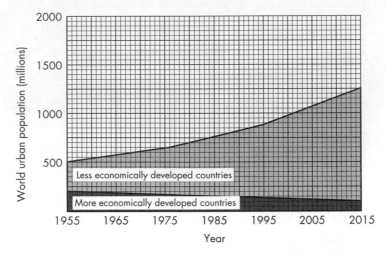

(i) What was the total world urban population in 1955? (1 line provided here)
(1 mark – Tier F only)

(ii) What is the estimated total world urban population in 2015?
(1 line provided here) *(1 mark – Tier F only)*

(iii) In which part of the world is there an increasing number of people moving to cities? (1 line provided here) *(1 mark – Tier F only)*

(iv) State **two** reasons why there is an increasing number of people moving to cities in Less Economically Developed Countries (LEDCs). (6 lines provided here)
(2 marks – Tiers F and H)

EITHER (TIER F)

(v) Suggest why some people think that is important to try to control the number of people moving to cities in Less Economically Developed Countries (LEDCs). (6 lines provided here) *(2 marks – Tier F only)*

OR (TIER H)

(v) Fig. 14.19 suggests that there will be nearly three times as many people living in urban areas in 2015 than there were in 1955.
How can the demands of such a rapidly increasing urban population be met?
(11 lines provided here) *(4 marks – Tier H only)*

(b) Study Fig. 14.20, showing urban models for a city in a More Economically Developed Country (MEDC) and a city in a Less Economically Developed Country (LEDC).

Fig. 14.20

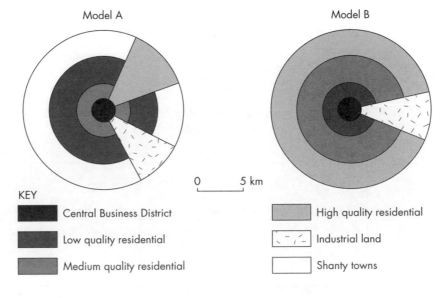

(i) Use Fig. 14.20 to complete the description of the main features of the urban models in Table 14.1.

Table 14.1

Main Features	Model A	Model B
Central Business District	city centre	
High Quality Residential	in a wedge shape around the edge	not present

(3 marks – Tier F only)

(ii) Which of the urban models is for a city in a Less Economically Developed Country (LEDC)? (1 line provided here) *(1 mark – Tiers F and H)*

(iii) State **two** reasons for your answer to part (ii). (6 lines provided here) *(2 marks – Tiers F and H)*

(iv) What is a 'shanty town'? (6 lines provided here) *(2 marks – Tier F only)*

(v) Choose *either* Model A *or* Model B and explain how its urban land use pattern has developed.
Model (1 line provided here)
Explanation (15 lines provided here) *(5 marks – Tier H only)*

(c) Study Fig. 14.21 which shows an area on the edge of the town of Bournemouth where there are new housing developments.

Fig. 14.21

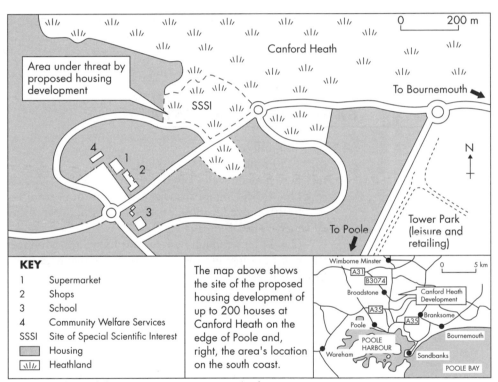

Source: adapted from *16–19: Core Geography* (Longman) 1994

EITHER (TIER F)

(i) What is the meaning of the term 'housing development? (1 line provided here) *(1 mark – Tier F only)*

(ii) State **two** features of the land shown on Fig. 14.21 as an 'area under threat'. (4 lines provided here) *(2 marks – Tier F only)*

(iii) Suggest **two** advantages of making Canford Heath into part of Bournemouth's Green Belt. (6 lines provided here) *(2 marks – Tier F only)*

(iv) State **one** disadvantage of making Canford Heath into part of Bournemouth's Green Belt. (3 lines provided here) *(1 mark – Tier F only)*

(v) What problems might arise from the building of supermarkets and leisure and retail parks, such as those shown on Fig. 14.21? (11 lines provided here) *(4 marks – Tier F only)* *(Total 25 marks – Tier F)*
(SEG)

OR (TIER H)

Fig. 14.22

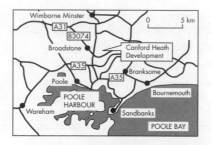

The map in Fig. 14.21 shows the site of the proposed development of 200 houses at Canford Heath and, above, Fig. 14.22 shows the area's location on the south coast. The Heath is home to some of Britain's rarest reptiles and birds, including the Dartford warbler, the smooth snake and the sand lizard. Conservationists will argue in the Courts next week that in allowing for these houses to be built the council failed in its legal duty to take conservation into account.
Source: adapted from *16–19: Core Geography* (Longman) 1994

(i)   Why is part of Canford Heath an 'area under threat'? (7 lines provided here)
(4 marks – Tier H only)

(ii)   What are the issues that arise from the building of supermarkets and leisure and retail parks, such as those shown on Fig. 14.21? (13 lines provided here)
(7 marks – Tier H only) (Total 25 marks – Tier H)
(SEG)

► EXAMINATION ANSWER

(a) (i)   500 million *(1) (Tier F)*
 (ii)   1250 million *(1) (Tier F)*
 (iii)   Less Economically Developed Countries *(1) (Tier F)*
 (iv)   (2 x 1) Seeking jobs; social attractions/opportunities; opportunities for better health care/education; problems in rural areas, etc. *(2) (Tiers F and H)*
 EITHER (TIER F)
 (v)   (2 x 1) Not enough houses/poor living and sanitation conditions; lack of jobs; risk of crime; increased pollution; relative neglect of rural areas; etc. *(2) (Tier F)*
 OR (TIER H)
 (v)   Level 1 – 1 mark
 Basic explanation:
 Need more food/jobs/better transport/infrastructure
 Level 2 – 2 – 3 marks
 Clear explanation:
 Housing and infrastructure investment necessary to provide at least modest standards of living and prevent outbreaks of diseases and social unrest
 Level 3 – 4 marks
 Full explanation:
 Development of a country; resources required in order to finance expansion and improvement; political will and expertise to ensure that the changes are supported and sustainable *(4) (Tier H)*

(b) (i)   (3 x 1)

Table 14.2

Main Features	Model A	Model B
Central Business District	city centre	**City centre**
High Quality Residential	in a wedge shape	**Around the edge**
Shanty towns	around the edge	not present

(3) (Tier F)

 (ii)   Model A *(1) (Tiers F and H)*

(iii) (2 x 1) More Economically Developed countries do not have shanty towns; more high quality housing; more medium quality housing, etc.   *(2) (Tiers F and H)*

(iv) (2 x 1) Poor, very low quality housing; made of any available building materials; usually lacking amenities and sanitation; unplanned/illegal; large sprawling area on edge of large city or near industrial areas/polluted areas, etc.   *(2) (Tier F)*

(v) *EITHER* Model A
Level 1/2 – 1–2 marks
Basic/clear explanation:
CBD at city centre/historic core/most accessible point; shanties on cheapest land outside city
Level 3 – 3–5 marks
Full explanation:
Shops/services developed at most accessible point and attract further development; land values nearest city centre are higher than further out due to accessibility, so better housing developed; industrial land along main transport arteries/major rivers with industrial sites on the flood plains, etc.   *(5) (Tier H)*
OR Model B
Level 1/2 – 1–2 marks
Basic/clear explanation:
CBD at city centre/historic core/most accessible point; industry on marshy/noisy/polluted land, etc.
Level 3 – 3–5 marks
Full explanation:
Shops/services develop at most accessible point and attract further development; industry started close to city with worker housing nearby, often high density and poor quality; better housing further out due to transport improvements, etc. *(5) (Tier H)*

EITHER (TIER F)

(c) (i) Planned area of residential land; housing estate   *(1)*

(ii) (2 x 1) Heathland/some trees; Site of Special Scientific Interest   *(2)*

(iii) (2 x 1) Protect it from further development; stop the urban area from sprawling too far; keep the area more open and attractive to nearby residents, etc.   *(2)*

(iv) Little other building land available; push up land/housing prices; stop the heath owners from making money, etc.   *(1)*

(v) Level 1 – 1–2 marks
Basic identification of problems such as:
Extra traffic/noise/litter; loss of trade for town centres
Level 2 – 3–4 marks
Clear identification of problems and development:
New roads take up land and bring traffic into edge of residential areas; large areas of land used up that could otherwise be used for residential/amenity/community; 'corner' shops and town centre shops lose custom and may face closure; problems of access for people without cars; less variety than normally available in a town centre, etc.   *(4)*
(Total 25) (Tier F)

OR TIER H

(c) (i) (4 x 1) Further expansion of urban area/demand for more houses; specific demand for new housing with associated amenities; lack of alternative accessible building land; relatively level land/low building costs; perceived by some to be of low value (especially agriculturally).   *(4)*

(ii) Level 1 – 1–2 marks
Basic recognition of issues:
Loss of town centre trade; large areas of land used; encouragement to car ownership, etc.
Level 2 – 3–4 marks
Clear recognition/understanding:
Because new retail areas are more accessible, with free parking, they are more attractive to motorists; town centre shops likely to decline as demand for their goods/services falls; the market becomes dominated by a few large retailers and smaller businesses suffer, etc.
Level 3 – 5–7 marks

Full understanding:
Above, plus recognition that new retail areas suit the wealthier, mobile, middle class leaving problems for others in society; less choice, less service and higher costs; arguably retail developments can relieve pressure on town centres, reducing the need for ugly multi-storey car parks, enabling pedestrianisation to proceed, leaving opportunities for more specialised shopping as rent falls – or 'ghost' towns develop, etc.

(7)
(*Total 25*) (*Tier H*)
(*SEG*)

SUMMARY

▷ An increasing proportion of the world's population live in urban areas. This urbanisation is strong in LEDCs.

▷ Counterurbanisation occurs in many MEDCs and has consequences for urban areas and the receiving rural settlements.

▷ Urban settlements are constantly changing; growing or decaying, generally or in areas, because of urbanisation, counterurbanisation, and other processes.

▷ Urban settlements usually have a pattern of land use. There is a tendency for similar land users, both commercial and residential, to concentrate in distinct areas of the town/city. These patterns and zones change and become very distinctly different.

▷ Urban change can bring problems for some people and for the quality of the environment. Change is often due to political or financial power.

▷ Urban planning strategies are often necessary to meet the challenges and problems created by urban change. They rarely meet everyone's needs and are often either ineffective or not attempted in LEDC cities.

▷ Urban settlements in LEDCs generally differ from those in MEDCs.

development

Chapter 15

Transport, trade and interdependence

⊳ **GETTING STARTED**

As the topic chart below shows, transport and trade have to be studied in all syllabuses to a lesser or greater extent. The movement of goods and people is vital for economic development, so clearly you should use this chapter alongside those on development and welfare (Chapter 9) and manufacturing industry (Chapter 12). Transport and urban settlements (Chapter 14) is another clear area of overlap and integration.

We live in an integrated and interdependent world. There is increasing global interdependence, especially through trade, and made possible by improved transport. This is an important idea at GCSE across the syllabuses, and often referred to as **globalisation**. A list of other terms with which you should be familiar is again given at the end of the chapter.

LONDON A	LONDON B	MEG A	MEG B	MEG C	NEAB A	NEAB B	NEAB C	NICCEA	SEG A	SEG B	WJEC	IGCSE	TOPIC	STUDY	REVISION 1	REVISION 2
✓	✓	✓	✓	✓	✓	✓	✓	✓	✓	✓	✓	✓	Road transport systems			
	✓	✓	✓	✓			✓		✓	✓			Urban traffic			
✓				✓	✓	✓	✓	✓	✓		✓		World trade patterns, and trade and development			
✓	✓	✓	✓	✓	✓			✓		✓	✓	✓	Trans/Multinational companies, and interdependence of industries and trading nations			

⊳ **WHAT YOU NEED TO KNOW**

 Transport
There has been a transport revolution, especially in MEDCs, over the past 30 years. The changes in transport and communications have had a major effect on the distribution of goods and on personal mobility. Airports and motorways have developed rapidly, and the number of cars has increased sixfold in 20 years. Transport **networks** have been built, extended and improved so that distance is now less of a barrier to the movement of people, goods and ideas. A network is the pattern formed as roads, railways, etc. connect places together.

Good transport is essential to economic development. Without a system of effective transport many of the industrial and commercial activities in the country would be strictly limited. A look at the differences in transport provision between an MEDC and an LEDC is revealing. It is hardly surprising that many LEDCs, e.g. Brazil, give such high priority to the development of transport networks.

Fig. 15.1 The route of the Trans-Amazonian Highway in Brazil

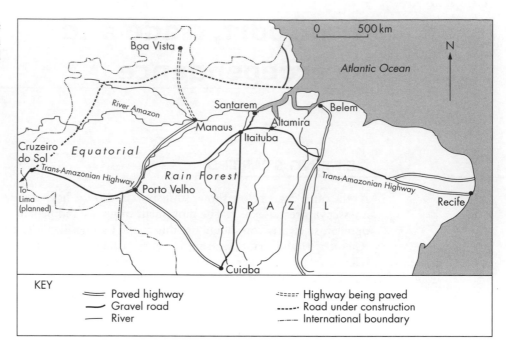

Accessibility

Transport is designed to make movement possible. Some places on a network are easier to get to than others. This idea is referred to as '**accessibility**'. It is a very practical idea with lots of applications in the real world. The best location for a superstore to serve a large region will be the one accessible to the largest number of people. It is interesting to note how the building of motorways has improved the accessibility of places, e.g. East Anglia as a result of building the M11. It is equally interesting to watch Ashford, Kent becoming a boom town thanks to Channel Tunnel transport developments; roads linking into Ashford International station on the Eurostar line (Fig. 15.2).

Fig. 15.2 Ashford, Kent – a booming town thanks to transport developments

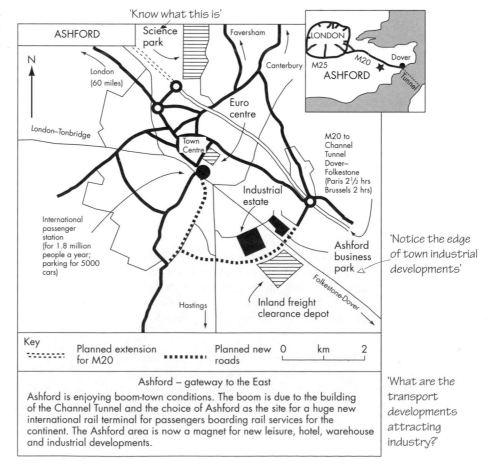

Ashford – gateway to the East

Ashford is enjoying boom-town conditions. The boom is due to the building of the Channel Tunnel and the choice of Ashford as the site for a huge new international rail terminal for passengers boarding rail services for the continent. The Ashford area is now a magnet for new leisure, hotel, warehouse and industrial developments.

Movement and transport are all about minimising distance. Distance can be measured in a number of ways. For example:

1 in kilometres or miles – this is known as **space-distance**
2 in minutes, hours – this is known as **time-distance**
3 in pounds – this is known as **economic-distance** or **cost-distance**.

Space-distance is fixed and cannot be changed by people. Time-distance and cost-distance have been changed by developments in technology. The world really is a smaller place today than it was in the past; it has been estimated that the development of air travel during the twentieth century has had the effect of 'shrinking' the USA by a factor of 200 in terms of time-distance over the past 50 years. Journey times are now about 200 times quicker than they were in the 1930s.

The world being a small place is behind the idea of the **global economy,** the world being 'a global village' and the use of the term, **globalisation.** Improvements in transport and communication have been the key.

The graph (Fig. 15.3) plots transport costs against distance for three forms of transport. Costs increase with distance for all forms of transport, but over short distances road transport is cheapest. This may help to explain the explosion in road transport over recent years, which can be seen as a transport-environment system (Fig. 15.4).

Fig. 15.3

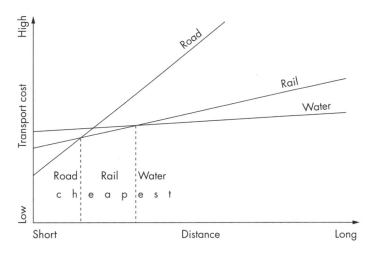

Traffic congestion

Urban road traffic congestion is perhaps the biggest issue and problem in the geography of transport, as the recent headlines have shown.

Move to 'bury' London's city traffic crisis

Traffic-choked city on the road to nowhere

The problem may, unless well managed, get worse as car ownership in Britain rises to the higher levels found in the USA and wealthier parts of Europe, e.g. Germany, France, etc.

Various transport improvements have been introduced into urban areas to help to solve this problem and the resulting concerns to people (e.g. delays to journeys, road traffic accidents, etc.). These include road-widening schemes, the building of inner relief roads and outer ring roads (urban motorways through the built-up area and around the suburbs or edge of the town/city), pedestrianising town centres so that they become traffic-free, turning town/city centre roads into one-way systems, developing tidal traffic flows along major roads, developing park-and-ride schemes (large, free suburban car parks with free bus services to and from the city centre) and the development of rapid transit systems (e.g. the London Docklands light railway, Sheffield's supertram and the West Midland Metro, joining Birmingham and Wolverhampton by tram-like vehicles).

Fig. 15.4   (a) INPUTS

Home produced oil
How many years supply?

Forties
Piper
Brent
Ninian
The North Sea

Imported oil
An accessible source?

× Oil fields

Syria
Iraq
Iran
Jordan
Kuwait
The Gulf
Saudi Arabia
Red Sea
U.A.E.

0 200 400 600
km

(b) PROCESSES

Burning of oil by
petrol-driven cars

diesel-driven trains
INTER CITY →

kerosene-driven planes

50% of all oil used in western Europe is used by cars

(c) OUTPUTS

Locally

lead

Internationally

oxidation in cloud,
nitric acid

carried by
prevailing winds

hot gases rise

Scandinavia
lake

oxides of nitrogen
e.g. UK

The road transport system and its environmental effects is shown in Fig. 15.4. The road transport system in many MEDCs is a source of conflict between different groups of people. The M25 motorway runs right round the edge of London, linked to roads from other parts of the country, making it much easier to drive between places on either side of London without going through the built-up area. Some people are in favour of the motorway (e.g. firms in towns north of London sending goods by road to places south of London, or people living in central London on streets that were used by heavy lorries), others are against it (e.g. people living alongside it now, or people who believe that rather than relieving congestion it has generated more traffic in and around London).

▷ World trade

Fig. 15.5

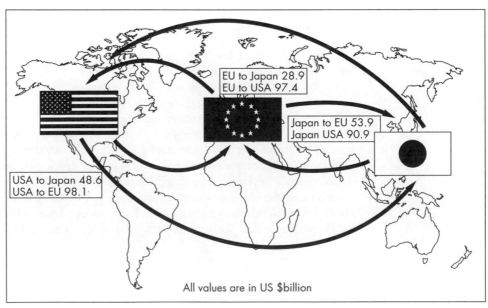

EU to Japan 28.9
EU to USA 97.4

Japan to EU 53.9
Japan USA 90.9

USA to Japan 48.6
USA to EU 98.1

All values are in US $billion

Three supra-national economic unions, i.e. the USA, the EU and Japan, dominate world trade; though the NICs (newly industrialising countries) to the west and south of Japan and around the Pacific, e.g. Taiwan, Hong Kong, South Korea and Singapore, are taking a growing share. Trade between MEDCs (e.g. USA, EU and Japan) and LEDCs remain characterised by the pattern shown in Fig. 15.6. MEDC manufactured goods are traded for LEDC primary products (food, drink, raw materials, etc.) at prices favourable to the MEDCs. LEDCs become dependent, as Fig. 15.7 for The Gambia shows, on a narrow range of poorly-priced primary products. Recent studies showed that LEDC farmers received no more than 20p for soft fruits they grew which were subsequently sold in British supermarkets for over £2.

Fig. 15.6 Primary and manufactured products as % of total imports and exports for selected regions

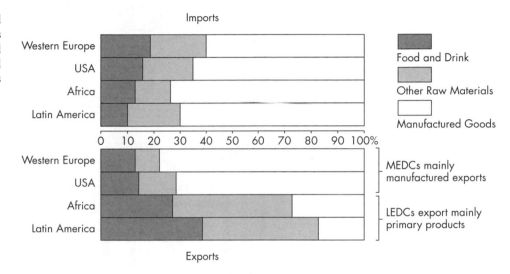

Fig. 15.7 The Gambia's trading pattern, 1995

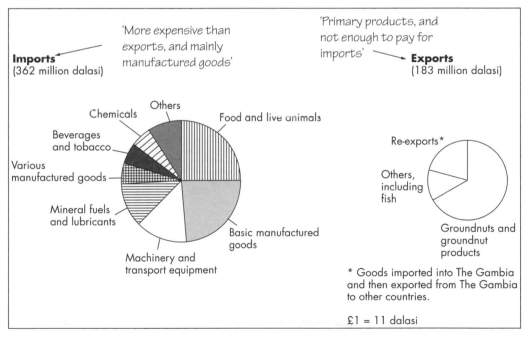

The nature of world trade means that both MEDCs and LEDCs are linked in a complex web of interdependency, as the cartoon (Fig. 15.8) depicts.

Countries are linked together, dependent on each other for help and have a shared responsibility for the world economy.

Fig. 15.9 tries to show the complex network of interlinking between the USA, EU, Japan, LEDCs and OPEC (Oil Producing Exporting) countries. Transnational or multinational companies with industries in different parts of the world, and so involved in international trade, are a key part of this network.

Fig. 15.8

Fig. 15.9

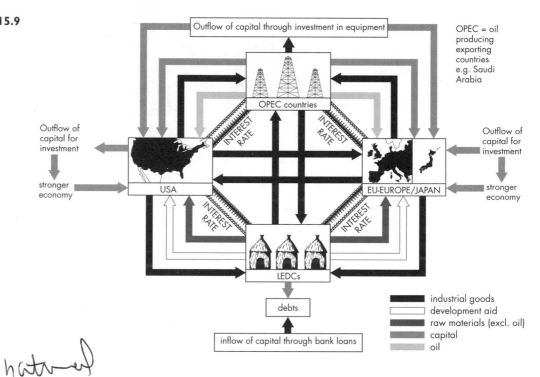

OPEC = oil producing exporting countries e.g. Saudi Arabia

Transnational companies

Transnational or *multinational* companies are large international firms operating across national boundaries, often in dozens of countries, and exerting enormous influence over our lives. The people in charge may have more influence on the shape of society than many of our elected politicians.

Transnational companies have grown particularly quickly since the 1960s. There are now more companies than countries with incomes greater than the GNP of Ireland. They include the giant oil and chemical companies such as Esso (Exxon), Royal Dutch/Shell Group, BP, etc., the great car producers (e.g. Ford, General Motors, Toyota), and corporations such as Unilever (food, detergents, etc.,) and IBM (computers).

The number and location of head offices of the 382 largest multinational companies are shown in Fig. 15.10.

Multinationals, as Fig. 15.10 reveals, are overwhelmingly MEDC (American, European and Japanese) companies. Japanese multinationals (e.g. Toyota, Honda, Nissan, Sony, etc.) currently invest large sums of money opening factories in other countries, especially in the USA but in most continents, including in Britain and the EU. Fig. 15.11 tells the story.

Fig. 15.10

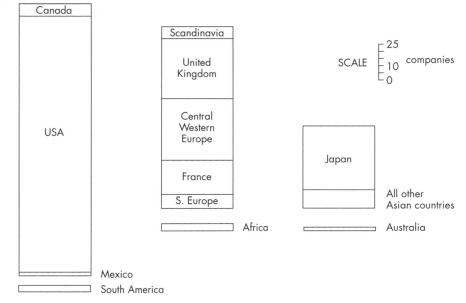

Fig. 15.11 Japanese industrial investment around the world

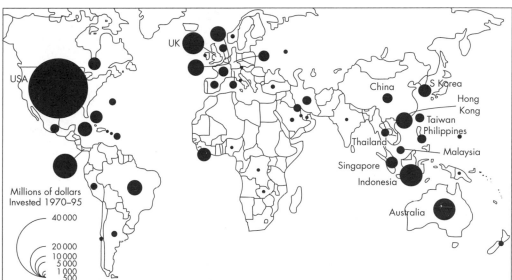

This can have both positive and negative effects. Table 15.1 shows the main advantages and disadvantages of the build-up of foreign companies in LEDCs. It is clear that the factories, farms and jobs of a transnational company in a country will be part of a larger organisation and so may depend on processes and workers elsewhere, and will depend on decisions made elsewhere.

Table 15.1 The advantages and disadvantages of transnational companies for LEDCs

Advantages of transnational companies	Disadvantages of transnational companies
provide money (capital and foreign exchange) for development	make profits in 'developing' countries, often sending more of them back home than they invest locally
provide jobs for local people	can undercut local prices and drive local firms out of business, so causing some job losses
introduce new technology	hire mostly unskilled local people, with many skilled and management jobs being held by foreigners
produce useful products for the local market which might otherwise have to be imported (e.g. oil, cars)	may produce goods not appropriate to 'developing' countries, but being foreign carry status, especially with rich (e.g., Nestle's powdered baby milk)
often pay higher wages than local firms	attracted by cheap, controllable labour, especially female, and pay less than to workers doing same job in 'developed' countries
are a cause of change, and progess (economic growth)	often borrow local capital rather than import it and so deprive local industry of finance
	technology is often imported, with Research and Development work staying in the 'developed' countries

▷ **Issue**   *International trade helps MEDCs and hinders LEDCs?*

Fig.15.12

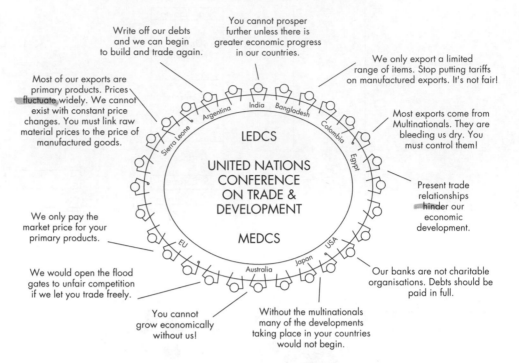

International trade is largely controlled by MEDCs and trans/multinational companies in their interests, and different trading arrangements between the two sets of countries may help economic development in LEDCs more than at present.

▷ **Case study**   *BART (San Francisco Bay Area Rapid Transit System)*

BART is a rapid transit system of computer-controlled lightweight electric trains which run under ground, under water and above the ground for 120 kilometres around the San Francisco region. It is quicker than travelling by bus, with trains running at speeds of up to 130 km per hour. The system is able to carry many more passengers than the previous bus system. Some 300 000 commuters a day are transported, and there are only 90 seconds between trains at peak periods. Fume and noise pollution levels from cars, and traffic congestion, have been reduced in the CBD.

Fig. 15.13

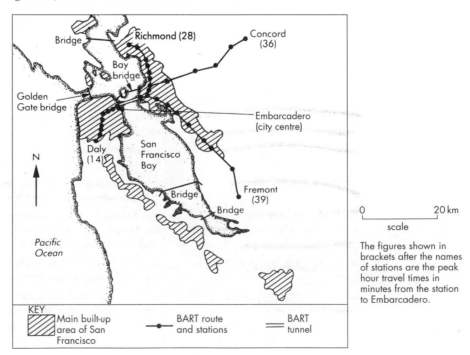

The development of electric tramway networks in some British cities (e.g. Manchester, Sheffield, etc.) which are integrated into the present transport system, e.g. tramway stops at important road junctions, has been inspired by systems such as BART as well as the London Underground.

▷ Key terms

Make you understand and can apply these geographical terms

Accessibility	The ease with which a place can be reached.
Aid	Gifts or loans of money or other forms of assistance by MEDCs to LEDCs.
Commuters	People who travel long distances from the countryside or from another town to their place of work.
Integrated transport	When different types of transport are knitted together into one system, e.g. park-and-ride schemes.
Interdependence	The interlinking of places, industries and countries through trade, aid and investment.
Outward/inward investment	Capital (money) invested in production (e.g. factories) in other countries.
Primary product	A raw material or fundamental product, e.g. food.
Rush hour	Period when majority of the population of large cities are making their journeys to work or home again.

Others such as **import**, **export**, **multinational (transnational) company** are defined and explained in the chapter.

Suggestions for further work

▷ Transport and traffic surveys are a favourite topic of field studies. Here are a few which involve such surveys:

   1 Where are the main traffic congestion points in your area and why?
   2 Does the town need a by-pass?
   3 Public bus services serve older residential areas better than new ones. Is this true?

▷ As with other topics, teacher-planned, classroom-based coursework units can be set, e.g. the effects of commuting, including 'rush hour' problems, on a large urban area, with possible solutions considered.

STUDENT ANSWER WITH EXAMINER'S COMMENTS

(a) Study Fig. 15.14 showing the number of buses on the roads in a British city.

Fig. 15.14

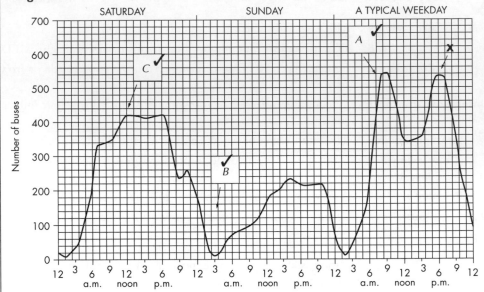

(i) Label **each** of the following in the correct box on Fig. 15.14.
Label **A** Buses taking people to work
Label **B** A quiet period during the weekend
Label **C** High number of buses probably used by shoppers   3 (3)

(ii) Suggest a label for arrow X

Buses taking people home ✓   1
_(1)_

'Well done! Good start'

(iii) Suggest a time when this city has a rush hour

7–8 a.m. on a weekday ✓   1
_(1)_

(b) Many schemes have been introduced to reduce traffic congestion in cities. These include Park-and-Ride, Urban Light Railways, Tidal Flow Systems and Ring Roads.
Describe any scheme to reduce traffic congestion in a named town or city that you have studied.

'Good, a real place!'

Named town or city _Newcastle_ ✓

'Better on problem than description of system'

The Newcastle Metro is an Urban Light Railway designed to reduce traffic congestion. The idea is that people, instead of taking the cars into the city centre, go instead to a station and take the train.

'Simple and clear'

It has been partly successful in reducing traffic congestion but many people have found problems in reaching the stations from their homes and as they have to drive the car anyway to reach the station are still driving into the city.   4

'A Level 2 answer'

_(6)_

Fig. 15.15 Fotherby bypass

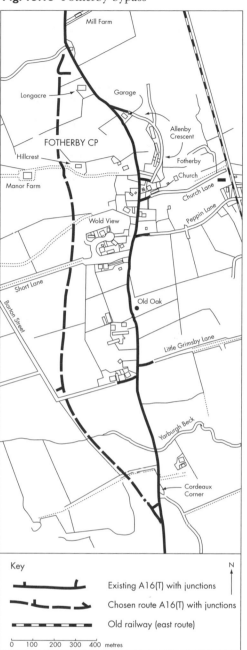

Key

⎯⎯⎯⎯   Existing A16(T) with junctions

⎯ ⎯ ⎯   Chosen route A16(T) with junctions

▪▪▪▪▪▪   Old railway (east route)

0   100   200   300   400 metres

Department of Transport officials showed plans for the new A16 Fotherby bypass.

Work is due to start in 1996 in a bid to cut down on the large number of accidents that have taken place in the village.

The Department says that over 200 casualties are expected to be saved over a 30 year period as a result of building of the road.

The choice of taking the route to the east of the village along the old railway line was ruled out because of the increased travel time and nearness to some houses.

Traffic using the A16 has grown throughout the 1980s and over 90% of the traffic is through traffic. Everyday over 9500 vehicles use the A16 and many are heavy vehicles.

'Fine reasons "lifted" from data'
'Heavy vehicles, through traffic, etc.?'

'Mention of increased time travelling and nearness to housing in data!'

'Either they are for, against or don't care but why?
(A reason needs giving!)'

'Pity, you didn't answer these and lost marks!'

(c)   Study Fig. 15.15.
(i)   State **three** reasons why the Fotherby bypass is needed.

    1 *There have been many road accidents in the village.* ✓

    2 *It will cut down the number of vehicles.* ✓

    3   2

                                                    (3)

(ii)   In what way is the chosen route better than the east of village route?   0
    (3 lines provided)   (2)

(iii)   What might the following people think about the new bypass?
    The owner of the garage in Fotherby (3 lines provided)
    A person who has retired to the village (3 lines provided)   0
    The farmer at Manor farm (3 lines provided)   (6)

                                              (*total* 22)
                                     11   (*NEAB*)

▶ **A TUTOR ANSWER**

Study Fig. 15.16 which shows Ghana's main imports and exports. Their values are shown in United States dollars ($).
Fig. 15.16

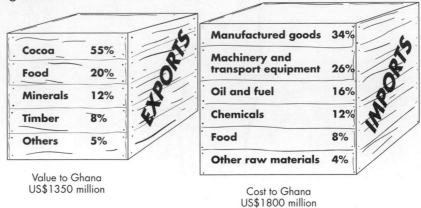

(a) What is the difference between the exports of a country and its imports?

The exports are the produce of the country being sent elsewhere, the imports are

goods from other countries which the importing country needs.

(b)

Use the information in Fig. 15.16 to complete the pie diagram showing Ghana's exports. (Fig. 15.17)   (2)

Fig. 15.17

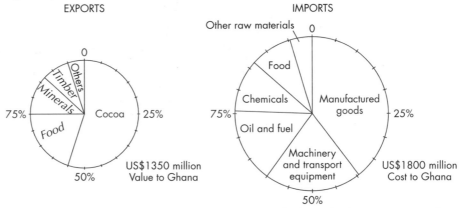

(c) Suggest a major difference between the kind of goods that are exported and those that are imported.

The exported goods are raw materials, the imported ones are mostly

manufactured goods.

(2)

(d) Ghana in an LEDC (less economically developed country). What economic problems does the trade pattern shown create for such a country?

It costs them more to import the goods than the income they make from their

exports. Balance of trade deficits and debt result. If one year the cocoa harvest

drops, this could cause further monetary problems, as they are very dependent on

cocoa. If the demand for raw materials drops this could also have damaging

effects on Ghana's economy. Cocoa could become less popular in, say, Europe.

(4) (*Total 10*)
(*NEAB*)

> **EXAMINATION QUESTION**

Tier F only

Study Fig. 15.18 showing changes in the volume of passenger traffic on a weekday in a major city in an MEDC (More Economically Developed Country).

Fig. 15.18

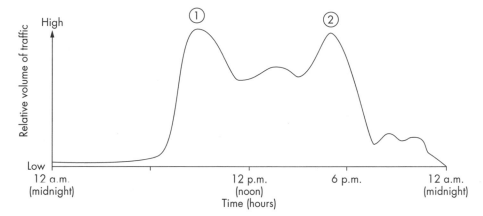

(a) (i) State the approximate times of points 1 and 2. (2 lines provided here) (*2 marks*)

    (ii) What is the name commonly given to these two times of peak traffic?
(1 line provided here)   (*1 mark*)

    (iii) Describe **briefly** the changes in volume of traffic shown by the graph.
(4 lines provided here)   (*2 marks*)

(b) Study Fig. 15.19 showing conditions common at the time shown by point 2 on Fig. 15.18.

Describe **three** problems travellers might have. (6 lines provided here)   (*6 marks*)

Fig. 15.19

(c) Study Fig. 15.20.

    (i) In which of these areas are you likely to see the conditions shown in Fig. 15.19?
(1 line provided here)   (*1 mark*)

    (ii) Explain why the streets in this area are often congested at peak times.
(5 lines provided here)   (*4 marks*)

(d) Four possible solutions to road traffic problems in urban areas are listed below.

    1. Pedestrianisation of the town/city centre.

    2. The building of ring or relief roads/motorways.

    3. The building of public tramways/rapid transit systems.

    4. The building of 'city airports'.

Fig. 15.20 The inner urban areas of this city

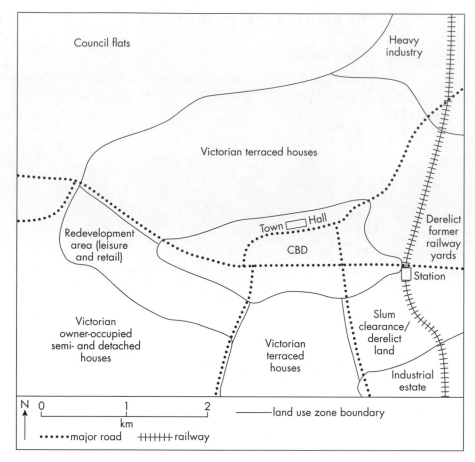

(i) Choose **two** of these possible solutions. What are the advantages and disadvantages of each?
Solution Number (1 line provided here) (7 lines provided for rest of this part)
Solution Number (1 line provided here) (7 lines provided for rest of this part)
(6 marks)

(ii) Many cities now use integrated traffic management schemes. In these schemes different forms of transport are used together.
Name a city with an integrated traffic management scheme. Describe the scheme.
Name of city (1 line provided here)
Description (7 lines provided here)
(3 marks)
(Total 25 marks)
(NEAB)

Tier H only

Study Fig. 15.18.
(a) (i) Describe what the graph shows. (3 lines provided here) *(2 marks)*
   (ii) Where within the city would the conditions shown for around 1800 hours be most likely to occur? What might happen to the passengers as a result of the conditions shown? (14 lines provided here) *(6 marks)*
(b) Explain why the streets in this area are often congested at certain times of the day.
(4 lines provided here) *(4 marks)*

Study Fig. 15.21, which shows a possible solution to urban traffic congestion.
(c) (i) Describe, with examples, **two other** possible solutions to the problem of traffic congestion in large cities.
   Solution 1 (6 lines provided here)
   Solution 2 (6 lines provided here) *(6 marks)*
   (ii) Many cities now have integrated traffic management schemes where different types of transport are used together. Name such a city and describe its scheme.

Name of city (1 line provided here) (9 lines provided for description)   (*4 marks*)

Fig. 15.21

Study Fig. 15.22 which shows actual and forecasted growth in urban road traffic in Britain, and a recent newspaper headline.

Fig. 15.22

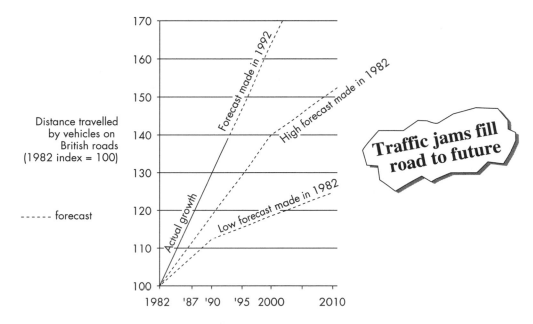

(d) (i) Use the information in Fig. 15.22 to describe how urban traffic problems in Britain may increase. (8 lines provided here)   (*3 marks*)
     (ii) Suggest reasons for these continuing problems. (12 lines provided here) (*5 marks*)
          (*Total 30 marks*)
          (*NEAB*)

▶ **EXAMINATION ANSWER**

Tier F only

(a) (i) 1 0900 2 1800 (2 x 1)   (2)
     (ii) Suggest 'rush hour'   (1)
     (iii) Level 1 – 1
           Gives two points about the oscillating pattern
           Level 2 – 2
           Gives the full 24 hour picture   (2)
(b) (3 x 2) Level 1 – 1–3
     Briefly states a valid consequence
     Level 2 – 4–6
     Extends and develops the consequence   (6)
(c) (i) CBD   (1)

    (ii) Level 1 – 1–2
      Suggests and perhaps develops one simple reason about the working day
      Level 2 – 3–4
      Develops explanation by expanding on process of movement involved, e.g.
      commuting   *(4)*

(d) (i) (3 + 3)
     Level 1 – 1–2 (x 2)
     Simple, brief argument supporting one or both sides
     Level 2 – 3 (x 2)
     Expect development of at least one side and /or introduction of examples *(6)*
  (ii) Level 1 – 1–2
     Expect basic description of how scheme integrated and named example
     Level 2 – 3
     Expect fuller description with working details and how it eases problems *(3)*
                        (Total 25)(*NEAB*)

Tier H only

(a) Level 2 – 1–4
   Writes about the obvious depicted by the data (e.g. stressful CBD rush hours)
   Level 3 – 5–8
   Describes fully three consequences   *(8)*

(b) Level 1 – 1–2
   Level 2 – 3–4
   As per (c)(ii) on Tier F   *(4)*

(c) (i) (2 x 3)
     For each solution proposed:
     Level 2 – 1–2
     Simple description with named example
     Level 3 – 3
     Extends description to illustrate why it may be a solution   *(6)*
  (ii) Level 1 – 1–2
     Level 2 – 3
     As per (d) (ii) on Tier F
     Level 3 – 4
     Extended description   *(4)*

(d) (i) Level 2 – 1
     Offers growth in traffic
     Level 3 – 2–3
     Expect detailed interpretation (e.g. forecast revision) and illustrative statistics *(3)*
  (ii) Level 2 – 1–2
     Expect 1–2 basic reasons
     Level 3 – 3–5
     Expect advantages and growing use of private motor car developed *(5)*
                      (Total 30) (*NEAB*)

SUMMARY

▷ Transport, especially by road is very important to modern industry and ways of life, particularly in MEDCs.

▷ The growth of traffic in urban areas requires strategies to manage the movement of people and goods.

▷ There are different patterns of trade in the world but they are dominated by few MEDCs.

▷ Industries and countries are increasingly interdependent through trade, investment and aid.

▷ International trade is closely linked to development. Trans or multinational companies are a major force in this trade as international trade is an essential feature of most industries.

▷ Asian countries on the western rim of the Pacific are increasing their share of world trade and their investment abroad, especially in the European Union.

▷ There is a growing awareness that interdependence of places means that we all have a shared responsibility for the development and welfare of the world and its people. 'Globalisation' has occurred as the world has become ever more interlinked.

Index

Index by Auriol Griffith-Jones

Longman - for all your study guide needs

Addison Wesley Longman publishes a wide range of curriculum-related books to help you with your studies. If you have enjoyed using this book and have found it useful, you can now order others directly from us - simply follow the ordering instructions below.

Don't forget to tell your fellow students about *Longman Study Guides* - they might find them useful too!

HOW TO ORDER

A full list of titles is given overleaf. Decide which title(s) you require and then order in one of the following ways:

by post
Fill in the quantity alongside the title(s) you require, select your method of payment, complete your name and address details and return your completed order form and payment to:
Addison Wesley Longman Ltd
PO BOX 88
Harlow
Essex CM19 5SR

by phone
Call our Customer Information Centre on 01279 623923 to place your order, quoting mail number: HESG1

by fax
complete the order form overleaf and fill in your name and address details and method of payment, and fax it to us on 01279 414130.

by e-mail
E-mail your order to us on awlhe.orders@awl.co.uk listing title(s) and quantity required and providing full name and address details as requested here. Please quote mail number: HESG1. Please do not send credit card details by e-mail.

Mail no: HESG1

Your Name _____

Your Address _____

_____

Postcode _____ Telephone _____

Method of payment

☐ I enclose a cheque or a P/O for £ _____ made payable to Addison Wesley Longman Ltd
☐ Please charge my Visa/Access/AMEX/Diners Club card

Number _____ Expiry Date _____

Signature _____ Date _____

(please ensure that the address given above is the same as for your credit card)

Prices and other details are correct at time of going to press but may change without notice. All orders are subject to status.

☐ *Please tick this box if you would like a complete listing of York Notes Literature Guides (suitable for GCSE and A-level English students)*

LONGMAN   Addison Wesley Longman

LONGMAN HOMEWORK HANDBOOKS (KEY STAGE 3)

£7.99 each unless otherwise stated

QTY *(0582)*

1	_____ 29330 8	English (KS3)
2	_____ 29331 6	French (KS3)
3	_____ 30423 7	French pack*(KS3) (£12.99)
4	_____ 30425 3	French cassette (KS3) (£6.00)
5	_____ 29329 4	German (KS3)
6	_____ 30427 X	German pack*(KS3) (£12.99)
7	_____ 30428 8	German cassette (KS3) (£6.00)
8	_____ 29328 6	Mathematics (KS3)
9	_____ 29327 8	Science (KS3)

LONGMAN GCSE STUDY GUIDES

£9.99 each unless otherwise stated

10	_____ 30481 4	Biology
11	_____ 31538 7	Business Studies
12	_____ 30482 2	Chemistry
13	_____ 31539 5	Economics
14	_____ 30484 9	English
15	_____ 30483 0	English Literature
16	_____ 30485 7	French
17	_____ 03839 1	French pack* (£14.99)
18	_____ 03836 7	French cassette (£6.00)
19	_____ 30486 5	Geography
20	_____ 30487 3	German
21	_____ 03837 5	German pack* (£14.99)
22	_____ 03838 3	German cassette (£6.00)
23	_____ 30495 4	Higher Level Mathematics
24	_____ 30494 6	Information Technology (£10.99)
25	_____ 30496 2	Mathematics
26	_____ 30497 0	Music
27	_____ 31540 9	Physics
28	_____ 28700 6	Psychology
29	_____ 31542 5	Religious Studies
30	_____ 30498 9	Science (£10.99)
31	_____ 22651 1	Sociology
32	_____ 22652 X	Spanish
33	_____ 24509 5	Spanish pack* (£14.99)
34	_____ 24511 7	Spanish cassette (£6.00)
35	_____ 23771 8	Technology
36	_____ 30545 4	World History

LONGMAN GCSE EXAM PRACTICE KITS

37	_____ 30381 8	Biology £4.99)
38	_____ 30383 4	Business Studies (£4.99)
39	_____ 31191 8	English (£4.99)
40	_____ 30384 2	Geography (£4.99)
41	_____ 30385 0	Mathematics (£4.99)
42	_____ 30379 6	Physics (£4.99)
43	_____ 30380 X	Science (£5.99)

LONGMAN GCSE REFERENCE GUIDES *£6.99 each*

44	_____ 05788 4	Biology
45	_____ 05790 6	Chemistry
46	_____ 05072 3	English
47	_____ 05077 4	French
48	_____ 05074 X	Mathematics
49	_____ 05794 9	Physics
50	_____ 05076 6	Science

GCSE SURVIVAL GUIDE *£2.95*

51	_____ 05078 2

_____**YORK NOTES LITERATURE GUIDES** *(see overleaf)*

LONGMAN A-LEVEL STUDY GUIDES

£9.99 each unless otherwise stated

52	_____ 22569 8	Accounting (£10.99)
53	_____ 31545 X	Biology
54	_____ 31652 9	Business Studies
55	_____ 31546 8	Chemistry
56	_____ 05782 5	Computer Science
57	_____ 27688 8	Economics (£10.99)
58	_____ 31656 1	English
59	_____ 05784 1	French
60	_____ 24495 1	French pack* (£14.99)
61	_____ 24497 8	French cassette (£6.00)
62	_____ 05173 8	Geography
63	_____ 31654 5	German
64	_____ 24498 6	German pack* (£14.99)
65	_____ 24508 7	German cassette (£6.00)
66	_____ 28702 2	Government and Politics (£10.99)
67	_____ 31549 2	Law (£10.99)
68	_____ 31550 6	Mathematics (£10.99)
69	_____ 31551 4	Modern History
70	_____ 27690 X	Physics
71	_____ 31655 3	Psychology
72	_____ 27691 8	Sociology

LONGMAN A-LEVEL EXAM PRACTICE KITS *£6.99 each*

73	_____ 30386 9	Biology
74	_____ 30387 7	Business Studies
75	_____ 30388 5	Chemistry
76	_____ 30389 3	Mathematics
77	_____ 30390 7	Psychology
78	_____ 30382 6	Sociology

LONGMAN A-LEVEL REFERENCE GUIDES *£6.99 each*

79	_____ 06394 9	Biology
80	_____ 06390 6	Chemistry
81	_____ 06396 5	English
82	_____ 06398 1	Mathematics
83	_____ 06392 2	Physics (£7.99)

LONGMAN HANDBOOKS *£7.99 each*

84	_____ 09965 X	Botany
85	_____ 08810 0	Chemistry

LONGMAN PARENT'S AND STUDENTS' GUIDES

£2.99 each

86	_____ 29971 3	Longman Parent's Guide to Pre-school Choices and Nursery Education
87	_____ 29975 6	Longman Parent's Guide to Key Stage 1 of the National Curriculum
88	_____ 29974 8	Longman Parent's Guide to Key Stage 2 of the National Curriculum
89	_____ 29973 X	Longman Parent's Guide to Key Stage 3 of the National Curriculum
90	_____ 29972 1	Longman Parent's Guide to GCSE and Key Stage 4 of the National Curriculum
91	_____ 29978 0	Longman A-level Survival Guide
92	_____ 29969 1	Longman Students' Guide to Vocational Education
93 to	_____ 29970 5	Longman Students' Guide to Returning Learning
94	_____ 29976 4	Longman Students' Guide to Higher Education

* pack = book and cassette